D0863914

The
Nature of
Co-operation

The
Nature of
Co-operation

John G. Craig

BLACK
ROSE
BOOKS

Montréal/New York
London

BLACK ROSE BOOKS No. W194
Hardcover ISBN 1-895431-69-7
Paperback ISBN 1-895431-69-9

Library of Congress No. 93-70391

Canadian Cataloguing in Publication Data

Craig, J. G. (John George), 1935–
The nature of co-operation

ISBN 1-895431-69-7 (bound) –
ISBN 1-895431-68-9 (pbk.)

1. Cooperation. 2. Cooperative societies. I. Title.

HD2963.C73 1993   334   C93-090102-9

Cover Illustration: Detail from *The Peaceable Kingdom*, by Edward Hicks, c. 1834.

Mailing Address

BLACK ROSE BOOKS   BLACK ROSE BOOKS
C.P. 1258   340 Nagel Drive
Succ. Place du Parc   Cheektowaga, New York
Montréal, Québec   14225 USA
H2W 2R3 Canada

Printed in Canada

A publication of the Institute of Policy Alternatives of Montréal
(IPAM)

TABLE OF CONTENTS

Chapter 1

INTRODUCTION

This book is about the evolution of co-operation as practised in co-operative organizations. These organizations are as varied as the imagination of their members. They are sometimes huge organizations with tens of thousands of employees and millions of members. They are sometimes very small with only a few dozen members. Some are very wealthy with millions of dollars in reserve, some are social organizations that require constant subsidies to exist. They originated in Europe in the early part of the nineteenth century and have been evolving since.

Co-operatives exist in one form or another in almost every country of the world. Farmers in the United States use them to market their harvest. Farmers in Nicaragua use co-operatives for the same purpose. White Afrikaaner farmers in South Africa purchase farm supplies from their co-operatives—so do black farmers in most other countries in Africa. Consumers in England and other western European countries spent over US$50 billion on groceries and household needs at the 14,000 local co-op stores, and consumers in eastern Europe also spend billions.[1]

Co-operatives are seen as the optimal organizational form to develop agriculture in such diverse countries as Israel, Algeria, India, Kenya, Tanzania, China and Thailand. Yet popular wisdom by international aid experts in industrialized countries, and politicians in less developed countries, is that they do not work. Literally tens of thousands of co-operatives were organized during the past twenty-five years and the vast majority were dismal failures. As one developer says, "The potential of co-operatives to promote broad-based development is undisputed, but in practice, results have often been disappointing."[2]

The purpose of this book is twofold: to provide an overview of how co-operative organizations function and how they have evolved around the world during the past 150 years; secondly to explore why they have been very successful in some places and dismal failures in others.

Co-operatives are organizations designed to enable people to co-operate in some facet of their lives. They may be co-operative communities where people spend most of their time. They may be a consumer-owned store or credit union or insurance organization, or they may be owned by producers to market products, like agricultural products or soapstone carvings. The wide range of types and processes make generalizations difficult. Before we start the analysis, the following are some current examples of how co-operation in co-operatives is being applied in highly diverse settings.

EXAMPLES

Israel: The Case of Ya'ad[3]

In 1974 the Israeli Government designated a tract of land in the Galilee region for rural development. The trees were striped centuries ago and the region is a rocky barren wasteland; the shortage of arable land and water means it is not suitable for agricultural settlement. The region known as the Segev was planned as a cluster of industrial villages operating within a regional framework. Sixteen settlements of 80 to 400 families each, for a total of 3,270 families or about 15,000 residents are planned when development is completed. A service centre will be located at the heart of the region and will provided: an educational centre combining schools and community activities; a medical centre; municipal offices; and a commercial centre.

An industrial park is being developed that will complement the light industry zones of each settlement, providing space for larger plants which require a central location in the region. It will also allow firms to share services such as training facilities, maintenance shops, computerized services and so on, thus reducing costs by avoiding duplication of industrial infrastructure. This area and the local government are controlled by the residents of the sixteen communities that are being settled. In the process, the settlers plan their communities to fit their needs and aspirations as they develop.

Ya'ad is one of the first settlements in the area and is formally incorporated as an Industrial Moshav Shitiffi. After several years of planning, the first settlers moved into the new town site in 1978 with housing, public facilities, and office space financed by the Jewish National Fund and sold to the settlers on a long-term mortgage. The social organization of each settlement is determined by the settlers and as a result, each of the sixteen settlements vary in the way they are organized.

The organizers of this settlement are all graduates with computer science, engineering or architecture degrees. They wanted to work together co-operatively but make consumption decisions in the nuclear family. As a result they have designed a community to do just that.

The community is based on industries rather than agriculture. The new industries include a computer software business, an electronics firm specializing in the development and production of electronically controlled weighing instruments and an architectural and civil engineering firm. As service industries, they have clients all over Israel with business activities taking place in Ya'ad and in the clients' offices.

Each firm is owned by all the residents of Ya'ad which now consists of forty-two families. All the adults work in the firms and make decisions as a group. The administrative jobs are rotated, allowing residents to pursue their professional careers, based on a division of labour and job specialization. But the major decisions of the group are made at the general assembly meetings held once a week.

Children automatically become members at birth. They are raised in their parents' home and looked after during working hours in a day-care centre operated by the parents. Because most of the adults prefer to pursue their professional careers, the group has decided that each couple must contribute one year's work in the day-care looking after the children, allowing the parents to decide when they will spend this concentrated period of time with their children.

Each worker is paid the same wage. Each couple must contribute eight hours and five hours per day of work. For example, in one family, the wife worked eight hours and her husband worked the five hour shift and spent the extra time with their small children. Since monthly salaries are paid, consumption in the community is determined by each family. Production decisions are made communally but consumption decisions are made by individuals and based on individual choice.

Like all the business activity in the settlement, the village shop is owned by the members of the co-operative. Each family has a key and records purchases when they are made. There are no employees, and shelves are restocked and supplies ordered in periodic, collective work-sessions. This decreases the cost and enables more workers to be engaged in productive work in income-generating co-operatives.

The community was begun by eight couples and now supports forty-two families. New members who are interested are made aware of the industrial plans and decide whether these provide the kind of occupational alternative they desire. They are then admitted for a six-month period during which they work and get to know the other members of the community. At the end of six months, the new member and the community make a decision. If both decisions are positive, then the newcomers are granted membership. Membership is voluntary and members can leave the community whenever they wish.

The community is prosperous and the businesses are working well at this time. The settlements take in new members as more workers are needed in the firms. Care is taken to develop compatible business activity; new members with different skills have the opportunity to develop business activity that are compatible with the existing ones. The intent is to create an expanding economic base so the community can grow to its desired size and members are able to utilize their professional training.

These communities have long-term financing that enables young people to settle, create employment and build a community. There is also plenty of scope to let the settlers determine their own lifestyles and their own destinies. These communities are interesting examples of how worker co-operatives can be used to provide employment and new settlements where they are socially desirable. Long-term mortgages enable the young people to build adequate housing and business premises, and are an important feature that helps the overall success of the project. The communities also allow for innovation and social experiment, and are not prescribed by distant bureaucrats. The settlers can discuss and think through the social organization of the businesses and communities.

Ya'ad has planted an olive grove and some gardening takes place. The regional government has also started a reforestation programme that will create 3,250 acres of forest recreation area. Over the next few decades, this once barren wilderness will be transformed into a productive community.

Nepal

On the edge of Katmandu, Nepal, there are several camps for Tibetan refugees. One of these houses about 500 adults and children, who have become self-supporting by raising sheep. The animals provide a source of food as well as income, for their wool is cleaned, spun, dyed and woven into beautifully designed, high-quality rugs. Some are sold to tourists, but most are exported overseas through commercial channels. The business has continued to grow and additional wool is now imported from India. This rug factory gives the refugees more than economic independence: it provides them with a sense of purpose and transforms their lives from a state of lethargy, sadness and boredom into one of cheerful activity. While the intermingled generations sit working at their tasks and passing on their skills, they also sing Tibetan songs and legends, keeping their culture alive. These people want to return to their homeland, but in the meantime they are working co-operatively to make the best of their present circumstances.

On the other side of Katmandu is another refugee camp. This group, which is not self-supporting, relies on handouts and the sale of souvenirs to tourists. Why have groups of refugees from the same country with the same opportunities responded to their plight in opposite ways? Why has one group co-operated in order to help themselves, while others have not? What are the conditions under which groups of people turn to mutual co-operation to help themselves?

There are a number of theories that attempt to explain the grounds for co-operation between people. They variously attribute the phenomenon to biological, psychological and cultural causes but no single theory satisfactorily provides a complete explanation of co-operative behaviour. Each, however, offers some insights into this fundamental process of human interaction.

WHY CO-OPERATION EMERGES

Mutual Aid

The theory of mutual aid, first developed by Peter Kropotkin around the turn of the century, is based on Darwin's theory of evolution — that is, the survival of the fittest or strongest of the species in the animal world. Kropotkin, who travelled extensively in eastern Asia during the late 1800s, observed the ways in which various animal species attempted to overcome threats to their existence. In particular, he was struck by their reliance on mutual aid and the significance of this pattern of behaviour to their ability to survive:

> The animal species in which individual struggle has been reduced to its narrowest limits, and the practice of mutual aid has attained the greatest development are invariably the most numerous, the most prosperous and the most open to further progress. The mutual protection which is obtained in this case, the possibility of attaining old age and the accumulation of experience, the higher intellectual development, and the further growth of sociable habits, secure the maintenance of the species, its extension, and its further progressive evolution. The unsociable species, on the contrary, are doomed to decay.[4]

In short, those that co-operate the most survive and flourish.

Turning to the human species, Kropotkin points out that man has been living in clans and tribes since the dawn of the early stone age and that, from that time, people have continued to build co-operative relations built on mutual aid. But the growth of the State has reduced, and in some cases eliminated, mutual aid, as the people in power have sought to control the behaviour of the masses. When State control weakens, mutual aid institutions reappear in all societies.

Kropotkin concludes from his study of the history of mankind that the practice of mutual aid has allowed people to develop the arts, knowledge and human intelligence. The periods when institutions based on mutual aid were strongest was also the period of greatest progress in arts, industry, and science. He notes that

> the study of inner life of the medieval city and of the ancient Greek cities reveals the fact that the combination of mutual aid, as it is practised within the guild, and the Greek clan, with a large initiative which was left to the individual and the group by means of the federative principle, gave mankind two greatest periods in its history.[5]

He dismisses the simple explanation that the industrial progress of the past two centuries was a triumph of individualism and competition. Rather, industrial progress was achieved by organizational mechanisms that forced co-operation (i.e., large bureaucracies and limited liability which allowed groups to pool investment capital). These are not mechanisms where individuals are struggling against other individuals, but rather groups of individuals competing with other groups. Mutual aid is practised internally.

According to mutual aid theory, co-operation is based on the premise that only the fittest survive, not individually, but as a species. The greater the development of mutual aid, the greater are the obstacles that any group can overcome, and the more they can develop, and conquer threats to their existence. The basic drive for survival leads to mutual aid. But why does the drive appear to be stronger in some species (including humans) than in others? Sociobiological theory attempts to answer this question.

Sociobiological theory

Sociobiological theory is compatible with Darwin's and Kropotkin's observations, but it goes further. Its proponents postulate that altruism or mutual aid is the result of genetic similarities between members of human and other animal species. Individuals provide mutual aid to each other because it increases the survival chances of the gene pool.[6] Thus, co-operation which is basic to humans and animals, is due not to culture or learning, but rather to biology.

Sociobiology is controversial and few experiments have been carried out by its proponents to verify crucial aspects of the theory. It has been adopted quickly and unquestioningly by those searching for social determinism, as it offers "A Genetic Defense of the Free Market."[7] These authors have summarized recent research that casts strong doubt on the theory and analyzed the reasoning and logic used by sociobiologists. They conclude that the basis for co-operation is "Not in Our Genes."

Behavioural Theory

Behaviourists have developed a theory of operant conditioning which stands in marked contrast to sociobiological theory. This theory assumes that most behaviour patterns in animals and humans are not predetermined but can be changed by a schedule of reinforcements.[8] Behaviour is a response to stimuli in the environment. If the response results in a positive effect, that particular form of behaviour is encouraged or reinforced, and will probably continue. If the effect is negative, a change in behaviour will likely occur.

This learning theory emerged after the famous experiments carried out on animal learning by behaviourists like Pavlov. They attempted to show that much of the behaviour believed to be instinctive could in fact be altered by learning. More recent behaviourists have focused on the question of whether behaviour may be controlled or changed by altering variables in the environment.

Behavioural theory such as operant conditioning would explain co-operative behaviour as follows. People learn, through trial and error, that what they cannot do individually can best be done by working with others. When individuals respond to a situation by co-operating and this behaviour is positively reinforced, they will co-operate in similar situations in the future. If, however, a co-operative response produces negative reinforcement, people will tend to avoid co-operation.

Thus, co-operative behaviour is directly related to the environment. It occurs in situations where the environment encourages co-operation and where the failure to co-operate may have unfavourable consequences.

Exchange Theory

Exchange theory is also a learning theory, but the explanation of why people co-operate is different from that put forward by behaviourists. Social exchange is seen as a basic human process, in which unspecified obligations result from social acts that help the entire group. It is understood by all that reciprocity will occur, but it is unknown when and in what form others will discharge their obligations. The social exchange of aid and assistance thus depends on trust and, in the process, helps to build trust both within a group and between groups. Provided that an atmosphere of trust and social exchange exists, co-operation will take place between individuals or groups. Because an act of co-operation helps others as well as the initiator, a pattern of co-operative behaviour will develop and continue over time.

Peter Blau provides a detailed elaboration of this theory.[9] Social exchange processes can explain differentiation of power and, also, the emergence of hierarchic and formal organizations that encourage a high level of competitive behaviour. As in the case of behavioural theory, behaviour is explained without reference to the effects of biological makeup and individual differences between people. It is primarily the processes within and between groups that determine the extent of their co-operative activity.

Functional Theory

Functionalism explains co-operation on the basis of the effect that such behaviour has for the wider whole. Functional theory suggests that the source of co-operative behaviour rests with the perceived needs of individuals and their group. If the perceived needs of a group are not being met, attempts will be made to rectify the situation. If individual action proves inadequate, the group may turn to co-operation as a means of satisfying these needs. Similarly, co-operative activity will not occur if it fails to meet individual and group needs or if they are already being met in some other way.

The above theoretical perspectives attempt to identify the origins of co-operation between people. They suggest that co-operation occurs under certain conditions and fails under others. But they do not specify these conditions; nor do they shed much light on why some Tibetan refugees have become self-supporting, rather than live on handouts. This book will explore this question and attempt to advance our understanding of why some co-operatives are successful and why others fail.

The book is divided into seven chapters. Chapter 2 reviews the roots of the co-operative movement from its start in England and Germany, and how its evolution through the past 200 years. This evolution has varied over the course of five periods, as co-operatives have developed a philosophical base and adapted their ideological base to fit the environment in many different countries.

Chapter 3 provides an overview of what the international movement now looks like, and examines the diversity of forms of service co-operatives. It also explores the contributions and limitations of service co-operatives in the economy.

Chapter 4 outlines the development of comprehensive forms of co-operation in western and eastern Europe, India and Israel. It then explores the dynamics of co-operation in these organizations in terms of a number of internal and external characteristics.

Chapter 5 explores co-operative development in less industrialized countries. Three countries — India, China and Tanzania — all have extensive co-operative development. The major problem of co-operatives stimulated by the State is made evident in these cases and discussed.

Chapter 6 addresses the questions, "What is the problem? Why does co-operation frequently get squeezed out of organizations?" The older paradigm is contrasted to the emerging paradigm, which is more compatible with the logic of co-operation. This presents a dilemma for managers and elected leaders to build organizations where co-operation can flourish rather than be squeezed out by the traditional bureaucratic approaches.

Chapter 7 introduces the problem of social inequality, namely class, race and gender. All organizations impact on these factors in their day-to-day activities and co-operatives are no exception. The chapter explores the research that has taken place in this area and addresses one approach, empowerment, as a way to address these problems in society. The theory of co-operation, like most theory, has been based on white males. What would organizations look like if they evolved having both men and woman as full partners? The research in this area is sparse but the anecdotal information suggests that women-centred co-operatives may evolve differently.

Chapter 8 provides a case from Japan where management is applying the logic of the emerging paradigm. These co-operatives are dominated by women members. They are growing rapidly as home-makers co-operate and exercise real power in the market place. How much of the difference is due to Japanese culture and how much is due to responsiveness to the needs and aspirations of the women members?

Notes

1. International Co-operative Alliance. 1992, *XXXth Congress, Tokyo, October, 1992 Agenda and Report*. Geneva: International Co-operative Alliance: 77-78.
2. Ledesma, A.L., A.Y. Ledesma, A.B. Quizon and A.M. Salinas. 1982, *The Cooperative Experience in Asian Cultures*. Manila: Centre for the Development of Human Resources in Rural Asia: 1.
3. This case was developed from information obtained from a visit to the area plus written material distributed to visitors. All errors are the responsibility of the author.
4. Kropotkin, Peter. 1989, *Mutual Aid: A Factor of Evolution*. Montreal: Black Rose Books: 246.

5. Kropotkin, 1989: 248.
6. Trives, Robert. 1971, "Evolution of reciprocal altruism." *Quarterly Review of Biology*, 46 (1): 35-40; and Wilson, Edward Osborne. 1975, *Sociobiology: The New Synthesis*. Cambridge: Harvard University Press.
7. Ross, Steven, Leon J. Kamin and R.C. Lewontin. 1984, *Not in Our Genes*. Harmondsworth: Pelican: 235.
8. Skinner, B.F. 1969, *Contingencies of Reinforcement*. New York: Appleton-Century-Croft.
9. Blau, Peter M. 1964, *Exchange and Power in Social Life*. New York: John Wiley & Sons.

Chapter 2

ROOTS AND EVOLUTION

Co-operation may be defined as any joint or collaborative behaviour that is directed towards some goal and in which there is common interest or hope of reward.[1] Co-operation may be voluntary or involuntary. It may be formal or informal, but it is always directed towards an end in which all participants have a stake. In its actual application in human groups, co-operation may become much more than a social process. It may become an end in itself, a way of life or an institutional structure.

Formally defined, co-operation can include almost all of those forms of human interaction that sociologists refer to as social organization. But the concept can also be broken down into a variety of types, with more specific and precise meanings. The analytical typology that follows is a conceptual construct, based on the social setting within which co-operation may occur. It is not suggested that these conditions exist in a pure form in the real world; in fact, different types of co-operation may emerge in various social settings. But the typology serves a useful purpose by providing a starting point for the development of a theoretical framework. Using social setting as a criterion, we can identify five conceptually discrete types of co-operation.[2]

TYPES OF CO-OPERATION

Automatic co-operation refers to co-ordinated activities or joint efforts of an impersonal nature, which take place between individuals in physical proximity to each other. It is unplanned and often unnoticed by its participants. It may occur as a group response to a common threat or simply as a response to an ordinary situation in which individuals have learned to co-operate.[3] Examples of automatic co-operation are queueing at bus stops and supermarket check-out counters, and the movement of people in and out of crowded elevators.

This type of co-operation occurs often in daily living. It becomes a natural response, and there may be little or no communication between the participants. They co-operate only because it is useful for them to do so in the circumstances in which they find themselves.

Spontaneous co-operation is perhaps the oldest and most natural form of co-operation in human interaction. It is also the most widespread in everyday life. Its basis is the friendly relationship that often exits between individuals, and it is unprescribed by tradition, contract or command.

This type of co-operation takes place within the family, in neighbourhood groups and play groups, and through other close personal forms of association. Small group research, family studies and research into friendship groups have provided considerable information on the occurrence of spontaneous co-operation in a variety of settings. In these settings, when common action is required, individuals are generally quick to co-operate because of the strength of the social ties between them.

Traditional co-operation is regulated, not by instinct, volition nor circumstance, but rather by the traditional social norms of the participants. It is often part of the moral fabric of the community and described in community traditions. Examples of traditional co-operation include the sharing of food in hunting and gathering cultures, community barn-raising, volunteer fire brigades as well as the organization of much of communal life. In these cases, co-operative behaviour may be regarded as simply the moral and correct way of living.[4] The neatly terraced fields in Bali are the outcome of co-operative work organized within a traditional way of life. Brooke describes how this work is organized:

> The symbol of these efforts — the bale bandjar — is seen by most visitors but noticed by few. This open-fronted pavilion is where men gather to train their fighting cocks; to hold gamelan (orchestra) rehearsals; to conduct council meetings or just to pass the time of day. And, the youngsters whom you see enjoying their frame of table tennis are playing in the bale bandjar. Twenty to thirty families generally belong to a bandjar. (In many ways the bandjar resembles the Israeli moshav which, in turn, is a modification of the kibbutz.) The bandjar usually owns a number of rice fields which are worked communally and enjoy absolute equality and all are compelled to assist each other with labour and materials. And, as a communal group, without financial reward, they attend to the repair of their temple and the upkeep of their roads. Membership of the bandjar is compulsory. After marriage a man is in-

vited to join. He is given ample time. He is thrice summoned but if he thrice denies then he is considered morally "dead." He is then ostracized from all social activities and, what is even more important, is denied the right to be buried (often a prelude to cremation) in the local cemetery.[5]

In Bali, co-operation is a way of life regulated by strong traditional pressures. Traditional life in India is similar. The Hindu family that observes the principle of being "joint in food, worship and estate" in effect recognizes the morality of mutual aid between family members, however remote in time and space they may be. The thread of traditional co-operation is very strong in most major religions and in most of the world's older cultures.

It is also strong in many developing nations, where attempts have been made to introduce Western forms of co-operation as a means of achieving social and economic progress. These experiments have been based on the assumption that Western co-operative structures, being similar to traditional ones, can be readily established in traditional societies. Unfortunately, as we shall see in Chapter 4, the relationships between different types of co-operation are not as simple as is sometimes believed, and the transition from a traditional to a contractual form is usually not easy.

Directed co-operation is based on demand. There is a clear and well-accepted goal, and individuals are directed to co-operate in order to achieve that goal. An important example of directed co-operation is found in a military organization whose goal is to win a battle. Soldiers are commanded to co-operate, in accordance with specific orders as to how they should organize and conduct themselves in the course of the battle. This type of co-operation is very prevalent in modern society, and is facilitated by an organizational hierarchy. The hierarchy provides a means of co-ordinating highly specialized work carried out by many individuals, so that it is directed towards the achievement of organizational goals. Co-operation is thus the result of formal structural arrangements with which the individual is expected to comply, by reason of his/her participation in the organization.

A number of countries have decided that co-operatives are desirable forms of business for the population. Where local citizens have not in the past shown a strong interest in voluntary co-operation, the government itself has assumed responsibility for setting up such organizations. In many cases, people have little choice but to join these co-operatives. Organizations of this type are an obvious form of directed co-operation.

Contractual co-operation is a prevalent form in modern industrial-ized society. In this case, co-operation is both voluntary and formal-ized, based upon an explicit agreement between individuals to work together towards the achievement of a common goal. Often a separate organization is established in which membership is re-quired, and legal sanctions are set out regarding the duration of the co-operative contract and the specific conditions of membership. The functions of the co-operative may be economic in nature, such as col-lective buying or selling of goods; or they may have a social or service orientation, as is the case with a local ratepayers' association.

Contractual co-operation is not confined to voluntary organiza-tions. It is also evident in many work-related situations. For example, in applying for and accepting a job, the individual in effect under-takes a voluntary commitment to co-operate in working towards the employer's goals and objectives. He/she also accepts certain terms and conditions of employment (the equivalent of membership in a voluntary organization).

An individual may participate in many co-operative contracts in his/her everyday life, and the scope of his/her involvement may vary considerably. In some cases, a co-operative may be used occasionally or for a very limited purpose. In others, it may meet most or all of the individual's daily needs. An example of the latter situation is the com-munity of YA'AD (see Chapter 1) which is organized entirely on co-operative principles.

Co-operative organizations, labour unions and other voluntary associations are organizational forms that are designed to facilitate contractual co-operation between the members of the group. These organizations have been the focus of much research and many case studies, and these will be analyzed in Chapter 4.

CO-OPERATION, CONFLICT AND COMPETITION

The concept of conflict is often seen as the opposite of co-opera-tion. In some cases it may be, but for most social situations these con-cepts have a much more complex relationship and need to be explored in more depth.[6]

All theories of society and human interaction must make some basic philosophical assumptions about the nature of man. Some theorists, such as Aristotle, perceive man as being essentially gregarious and a "social animal"; others, like the seventeenth-century philosopher Thomas Hobbes, believe that the natural state of man is characterized by conflict and "the war of all against all." The latter view was carried forward into the nineteenth century, in the form of three major assumptions about human relationships. The first was the belief that all behaviour was a product of self-interest, as individuals tried to maximize pleasure and minimize pain. The second, embodied in classical economic theory of Adam Smith, proposed that society consisted of "discrete, self-interested individuals, united chiefly by ties of impersonal competition." Finally, the doctrine of natural selection affirmed the primacy, and even the exclusiveness, of competition and conflict in the whole evolutionary process.[7]

The emphasis of nineteenth-century thought on conflict and a struggle of all against all produced a reaction among social reformers, who perceived that the masses were placed at a disadvantage in a competitive economic environment. There emerged a new interest in developing co-operative communities to provide people with an escape from deprivation; and underlying this trend was the assumption that co-operation was the opposite of conflict and competition. This conclusion was unfortunate, for it oversimplified the relationship that exists between the three forms of human interaction. Coser has defined social conflict as follows:

> Social conflict may be defined as a struggle over values or claims to status, power, and scarce resources, in which the aims of the conflicting parties are not only to gain the desired values but also to neutralize, injure, or eliminate their rivals. Such conflicts may take place between individuals, between collectivities or between individuals and collectivities. Inter-group as well as intra-group conflicts are perennial features of social life. Conflict is an important element of social interaction. Far from being always a negative factor that tears apart, social conflict may contribute in many ways to the maintenance of groups and collectivities as well as to the cementing of interpersonal relations.[8]

Conflict is a concept that is independent of co-operation; not always opposite to it. In certain circumstances, conflict may be an integral part of inducing and sustaining co-operative behaviour, and the two may coexist in various social settings. Sometimes a low level of conflict is matched by a low level of co-operation. An example of

Figure 2.1

RELATIONSHIP BETWEEN CO-OPERATION AND CONFLICT

Co-operation	Conflict	
	Low	High
Low	Little Interaction	Unstable relations
High	Stable and comfortable	Unstable, intense, sometimes creative

this situation might be the relationships between people living in a high-rise apartment building in an industrialized city. Similarly, there are situations where the conflict between people is intense, but the intergroup co-operation to achieve other goals also is very intense. Some people view this as the ideal state of affairs for a modern corporation.

If these two concepts are dichotomized, they can generate a two-by-two table (see Figure 2.1) in which there is a logical combination of four types. All of these logical combinations could occur in social settings and in social organizations, and at different times in a given situation. Both concepts, conflict and co-operation, are dynamic processes. Thus, at various points in time and space, social groups may experience high conflict and low co-operation or high conflict and high co-operation. The latter condition is very intense. There is a strong commitment to achieve a goal by the participants, but there may be equally strong disagreement over the precise definition of that goal and particularly over the means of achieving it. The research of human groups, however, suggests that this is not a stable state. Groups with intense relationships of high co-operation and high conflict change over a period of time, so that their behaviour comes to resemble the conditions in the other three cells in Figure 2.1.

As conflict and co-operation processes may occur simultaneously within a group, so they may also arise between groups. In a study of the co-operative movement in western Canada, Bromberger documents the emergence of prairie co-operatives as a direct result of dissatisfaction and conflict with eastern-owned businesses, which dominated the economy. The wheat marketing co-operatives were a response to grain monopolies and the ownership of the transportation network by eastern railway companies. The credit union movement was a response to the inadequacy of banking services, which also were controlled by eastern interests.[9] It has been well documented that internal co-operation is often encouraged when groups are faced with a conflict provoked by other groups. In other words, external conflict can enhance internal co-operation.

Competition is a sub-type of conflict, and the observations made about conflict also apply here. Competition implies a win-lose situation. In groups of two people, the interaction will be either co-operative, in which both participants can win if the goal is achieved; or competitive, in which the fact that ones win means that the other necessarily loses. In such a situation, it appears that competition and co-operation are opposites. This is true for dyads or very small groups, but in situations involving many individuals the two concepts are independent and related in a much more complex way. A sports team may use a high degree of co-operation in order to develop effective plays against another team. The process within the team is co-operative, and the process between the teams is competitive. But there may also be an element of competition among the players in the co-operating unit, where they are vying with each other for personal gains (such as prestige or salary increases). Competition of this kind does not need to detract from the team's co-operative effort, and it may well increase its chances of winning. Similarly, people in organizations may compete for high status roles, yet maintain a high degree of co-operation to achieve the goals of the organization. The conflict of ideas is a very important aspect of participation and co-operation. Competition for the best ideas raises the quality of the output from the lowest common denominator to the group achieving excellence. To view these two concepts as opposites may therefore be useful for groups of two, but it is fallacious in larger human groups.

When co-operation is viewed as an ideology or an ethical value, competitive individualism (also seen as an ethical value) is rejected and seen as the opposite to co-operative behaviour. Kohn distinguishes between structural competition and intentional competition. Structural competition is characterized as "situations of mutually exclusive goal attainment." This is a zero-sum game where if one wins the other loses. This exists in situations of scarcity and in situations where competition is itself the goal and scarcity is artificially created.

This is the logic behind sports and other situations where only one team or one individual can be number one.[10]

Intentional competition is an individual's competitiveness, his or her proclivity for beating others. This can be contrasted to intentional co-operation where someone has the proclivity for working with others to attain similar goals. These behaviours function at the level of culture or values, in an area where the proclivity of individuals in terms of competition and co-operation bring forth differences in organizations and societies in general. It never means that only one behaviour is present. Both are usually mixed in the complex web of social interaction. In practice, we would expect to find both processes occurring to some degree over time in any particular group.

As Kohn points out, co-operation should not be confused with altruism.

> Co-operation is a shrewd and highly successful strategy —
> a pragmatic choice that gets things done at work and at
> school even more effectively than competition does. ...The
> 1980s have brought forth this realization in many North
> American organizations. Those organizations that have
> maintained a competitive individualism with in the work
> setting have had a hard time competing with organizations
> that build a co-operative environment in the work setting
> and between stakeholders or sets of organizations. The ad-
> versarial model of labour management relations in North
> America has put these industries at a disadvantage when
> compared to countries like Germany, Japan and Sweden
> that have a co-operative approach to labour management
> relations. We are slowly learning this lesson.[11]

The case for competition over co-operation has been based on four myths which are explored in depth by Kohn. They are: 1) competition is an unavoidable fact of life, part of human nature; 2) competition motivates us to do our best — or, in a stronger form, that we would cease being productive if we did not compete; 3) contests provide the best way to have a good time; 4) competition builds character, it is good for self-confidence.

Contractual co-operation implies voluntary membership in a group. Usually it requires the direct participation of members, and it may involve them in democratic decision-making. Democracy and co-operation also are independent concepts, which are intertwined in a complex way. They may co-vary, or there may be cases where contractual co-operation is high but participation and democracy are low in any given organizational setting. The relationship between these processes will be explored further in later chapters.

CO-OPERATION AND SOCIAL MOVEMENTS

Some forms of co-operation may take on a significance far beyond their functional role. They may in fact be closely associated with that broad social phenomenon known as social movement. In the case of contractual co-operation, the link is particularly strong. It is therefore useful to examine some of the principal components and characteristics of social movements as a form of human interaction.

A social movement may be defined as a collective attempt to bring about or resist change in social institutions or to create an entirely new order by non-institutionalized means. It is different from a protest movement in that it is directed towards a specific and verbalized goal; that is, a social movement articulates the state or condition that it aims to establish, while a protest movement focuses on the things that should be changed, without proposing actual solutions. In addition, social movements always possess a sense of mission.

Three factors are usually present in the emergence of social movements. The first factor is shared frustration with the existing order. This is not, however, sufficient in itself to account for the development of a social movement. Shared frustration may in fact result in a protest movement instead. A second and very important factor, is the development of a vision or a belief in the possibility of a different state of affairs, which leads to the articulation of a goal or ideology. The third factor is the emergence of organizations that are devoted to realizing the vision or the mission of the social movement. These organizations do not usually encompass all the people who identify with the cause, but they may become a focal point for further articulation of the vision, as well as for attracting wider support of the movement.

Social movements are characterized by the development of shared values, which results in a sense of membership and comradeship between individual participants. The existence of shared values or a goal is vital to generating and sustaining an ideology.[12] Anthony Downs has defined an ideology as "the verbal image of the good society and the means of achieving it."[13] Protest movements rarely embody such an image when they first arise. But if a protest movement is to change to a social movement, an articulated image of the good society must evolve, which in effect amounts to the development of a systematic set of beliefs supporting the creation of institutions. The ideology identifies social "heroes" and "villains," and it provides the justification for the values of the movement.

Values may vary along a number of dimensions. They may be forward-looking and progressive. They may be reactionary, in that they attempt to restore social institutions and values that have been held in the past. They may be conservative, in that they wish to preserve existing institutions. Social movements with conservative values are usually counter-movements that have emerged in opposition to movements that seek to change society.[14]

The scope of the values also may vary considerably between social movements. They may be comprehensive and focus on many aspects of society, or they may be quite restricted and aimed at a few specific areas. In addition, there may be variations in the clarity of values, as they are expressed by leaders and as they are understood and interpreted by adherents of a social movement. Leaders often communicate values in the form of slogans. These slogans may be simple and direct statements, or they may be allusive, reflecting very complex values. Values that can be made explicit are often easily understood, but those that remain implicit may be comprehended by adherents only after a long period of socialization. In most social movements, differences arise in the interpretation of values, and subgroups of the membership engage in continuing debates over which interpretation is right.

The specification of values presents a major dilemma for social movements. They need a large membership in order to be successful, yet many potential members may be concerned with presenting themselves to others in a socially acceptable manner. If the values of a movement appear to be radically different from those that are currently in society, the chances of gaining adherents may diminish considerably. But if these values are made more socially acceptable, they may distort the essential mission of the movement, so that it gains many adherents at the cost of losing its thrust.

To be successful, social movements need to develop strategies for attracting new recruits. Membership is generally based on personal identification with the cause and values of a social movement, and individuals may decide to formalize their commitment for a number of reasons. Joining the movement may be expedient, or it may be the path of least resistance in a pressure situation; or the individual may be convinced of the absolute rightness of the purpose of the movement and may join out of a sense of duty or responsibility. Because of these differences in motivation, in any social movement there will be members who are active and enthusiastic supporters and members who are passive. The movement must reflect values and practices that will satisfy the expectations of both groups.

Cultural variations may occur in social movements, since members are part of a broader culture and a product of its society.[15] As the social movement gains acceptance among a wide range of cultural groups, the shape and the emphasis of some values may change. For example, when the expression of values is translated into another language, differences in connotation and perception may lead to the reinterpretation of the values themselves. The conceptualization of a value in one language may not have an equivalent in another language; thus, through translation, the values that are central in a social movement in one society may be slightly changed in another.

The values of a social movement determine the nature and scope of its activities, or the means by which it attempts to achieve its goals. Obviously, a pacifist movement cannot use violence to attain its ends. The only means that are justified are those that are consistent with the basic values of the movement.

The values also shape the norms of the social movement. These are the rules of conduct that govern the behaviour of members towards each other and towards members of other groups, particularly those with which the movement is or may be in conflict. Norms are usually communicated early to members to ensure that new recruits conform to the movement's values during the period when they are learning its ideology. The norms also help to develop loyalty to the movement among members and strengthen its identification to them and to outsiders. For example, members may adopt a special vocabulary or accept special concepts, which immediately identify individuals associated with and sympathetic to the movement.

The norms of the movement help to define its subculture. they bind the followers and the leaders. Norms prescribe the behaviour that sets members apart from non-members, and provide members with guidelines as to how they should act and interact. Perhaps most importantly, norms exert constant pressure to give the movement continuity, and a direction that is consistent with its basic values and goals.

The values of a social movement influence the structures that link its members and provide a framework for action. For example, social movements that place a high value on equality and participation establish structures that permit and encourage member involvement in decision-making. The structures that develop in related organizations within the movement may or may not be hierarchical; they may be informal or highly formal. Whatever their form, they are important in facilitating the growth and development of the movement towards the achievement of its objectives.

Structures make it possible to define roles and arrive at an appropriate division of labour. They also enable leaders to emerge.

Leaders verbalize the ideology and communicate the values of the movement to members. They also analyze and interpret events, offering their own explanation of problems and proposals for solutions. The leadership group is very important in generating consensus and a feeling of unity within the social movement. Banks observes that various types of leaders emerge with the division of labour. The organizers and the enthusiasts are both needed, but conflicts may occur between these two fundamentally different types of leaders. This is a crucial problem for movements to resolve.[16]

As necessary as strong leadership is to the success of a social movement, it can create problems, particularly if the movement espouses an egalitarian philosophy. There is a danger that a small elite will develop, which — intentionally or otherwise — may come to exert extraordinary influence over the membership. Organizations may become monolithic, with decision-making authority concentrated among a few individuals at the top of the hierarchy. Such a situation contradicts the basic values of the movement, but it may be very difficult to prevent. The emergence of elites and the development of monolithic organizations are of great concern in many egalitarian movements, and they are a source of theoretical problems in the development of a sociology of co-operation.

Social movements may be sustained for centuries. Their ideology is conveyed from generation to generation and restated periodically, depending on the circumstances within various cultures. Also, the values and norms of the movement are reassessed and redefined from time to time, in accordance with changes in the broader social and cultural environment. The membership may expand and shrink at various places and at various times; but most social movements periodically exhibit great bursts of energy and rapid increases in member participation.

If a social movement enjoys initial success and growth, it often splits. Some radical and aggressive members may seek more change and more purity in form; others may be more conservative and content with the achievements already made or in-progress. The movement may survive such internal conflict, but eventually, having run its course, it will come to an end.[17] It may or may not have made a significant impact on the social institutions it has confronted, and rarely are the changes as complete and sweeping as those envisaged in its ideology. The extent of the movement's apparent achievements is often disillusioning to idealists; but in many cases, these individuals may underestimate the progress that has been made.

Many of the non-technological changes that have emerged in society over the past 200 years are the result of the efforts of various social movements to reform existing institutions. Some of these movements have applied the concept of contractual co-operation as a means of attaining their objectives, and one the co-operative movement has adopted a basic philosophy of co-operation to provide a framework for its activities.

This book is concerned primarily with developing a sociological theory that explains the form and evolution of the co-operative movement. The focus on this movement does not mean the theory is limited to only these co-operative organizations. Contractual co-operation is a much broader concept, and the theory in this book should apply to other situations where groups of people are attempting to co-operate contractually.

> Science explains the real, social philosophy judges the real and proposes several changes in order to improve it. Science at the most, does not go beyond the strict and pure intelligence of the real, but, it attempts to seek and to co-ordinate adequate means in order to reach the aims that are given to it by social philosophy or policy.[18]

Social philosophy is the starting-point in developing any theory of social behaviour. Thus, the study of the co-operative movement must begin with an examination of the philosophy on which it is based.

The social philosophy of co-operation is based on collective solutions to human problems. It encompasses the philosophies that emphasize co-operative action in the solution of economic and social problems. The non-exploitation of humans by humans is fundamental. This is also a philosophical position of most of the major religions of the world. Consequently, when the social philosophy of co-operation was being articulated by social philosophers one and two centuries ago, it was closely related to the core philosophical positions in religion and could be viewed as a secularization of these morals into business and economic life.

We can find examples of co-operative activity among mankind prior to written history.

> In one form or another, speculative or reflective interest in co-operation is as old as human thought. Some of the most ancient proverbs and legends embody man's realization not only of the importance but also of the elements of co-operation. From Confucius, Lao-tzu, and Gautama in the Far East, as from the prophets of the Old Testament, the

centrality of the ethic and psychology of co-operation may easily be inferred. For both Plato and Aristotle, co-operation was the keystone of the good state, and what Aristotle called 'status', or political factionalism, was the infallible sign of civic degeneration. In the writings of the Christian fathers, the imperative of co-operation was based in part on their organismic image of the world and society, but also on the remembered reality of early Christian co-operative communities — often indeed communistic — and on the kinds of brotherhood and interest associations that flourished throughout the Middle Ages. The theme of co-operation was a powerful one in medieval religious thought, and a great deal of modern thought on co-operation is but a secularization of this theme.[19]

The type of co-operation to which Nisbet refers was mainly traditional. We are concerned primarily with contractual co-operation. The philosophical values of contractual co-operation emerged out of Europe's changing society in the mid-eighteenth century. Great Britain and Europe at that time were scenes of considerable social change. Feudalism had crumbled. The sheep enclosures had forced serfs off the land and crowded them into the cities. A market economy was emerging, and the industrial revolution was transforming the entire commercial structure for the production and sale of commodities. Many people lived in circumstances of extreme deprivation, as wealth accumulated in the hands of industrialists, corporations and the aristocracy. Gradually, social reformers began to seek solutions to the problem of the destitute and disadvantaged. Their goal was to eliminate poverty and to create an ideal society. Co-operation was one approach that was explored. A social philosophy of co-operation was developed, and attempts were made to put it into practice in everyday life. From the emergence of the movement in the early 1800s to the present, five stages of development can be identified.

STAGES OF CO-OPERATIVE DEVELOPMENT
Stage One: 1817 to 1840

In the first stage of development, philosophers and practitioners struggled to develop the co-operative vision of the good society, and to establish organizations and communities in which this image could be realized. Comprehensive communities, as well as service organizations were conceived and tried. This was an enthusiastic period, when many believed that co-operation was the gateway to the millennium. Their hopes, however, were not to be realized — at least, not in their lifetime.

In England, interest in the movement was triggered by Robert Owen's famous "Report on the Poor," in which he advocated the establishment of co-operative communities.[20] In France, Charles Fourier's proposals for the establishment of phalanxes gained considerable support by practitioners.

> The occasion for Robert Owen's report ... was one of those major crises which have since become an apparently inevitable feature of capitalist economy. Bad as the conditions had been for the industrial workers in Great Britain around the turn of the century, they became literally disastrous with the end of the Napoleonic Wars. The production, geared to the deceptive prosperity of the war years, was now throttled and came to a virtual standstill ... Workers by the thousands were laid off, and the returning soldiers swelled the army of the unemployed. Worst hit was agriculture and the textile industry.... Farms were abandoned and, even if offered for rent free, found no takers. The unemployed were destitute: but even those who still had work could hardly survive on drastically reduced wages... Rioting, demonstrations and machine-wrecking were rampant. The government clamped down on the unruly and the desperate ... (with force).
>
> It was then that a Select Committee, appointed by the House of Commons to report on the poor laws, asked Robert Owen, the industrialist, well known for the philanthropic reforms he had introduced at his factory at New Lanark, to give the Committee the benefit of his counsel. Owen, with a great deal of zeal, summed up his ideas in a report that made co-operative history. Although a successful capitalist himself, Owen saw clearly the shortcomings of the system and was convinced of the need for 'fundamental changes'. As things stood, every increase in production, every step forward in technological progress, he knew from direct experience, served only as an occasion to deepen the gulf between the wealthy and the poor and to make rivalry among the industrialists themselves more brutal. The cure Owen proposed consisted essentially in the creation of conditions that would make it possible for people to work together and live together in 'mutual confidence and kindness', a social

order based on co-operation instead of on competition. The question as Owen saw it could not be one of puny relief measures but rather of a complete transformation of the attitude towards the poor. To safeguard their dignity, he felt, they should be given not charity but an opportunity for self-rehabilitation. Since the means were necessarily limited, he recommended concentration of facilities and personnel. Seeing supervision as the main problem, Owen concluded that it would be more economical to care for the poor in groups than individually. It was thus that he came to conceive his famous plan of the 'villages of co-operation'.[21]

According to Owen's plan the government was to settle the unemployed in groups of from five hundred to fifteen hundred. It was to provide them with land and tools, making them as self-supporting as possible. Both agriculture and basic manufacturing were to be pursued. Everyone was to be free to choose his occupation, but bound to apply himself to it earnestly. Only the children were to be exempt from work. They were to attend school until they grew old enough to take up manual labour, which they were to do gradually, beginning with only a few hours a day.

The Committee rejected Owen's plans and in its report warned the government about the dire consequences if it ever tried to provide work for all. Owen then appealed for public support of his ideas, thus launching the movement in Great Britain.

By 1821, the Co-operative and Economical Society had been formed, proclaiming as its ultimate objective the establishment of a village of unity and mutual co-operation, which combined agriculture, manufacturing and trades upon the plan projected by Robert Owen. The co-operative community (known as New Harmony) was intended to provide universal relief for the suffering of humankind. Everyone was urged to adopt this new scheme and to make themselves part of it. "Owen himself proclaimed that he could not think of any better way of ending his days than as an undistinguished member of one of these happy villages, satisfied with an income of twenty pounds a year, and earning it."[22]

The conduct of the New Harmony experiment was strongly influenced by Owen's experience as a reformer at New Lanark. The great discovery which he disclosed in his 'A New View of Society', and which he claimed to have made by dint of this experience, was that man's character was formed not by him but rather for him. Or, in other words, that man's character was a product of his social environment. Captivated by his discovery, Owen did not stop to consider the several other factors that help shape human character, such as heredity, geographic-climate conditions, nutrition, and so forth. If the bad environment of industrial competitive society produced bad character, all that was needed to produce good character, he reasoned, was an environment of an opposite nature. The fact that man created his social environment as much as he was conditioned by it did not enter into Owen's considerations. He was satisfied that environment was an entity in itself and, true to his role as a manufacturer, he proceeded to treat it like a commodity to be cut to any desired size and shape. His discovery provided the theoretical framework for his approach to community. Being at best only a half-truth, it became the principal cause of all the fumbling that marked the conduct of the New Harmony experiment.

Proceeding from a faulty assumption he kept heaping mistake upon mistake. Heedless of the fact that community at best can be nurtured but never manufactured, Owen spent a great deal of time and effort on blueprints and wooden models. The exaggerated concern with the details of the lay-out proved to be not only of no practical value but it served to befog his whole approach to the problem of organizing the community. Instead of giving first place to the primary requirement of community, the group of people who are to form it, he concentrated all his efforts on securing a place, buildings and other physical facilities, and only then began to look for the people to occupy them, without making any reasonable provisions for selection or guidance.[23]

Meanwhile Charles Fourier was devising detailed plans for co-operative communities in France. Unlike Owen, he was not a man of action, but he inspired others to put his plans into practice. Paul Lambert describes these plans:

First of all he proposes the association be formed in phalanxes, less to solve a problem of distribution and social justice than to solve that of production. He is one of the first reformers who laid stress on the fact that the struggle against pauperism depends more on the increase of production than on better distribution; provided such an increase of production occurs in a social context which would at least secure a proportional distribution of the growing national income. By using such a phrase, I am simply transcribing in our present day language an idea that was already entirely contained in Fourier's works.

The different members of a canton would associate, pool their properties, and first of all their lands, would remove the boundaries that separate them and live, I shall not say in common, for it would be untrue, but within a rationally constructed community called the phalanstery....

The tasks to which the members of the phalanstery devoted themselves related primarily to agriculture and subsidiarily to crafts. Fourier had not been struck by the industrial revolution to the same extent as Owen and Saint-Simon were.[24]

Hirschfeld adds that Fourier "foresaw a transitory mode, a partial realization which was ultimately to lead to phalanstery ... it was these associations which, at least as much as the phalanstery, retained the attention of a number of his disciples."[25] These disciples published a journal to popularize his ideas and in 1833 and set up a phalanx in France. It remained in existence for only a brief period.

Owen and Fourier are considered the fathers of modern co-operation. Their plans were elaborate, and they inspired many with their vision of the good society. Communities were established, but within a few years they all failed. Although the concept continued to inspire people, the possibility of successful implementation seemed remote and disillusionment prevailed.

Owen and Fourier were followed in this first stage of the co-operative movement by Dr. William King. He wrote extensively about co-operation and established a consumer co-operative at Brighton, England.[26] This experiment paved the way for the development of a co-operative movement dominated by service organizations. Service co-operatives are a form of segmental co-operation. Members do not interact as a community involved in a wide range of daily activities; rather, they co-operate only in one limited area of their lives — for example, in the procurement of food.

King's contribution has been summarized as follows:

Even more than Owen, Dr. King was purely a reformer. Even less concerned with all-encompassing ideas than with practical self-help, he became the first determined ad-

vocate of segmental co-operation and helped launch what
became the first vogue of consumers' stores, then called
Union Shops. It is interesting to note, though, that he too
saw in the co-operative community an ultimate goal.

That Dr. King's approach was much more matter-of-
fact than that of Owen can be seen from the following
quotations taken from the first issue of his magazine *The
Co-operator,* May 1828: 'Co-operation means, literally,
working together. Union is strength in all cases, and
without exception. Many hands make short work. What
one man cannot, two may. What is impossible for a few, is
easy for many. But before many can work, they must join
hand in hand; they must know their object, and feel a common interest and a common tie ... at present, in working
for others, we get for ourselves only a small whole'. He
asks 'how is this to be done?', and he answers: 'We must
form ourselves into a society for this special purpose; we
must form a fund by weekly deposits; as soon as it is large
enough, we must lay it out in various commodities which
we must place in a common store, from which all members
must purchase their common necessities, and the profit
will form a common capital to be again laid out in the commodities most wanted'. This, as can be seen, is a perfect
formulation of the way in which a consumers' store is
formed and functions. The method recommended by Dr.
King was first applied by a Society in Brighton and then by
similar societies elsewhere, with so much success that by
1832 there were reported to be in existence four to five
hundred of the new Union Shops. However, two years
later 'the whole movement collapsed'. Chiefly responsible
for this quick disintegration were, probably, the queer
rules which some of the societies adopted. In some instances, a woman was not allowed to withdraw money
without her husband's consent. The Brighton Society itself
broke up, interestingly enough, because of its 'success in
accumulating capital'. When the Society made good, 'the
majority' according to Beatrice Potter, 'wished to realize
their original intention and became communists, while a
more individualistic minority departed with their share of
the capital and ... built themselves a fishing boat'. An experience, by the way, that would seem to indicate that
consumers' stores are beset by the same dangers as Co-
operative Colonies which, as Gide contends, 'are

threatened as much by success as by failure'. As to the 'communists', or as we would say today 'communitarians' and their original intentions, let us note a part of Dr. King's programme usually glossed over by historians. In theory at least, he looks beyond the consumers' store, as the following passage from his programmatic essay shows: 'When the capital has accumulated sufficiently, the Society may purchase land, live upon it, cultivate it themselves, and produce any manufacture they please, and provide for all their wants of food, clothing and houses. The Society will then be called a Community.' How seriously Dr. King himself took this possibility can be seen from the attention he pays to the advantages inherent in community, such as, for example, care for the aged and the widows, the education of the children, and so on. This is worth noting because Dr. King, whose writings fell into oblivion for almost a century, is being hailed by the advocates of segmental co-operation as one of their authorities. The above quotation should offer sufficient proof that his own conception of co-operation, like that of Owen, was all-inclusive.

There is, however, one fundamental difference between the two. While Owen favoured philanthropy, Dr. King insisted on self-help. The money earned by a Union Shop appeared to him to offer a sounder basis for community than did paternalistic bounty, even of a Robert Owen. This view anticipated, and probably influenced, the theory and practice of the Rochdale Pioneers. As to Dr. King's own efforts, their fate was not very different from those of Owen. By 1840, of the hundreds of Union Shops there remained only a few struggling survivors.[27]

During the same era in France, Michel Derrion of Lyon also established a more limited co-operative that was similar to those of King. Lambert points out:

> In 1835, Derrion sets up in Lyon the 'Commerce véridique et social: Derrion et compagnie' (True and Social Trade, Derrion and Co.); this society opened seven or eight retail shops but survived only three years. Derrion applied to the consumer the principle of return, but limited it to 25% of the profits and which was to be 'distributed proportionally each year according to the total amount of the purchases made in the various stores'. Of the remaining three

quarters, following one of Fourier's ideas, one quarter was allocated to share-holders; another quarter to managers and shop-assistants, official workers; a fourth quarter to charitable institutions.

Derrion's major weakness is that he took over from his master a particularly decadent idea, that of the variable return on the capital of the business. Later he continued to be active among the 'dissident fourierists', those who intended to carry out some of Fourier's projects, but who would not consider joining in phalanxes and setting up phalansteries.[28]

Thus, the first stage of the co-operative movement may be characterized as one that put both comprehensive (communities) and segmental (service) co-operation to the test. Both forms failed, but much had been learned which set the stage for more development.

Stage Two: 1844 to World War I

The onset of the second stage in the development of the movement is clearly marked by the appearance in 1844 of the Rochdale Society of Equitable Pioneers. The Society was formed by a group of people in Rochdale, England, who had been meeting regularly for about a year to discuss wages and ways to improve them. They failed to obtain the wage increases they sought from their employers, but they decided to continue meeting and to plan some form of action. A subscription was started in which each contributed two pence a week. They considered migrating out of England, as well as organizing a political lobby, but finally they chose co-operative action.

The detailed story of the Rochdale's Pioneers has been told often and well;[29] therefore, this analysis will be short, drawing out only the essential points. The aims of the group reflected the influence of both Owen and King: ultimately the intention was to establish co-operative communities, but the first step was to set up a co-operative store. These objectives were clearly stated in Article One of the Society's statutes:

> The objects and plans of this society are to form arrangements for the pecuniary benefits, and the improvement of the social and domestic conditions of its members, by raising a sufficient amount of capital in shares of one pound each, to bring into operation the following plans and arrangements.
> • The establishment of a store for the sale of provisions and clothing, etc.

- The building, purchasing or erecting of a number of houses, in which those members desiring to assist each other in improving their domestic and social conditions may reside.
- To commence the manufacture of such articles as society may determine upon, for the employment of such members as may be without employment, or who may be suffering in consequence of repeated reduction in their wages.
- As a further benefit and security to the members of this society, the society shall purchase or rent an estate or estates of land which shall be cultivated by the members who may be out of employment, or whose labour may be badly remunerated.
- That as soon as practicable, this society shall proceed to arrange the power of production, distributions, education, and government, or in other words to establish a self-supporting home colony of united interest, or assist other societies in establishing such colonies.
- That for the promotion of sobriety, a Temperance Hotel be opened in one of the society's houses, as soon as convenient.[30]

The Rochdale Pioneers also developed a set of rules of principles that attempted to capture the essence of the social philosophy of co-operation. These principles were not new, for they had been applied in previous co-operative experiments, but they were unique in the manner in which they were combined. In setting out guidelines for the operation of the Society, the Pioneers hoped to avoid some of the pitfalls encountered by their predecessors. For example, they recognized that, without the dividend principle, King's Union Shops had been unable to accommodate financial success; and other co-operatives that had used the dividend principle had been undermined by their practice of dealing in credit. The rules laid down by the Rochdale Society may be summarized as follows: 1) democratic control; 2) freedom for new members to join; 3) payment of limited interest on capital; 4) distribution of the surplus among the members in proportion to their purchases; 5) cash trading; 6) purity and quality of the products; 7) education of the members; and 8) political and religious neutrality. Two further principles were added at a later date: 9) sale at market prices and 10) voluntary membership.

The Society quickly succeeded, far beyond its founders' expectations. It also came to have a strong influence on the development of the co-operative movement, through its evident success and, more importantly, through the specification of the philosophical principles that must be applied in an economic co-operative organization. The Rochdale Society became the model for similar stores and related enterprises throughout the world. Co-operatives also became more diversified with the establishment of wholesale (in 1862), as well as factories to supply the stores. Farms were purchased, and some attempts were made to implement the more comprehensive co-operative endeavours outlined in the Society's first law. But these more ambitious efforts were only moderately successful, and the British movement concentrated its efforts on developing stores. These stores federated in order to broaden the supply of commodities required by their members. They also developed central institutions to consolidate the movement on the inside, to disseminate information about it, and to defend it from outside attacks. With the emergence of similar consumer movements elsewhere in Europe, the International Co-operative Alliance was established in 1895. It was charged with the task of co-ordinating the activities of affiliated co-operative federations in various parts of the world.

The co-operative movement was not confined to the operation of consumer co-operatives. The other branches, agricultural marketing co-operatives and savings and loans were started in the Raiffiesen movement in Germany. It began in the 1850s, and by 1880 it was well established among the farm population. It was so successful that similar movements soon developed in Austria, Switzerland and Italy. Worker-organized production co-operatives (particularly in France) were also growing. The debates over superior and inferior forms of co-operation were numerous and often heated. Infield observes:

> At this 'more advanced' stage, the co-operative movement witnessed the rise of conflicting ideologies that divided its ranks into a 'more radical, aggressive and a more moderate, conservative wing'. This division resulted from the issues of segmental versus comprehensive co-operation. Those in favour of the latter type of co-operation were strongly influenced by the socialist ideas of French co-operators like P.J.B. Bucher and the example set by Louis Blanc with his National Workshops. Thus, it was co-operative production that became the bone of contention. Essentially, there were two possible ways in which such production could be managed. The moderate wing, for the sake of efficiency, favoured the employment of hired labour; their opponents insisted that only an organization based on 'mutual self-

employment' was compatible with the true meaning of co-operation. The advocates of a 'co-partnership of the workers', the so-called Christian Socialists, found their most articulate exponent in E. Vansittart Neale. That it was not so much the management of production as the form of co-operation that concerned them, can be seen from the argument on which Neale based his appeal for aid in promoting what he called the Labour Association. Denouncing his opponents as nominal co-operators, he accuses them of an attitude utterly against that originally taken by the justly celebrated Pioneers of Rochdale who, as he points out, held out as their ultimate and real object the formation of home colonies, where the workers, sustained by the fruits of their own labour, might be able, by wisely organizing institutions, to secure to themselves, and their belongings every advantage — educational, intellectual, moral, and social number — which this work, aided by all the labour-saving marvels of modern industry, could attain. And, taking the success of their store as a testimony of the foresight of these poor weavers, he declares himself satisfied that they were not less wise in regard to their ultimate object.

Correct as this argument is in itself, it failed because it rested on an untenable case. Like so many who favour producers' co-operatives, Neale apparently confused the principle of profit elimination ... with that of profit sharing. Comprehensive in intent but segmental in practice, the producers' co-operatives suffered from this internal contradiction and were unable to make an impressive showing.[31]

The second stage of co-operative development saw the dominance of consumer co-operatives over other forms more comprehensive in nature like worker and housing co-operatives. Agricultural co-operatives were also looked down on as inferior, as they were seen as cartels for farmers to increase their incomes at the expense of consumers. Implicit in the supremacy of the consumer ideology was a denial of basic class conflicts. Class analysis was not seen as relevant to the co-operative theorists of the day.

Stage Three: World War I to the 1950s

In 1911, another set of co-operatives made their appearance; and by the end of World War I, their development marked the successful beginning of co-operative communities. The kibbutz (initially called *kvutza*) is a comprehensive form of co-operation, and its impact is different from that of segmental co-operatives. Infield describes it as follows:

This extreme type of co-operative community grew out of unique enterprise of resettlement, the Zionist return of Jews to their homeland. The first Kvutza, Dagania Aleph, came into life under circumstances which, in the sense of the dynamic forces at work, were essentially identical with those that prompted the establishment of the Rochdale Store. But in this case, the forces are traceable on two different levels: one, the immediate situation out of which the Kvutza grew, and the other, the conditions out of which grew the Zionist movement. In Eastern Europe, whence came the bulk of pioneers, political, economic, and social discrimination barred the Jews from virtually all normal satisfaction of their basic needs. Zionism, aiming at emancipation through building of a Jewish National Home in Palestine, offered a way out. Once in Palestine, the new settlers faced the imperative need for a sound economic basis. Only agriculture could offer a basis of this kind. Again, two grave difficulties had to be overcome: the desolate condition of the land and the pioneers' own lack of agricultural experience and skill. When traditional individual farming seemed doomed to failure, the pioneers, unwilling to resign, resorted to co-operation.

The first attempt at co-operative settlement, made to specifications furnished by the sociologist Franz Oppenheimer, failed. The original colony Merchavia, it is interesting to note, like so many other socio-reformistic communities, floundered for a while and came to nothing. Setting out, in contrast, without any preconceived plan and animated only by their conviction that group farming would succeed where individual efforts had failed, the ten men and women who established the first Kvutza, Dagania Aleph, formed themselves to begin with, merely into a loose farming co-operative. At the end of the first year, when the time came for sharing the profits there were none to share. Out of necessity they decided to do away with all distinction of assets. They agreed that each should work according to his best abilities and receive all that he/she needed that the common purse allowed.[32]

Thus, in 1911, was laid the basis for the first modern co-operative community. The fundamental change in attitude engendered a spirit of experimentation. New ways of working and living together were explored. In order to free hands for work on the land, one basic activity after another was reshaped along co-operative lines. First the nursery, then the laundry, the kitchen and the dining hall became communal enterprises. In each case the proposition was first thoroughly dismissed, tried and, if beneficial, accepted for good. Truly trial by error, this community grew from practical experience, not from a blueprint developed by a social planner.

Interestingly, as mechanization freed people from the fields, many of the communal activities have moved back to the family. In order to create work for all, the kibbutzim movement in Israel has developed manufacturing industries in conjunction with co-operative farms. These enterprises account for 6% of the industrial output of Israel and 10% of its manufactured exports.

The era from 1911 to 1950 was important for the development of co-operative communities. Voluntary communities were successfully established in Mexico, the United States, Canada and Europe. The co-operative principles as specified by the Rochdale Pioneers for consumer co-operatives were obviously not applicable, and new rules were devised by trial and error. Nevertheless, these communities upheld the fundamental values of contractual co-operation, and they perceived themselves as part of the co-operative movement.

Meanwhile in North America agricultural marketing co-operatives were taking root. The concept of farmers pooling their products through marketing co-operatives in North America was viewed with suspicion by co-operators who saw the consumer as supreme. The principle of voluntary membership was modified with the marketing contract. Once signed, farmers had to deliver all their produce to the co-operative. The principle of democratic control, limited interest on capital and patronage refunds were applied. The principles of cash trading and supplying pure unadulterated goods were irrelevant.[33]

The first half of the twentieth century was marked by the establishment of a solid base for the co-operative movement around the world. Segmental co-operation was firmly rooted in Britain and Europe by the late 1800s, but it had not yet developed on a wide international scale. During the third era, the growth and expansion of consumer and agricultural marketing and supply co-operatives developed strong organizations in many countries. Comprehensive co-operative communities demonstrated their possibilities in a variety of setting, and became established as a viable organizational form.

Another force, centralized socialism (communism), was established in the U.S.S.R. and subsequently in other countries in western Europe and Asia. The Marxist-Leninists in power established government-directed co-operatives. These organizations reflected some similarity in philosophy with the earlier movement. Contractual co-operation was replaced with directed co-operation. As a result of this development, the international co-operative movement was forced to reassess its philosophy and principles. Another cause for concern for the International Cooperative Alliance (ICA) members was modification of the Rochdale rules by the large agricultural marketing co-operatives that had developed in Europe, Canada and United States, as well as by the comprehensive co-operatives (both agricultural and worker production organizations). The ICA officials saw the development of wheat pools in Canada as an aberration and refused to recognize them as co-operatives. This was changed by inviting ICA officials to meet the leaders and groups of members.[34] They appreciated that these were dedicated co-operators and the Rochdale Principles developed for retail co-operatives just didn't fit all circumstances. They acted:

> From 1931 to 1934, a committee of the International Co-operative Alliance (ICA) studied for Present Application of Rochdale Principles with a view to assisting the ICA authorities to determine their precise application when identifying a co-operative of any type, from any part of the world, as being eligible for membership of the ICA and in consequence being considered a true co-operative suitable for membership....[35]

The report of the committee, released in 1934, triggered a number of responses from specific movements. These responses were studied, and a final report was made in 1937. The report recognized seven principles, but concluded that only four of these could be applied universally to all forms of co-operatives. These four were voluntary membership; democratic control; distribution of surplus to the members in proportion to their participation in the transaction of their society, and limited interest on capital. The other Rochdale principles were not formally discarded, but were considered to apply primarily to consumer co-operatives. As a result of this process of re-examination, the organizational variations within the movement were recognized. Yet the similarities continued to be emphasized in co-operative literature. This emphasis on similarity at the international level, rather than an in-depth attempt to establish distinctive types and to study these types, slowed the development of co-operative theory.

During this third stage of development, the supremacy of consumer co-operatives was successfully challenged, but the ideology of the movement — a new world order in a co-operative commonwealth — was only partially accepted. A growing proportion of movements accepted the position set forth in the 1930s by Fauquet to the effect that co-operatives represented a "co-operative sector" of a nation's economy, which was fundamentally different from the capitalist or the State sector but which, significantly, was not a new world order.[36] Another group clearly saw co-operatives in a supportive role to centralized planning and direction from the State. Ideological debates continued in some forums; but for the most part, the various movements went their own way, struggling to solve the immediate problems faced by their organizations.

Stage Four: The 1950s to the 1970s

The fourth stage is marked with a new dimension: the extension of government-directed co-operation. The world-wide co-operative movement is still struggling to come to terms with the change. Before World War II, the formation of co-operatives usually occurred with very little governmental encouragement and often in the face of hostility from the social and economic establishment. But after World War II, the race for quick development was pressing in the newly independent countries in Africa and Asia, and directed co-operation was widely adopted by the governments in the emerging nations. As colonialism crumbled by the end of the war, co-operation was accepted as good and desirable by many of the independence movements. After independence, co-operatives were started by the governments, with considerable assistance from "outside experts." The social environment shifted: co-operatives were now promoted by the United Nations agencies,[37] in bilateral aid programmes, through grassroots projects like the U.S.A. Peace Corps, and those sustained by volunteers from other countries. Church missionaries representing various denominations also promoted co-operatives. Co-operatives became popular organizational forms with numerous social reformers.

At the same time, the new prosperity of industrialized countries resulted in a dramatic growth of all forms of service co-operatives. By the 1960s, co-operatives in general, and agricultural co-operatives in particular, had become a major force. Amalgamation of smaller primary societies occurred in most of the industrialized countries; and by the end of the 1960s, service co-operatives in Europe, North America and

Japan were forming international business linkages. Multinational co-operatives had emerged.[38] The social upheavals of the 1960s meant a rediscovery of co-operatives by youth looking for an alternative. In North America The North American Students of Co-operation Organization (NASCO) was formed to be a clearing house for new student housing co-operatives, new types of food co-operatives and other co-operatives formed as alternatives to the corporate world. Co-operatives became the in thing for reformers, and expectations were created that they could solve all kinds of economic and social problems.

By the end of the 1970s the research was showing a clear pattern.[39] Most of the government-directed initiatives had created co-operatives that were dominated by the government's logic and not seen by the members as their organizations. Studies by the United Nations Research Institute for Social Development (UNRISD) showed this very clearly.[40] The picture at the end of the 1970s was one of contrasts. Co-operatives in the developed countries were facing strong competition. To survive they merged and formed larger and larger organizations. Management practices followed those in the private profit sector and the distinctiveness of the organizations was being lost. In the developing countries, the picture was also not encouraging, as government sponsored co-operatives were often inefficient and not respected by the members. The movement appeared to be in decline. Social reformers were looking for other organizational forms to promote. A closer look however showed some bright spots, which formed the social energy for the next era.

The Present Stage: The 1980s to the Present

By the end of the 1970s studies were starting to show that in developing countries a new wave of co-operatives was growing beyond the influence of the government ministries. The use of participatory action research and community development techniques meant co-operatives were developing in local communities without the top-down paternalistic approach, and a new wave of organizations was emerging. Laidlaw outlines the state of the world movement at the end of the 1970s. He found that commitment by members was declining along with their participation, the neglect of member education was taking its toll, and the potential of co-operatives was not understood by the general public. The movements around the world had an image problem and were in crisis and struggling.[41]

He concluded his global study with four recommendations:

1. In the years ahead, co-operatives everywhere should concentrate especially on the world problem of FOOD, all

the way from farming to consumer. It is an area of great human need in which the co-operative movement is in a position to give world leadership.

2. Workers' productive and industrial co-operatives are the best means to create a new relationship between workers and the workplace, and to bring about another industrial revolution.

3. The traditional consumer co-operative should be orientated in such a way that it will be doing something more than merely trying to compete with a capitalist business. It will be known as a unique and different kind of business and will serve only members.

4. To serve the urban population, there should be a cluster of many different kinds of co-operatives that have the effect of creating villages within the city.[42]

Interestingly, these trends Laidlaw saw as critical in 1980 have continued to develop and are gaining strength in the 1990s.

The agricultural co-operatives that developed independently of governments have made dramatic progress in addressing the food problem. Farmer-centred enterprises are once again emphasized by developers.[43] The Chinese reforms in 1978 allowed co-operatives to develop. By the mid 1980s, 141 million farm families were members of 35,000 agricultural marketing and supply co-operatives. India became self-sufficient in milk in two decades as Operation Flood developed a network of co-operatives owned by milk producers. These two countries represent nearly one half of the world's population!

The privatization drive by many governments in the 1980s meant that people were faced with either waiting for individuals to provide the services being abandoned by government or providing them for themselves in their communities. Day care, nursery, and other service co-operatives have been incorporated in record numbers. Community health clinics with an emphasis on preventative medicine have provided an alternative for increasingly expensive health costs.[44]

Worker co-operatives stimulated by the outstanding success of Mondragon co-operatives in Spain and elsewhere in Europe are emerging as a movement in Europe and North America.[45] This development is complemented by the transfer of manufacturing to lower-wage countries and the attempt by communities and workers to retain jobs. Communities are facing the reality that big government and big business cannot resolve their problems. Participatory development at the community level is gaining importance and co-operatives are being rediscovered.[46] Other forms are also developing; ESOPs (Employee Share Ownership Plans) are widespread in the United States and growing in Canada. These are not worker co-operatives but can be seen as a first phase in worker ownership. In Canada the Co-operators Data Services Limited was converted to a multi-stakeholder organization that has given voice to the workers, users and capital suppliers.[47]

These newer developments will be explored in more detail in later chapters. The point is that the current era of co-operative development has seen a new emphasis on community involvement and organizing.[48] The needs are different from the last century or from the first half of this century, so the organizations are different, but the goal of people co-operating is still strong.

CO-OPERATIVE PRINCIPLES AND VALUES

The developments in the fourth phase prompted another look at the principles and philosophy of the world movement. The International Co-operative Alliance Congress of 1963 decided to instruct the Central Committee to appoint a commission to examine the current application of co-operative principles. The study was to include different types of societies in different political and economic spheres. The intent was to obtain advice on the right formulation of co-operative principles in light of their application throughout the world. In March 1966, the Commission reported to the Central Committee and to the 1966 Congress. The Commission of five represented the movements from Great Britain, the United States, Germany, India and the U.S.S.R. It involved spokesmen from service co-operatives, comprehensive community co-operatives, voluntary movements and government-directed movements. After long deliberations, this group agreed on the six principles set out in Figure 2.2. These principles were subsequently adopted by the Congress, with wide acceptance among its membership.

The principles that distinguish co-operative from non-co-operative organizations are a translation of the philosophical values of the movement, rather than a literal statement of the values themselves. It is suggested here that the social philosophy of co-operation is founded on three basic value sets of equality, equity or economic justice and mutual self-help.

The value base of co-operatives comes from two sources. From the inherent logic of co-operation and secondly from the aspirations

Figure 2.2

THE ESSENTIAL PRINCIPLES OF CO-OPERATIVE ORGANIZATIONS

1. Open and Voluntary Membership

Membership of a co-operative society should be voluntary and available, without artificial restriction or any social, political or religious discrimination, to all persons who can make use of its services and are willing to accept the responsibilities of membership.

2. Democratic Control

Co-operative societies are democratic organizations. Their affairs should be administered by persons elected or appointed in a manner agreed by the members and accountable to them. Members of primary societies should enjoy equal rights of voting (one member, one vote) and participation in decisions affecting their societies; in other than primary societies the administration should be conducted on a democratic basis in a suitable form.

3. Limited Interest On Shares

Share capital should receive only a strictly limited rate of interest, if any.

4. Return of Surplus to Members

Surplus or savings, if any, arising out of the operations of a society belong to the members of that society and should be distributed in such a manner as would avoid one member gaining at the expense of others. This may be done by a decision of the members as follows:
(a) by provision for development of the business of the co-operative.
(b) by distribution among the members in proportion to their transactions with the society.

5. Co-operative Education

All co-operative societies should make provisions for the education of their members, officers and employees, and the general public, in the principles and techniques of co-operation, both economic and democratic.

6. Co-operation Between Co-operatives

All co-operative organizations, in order to best serve the interests of their members and their communities, should actively co-operate in every practical way with other co-operatives at local and international levels.

(Formulated by the ICA Commission on Principles and adopted at the 23rd ICA Congress in Vienna, September 1966.)

of the groups that organize co-operatives to achieve their goals. In both cases "values correspond to the orientation of human action in terms of final targets. In the ideological sense, value means an attitude to what is good and desirable or ideal."[49]

It is widely accepted that the co-operative principles are based on the basic fundamental values that underlie the idea and ideals of co-operation. The actual principles themselves are statements to guide co-operators in creating co-operatives and are not statements of the core values of co-operation. The individual core values of co-operation may not be unique to co-operatives or co-operators but may be shared with other movements or groups.

These values are the moral basis of co-operation and are embodied in the essence of co-operation. They may not be achieved in any given organization but are being striven for in many organizations. We would expect that the various values will vary in importance both within and between different parts of the world movement and in different eras. Values held by co-operators will be influenced by the major issues and cultural heritages that members bring to their organizations. For this reason values must be general in nature, yet understandable to ordinary members within a socio-economic cultural context.

The essence of co-operation may be summarized as follows:

> Co-operation is the free and voluntary association of people to create an organization which they democratically control, providing themselves with goods, services and/or a livelihood rather than profiting from others, with an equitable contribution of capital and acceptance of a fair share of risks and benefits generated by the joint activity. To sustain their endeavour they must develop individuals and build a solidarity relationship with other co-operators and like minded people.[50]

If there is agreement on the statement of the essence of co-operation then we need to unpack it and discuss the ideals or the final targets of what co-operative activity is about.

Junani Laurinkari sees the basis for co-operation as a search for justice, and the basic values must be seen in this light. He analyzes solidarity as justice, freedom as justice and equal rights as justice. Since the basis for co-operation is a quest for justice, Laurinkari (1986) is rightly critical of Craig for analyzing the basic values of co-operation in isolation from the basic value of justice. Justice for individuals through mutual assistance is the basic cornerstone of

Figure 2.3

RELATIONSHIP OF PRINCIPLES TO THE UNDERLYING VALUES OF
CO-OPERATION

Principles	Value Sets
1. Open and voluntary membership 2. Democratic control	2) Equality, human rights and freedom
3. Limited interest on shares 4. Return of surplus to members	3) Economic justice
5. Co-operative education 6. Co-operation between co-operatives	1) Mutual assistance

co-operation and the academic analysis of the underlying values. In short, it becomes impossible to isolate the values without acknowledging that most values cannot be realized without focusing on a set of related basic values.

There is no complete agreement on the essential values of co-operation. Lambert defines the essential nature of co-operation as follows: self-help; voluntary nature; mutual aid; democratic autonomy; elimination of profit; educational purpose; socialist nature; and striving to conquer. W.P. Watkins identifies seven fundamental principles of co-operation: solidarity; economy; equity; democracy; liberty; mutual responsibility; and education. Maurice Colombain builds on Fauquet's differentiation of co-operation in terms of association and its economic features. He lists five principles: solidarity or mutual commitment; equality in relation to the economic undertaking; service function; equity; and co-operative education. All three writers have attempted to specify the principles behind the rules. Watkins states that "the principles are well grounded in the concept of mutual aid." Mutual self-help implies solidarity and mutual commitment. The equality value is implicit in democracy, and the equity or justice relates to the economic nature. These three value sets are basic to the principles elaborated above by Laurinkari, Lambert, Watkins and Colombain.

Laurinkari argues that the first principle of co-operation is based on the outcome of freedom. This is insightful and very helpful in grasping the basic values. Figure 2.4 indicates that the values that have been identified by several scholars can be clustered into value sets

Figure 2.4

COMPARISON OF BASIC CO-OPERATIVE VALUES IDENTIFIED BY SELECTED SCHOLARS, VALUE SETS

VALUE SET	Laurinkari (1986: 309-315)	Craig (1980: 7-13)	Lambert (1963: 239-241)	Watkins (1986: 18-138)	Colombain (1976: 5-18)
1) MUTUAL ASSISTANCE	Solidarity as justice	Mutual self-help	Self-help Mutual aid Education Socialist nature Striving to conquer	Association or unity Economy Education Responsibility	Solidarity or mutual commitment Cooperative education
2) EQUALITY FREEDOM	Equal rights as justice	Equality	Democratic autonomy	Democracy	Equality in relation to the economic undertaking
3) ECONOMIC JUSTICE	Freedom as justice	Equity	Voluntary nature Elimination	Equity Liberty	Service Equity

which share a common unity and relate to the "Essential Principles of Co-operation." I have identified three sets which keep reappearing in the literature and relate to the six principles of co-operation. They are illustrated as follows in Figure 2.3 and the values are summarized in Figure 2.4

Academics could continue to debate the intricate details of which values are more global, most basic and most important. However for most co-operators this is unnecessary. They would prefer that all the values that reflect their fundamental ideals be clearly stated and captured in the discussion.

The International Co-operative Alliance at its Congress in Tokyo, 1992 did just that. They identified three kinds of basic values that are a part of the basic values. These are BASIC IDEAS, BASIC ETHICS and BASIC PRINCIPLES.

The basic ideas that are central to the concept of co-operation are listed in Figure 2.3 as value sets. They acknowledge that these can be interpreted in a variety of ways in the world on the basis of different political economic and cultural conditions.

The basic ethics are close to the basic ideas and are stated as personal characteristics of co-operators. They represent the co-operative culture or co-operative spirit for the organization as a whole. These include values of honesty, caring, pluralism (democratic approach) and constructiveness. They conclude with the observation that the principles set down in 1966 need to be restated in order to better reflect basic values. This is a task that will be addressed during the 1990s.

The three value sets are matched with specific principles in order to illustrate the relationships between them. But all three value sets are reflected to some degree in all six principles, and they should be thought of as a whole, rather than as separate and discrete entities. Collectively, they contain the spirit of the philosophy of co-operation.

By identifying the common sets of basic values we can list statements that seem to capture the essence of the basic values that various co-operators around the world experience in the movements in which they are involved. It would help to sharpen contradictions and in the process give us a better feel for the basic values inherent in co-operation.

The following is a list of value statements that have been deduced from the logic of co-operation and made in the literature. They are listed under the three value sets. No claim is made that they are exhaustive or listed in order of importance. An exhaustive list can only be done as an outcome of the discussion within the various co-operative movements around the world.

Mutual Assistance

a) Association or unity. The idea of individuals or entities joining together, combining, integrating and remaining united in order to satisfy common needs, achieve common ends, or derive mutual advantage from their association.

b) Economy. The essence of Co-operative Economy is the assumption by an association of the functions of ownership, organization and risk-bearing usually discharged by an individual.

c) Education. A movement must begin and continue in the minds of men and women. There can be no co-operation without co-operators, and co-operators must learn. People also need to have a mental set that when faced with problems they can not solve individually, they work together rather than fighting in frustration.

d) Social responsibility. An association of persons means individual have rights and responsibilities. The ideals in co-operation means co-operators everywhere are responsible both for and to one another. This value would encompass statements around the following:

i) Peace and disarmament. "The causes of war are economic."[51] It is argued that the proliferation of co-operatives reducing economic exploitation of the masses will reduce the support for leaders advocating war and hatred.[52]

ii) Honesty Trust and Openness. Co-operatives are by nature forced to be honest and quality minded because otherwise they cannot serve their members.

iii) Caring about others. This is a basic value that stems from our nature as a self-help organization.[53] Caring doesn't mean co-operatives are philanthropic or charities. They are businesses, but care about members and potential members and try to address changing needs. Mutual assistance implies that people can be masters of their own destinies by working with their neighbours rather than against them. This value is fundamental to the last two co-operative principles; co-operative education and co-operation between co-operatives.

Equality, Equal Rights and Freedom

a) Member Participation. Co-operatives are only strong if they are able to mobilize people. Participation is to basic the ideas of co-operatives and may take many forms, both formal and informal.

b) Democracy. A pre-requisite for member participation is democracy.[54] "A means for ascertaining and expressing the general will of the members."[55] Once again the idea of democracy is basic, but the way it is operationalized will vary considerably. In small organizations it is often direct, with members making day-to-day decisions. In large organizations it may be mainly representative, where members' main responsibility is to elect directors that make decisions on behalf of the members. The organization may evolve elaborate structures, as in the Han groups in the consumer co-operatives in Japan, or may be very simple, as in many European co-operatives. The test is whether the process is democratic in the eyes of the members.

c) Liberty. "The freedom to become members and the freedom of thought and action while they are members" is basic.[56] Once again the perception of freedom by those involved is an important dimension in this value, and circumstances will vary in time and place.

The equality, equal rights and freedom value set recognizes that people are important because they are people. It does not imply that all are equal in abilities, intelligence or other resources; rather, it is related to potential. Because of our humanity, all should have equal access to resources and all should have equal opportunity to control the forces that shape our lives. It is not suggested that all must find an equal level of mediocrity; equality is a liberating concept which proposes that all may aspire to achieve excellence. The value of equality is reflected in the first two principles of co-operative organization: open and voluntary membership, and democratic control.

Economic Justice

These are values that flow from the working of co-operatives both within a market economy and in a planned economy.

a) Equity. As a value, equity requires that "substantial justice shall be done to all the interests."[57]

b) Pooling. William King stated in 1929 "Co-operation affords to the workman a near prospect of independence" by pooling his capital.[58] By pooling, capital, or marketing power, or purchasing power, or labour co-operation may be achieved and may provide benefits to those co-operating.

c) Improving the quality of life in members communities. This would comprise many specific activities, including a respect for the physical environment. This has been raised by a number of scholars in addressing the values of co-operation.[59]

Economic justice or equity is another fundamental value of co-operation. It means being fair and just. Its connotation is one of distributive justice. Slogans such as a "just society" and "justice for all" reflect this value. The application of the equity and equality values creates situations where people respect and trust each other and where a sense of community can emerge. Equity is the essential value reflected in the third and a fourth principles of co-operative organizations: limited interest on shares and return of surplus to members.

The three values have been separated out and matched with specific principles in order to define them clearly and illustrate the relationships between them. But all three values are reflected to some degree in all six principles, and they should be thought of as a whole, rather than as separate concepts. Collectively, they contain the spirit of the philosophy of co-operation.

ASPIRATIONS OF THOSE ORGANIZING THE CO-OPERATIVE

An analysis of the value and mission statements of various co-operatives shows more values than those implied in the logic of co-operation. For example the Mondragon co-operative movement has the explicit value of creating jobs for the people in the Mondragon region of Spain. Similarly the Québec-based Desjardins Confederation holds to the basic value of "Solidarity with the local community which implies investment to create more job creating enterprises when unemployment exists." This solidarity with the local Québec population means that the local population can see the movement as a vehicle to further their nationalist aspirations. The farmers in western Canada organized the Wheat Pools to achieve orderly marketing of wheat. The values of working together are reflected in creating organizations with the mission to change the marketing system.

Co-operatives are not isolated from the socio-economic and cultural context of the members. They are a useful organizational structure to further the aspirations and values of a particular group. As a result it is possible to find co-operatives with values where racial discrimination may be practised (e.g., South Africa), or where there is violence against another group, even though the values inherent in co-operation are in conflict.

Finally, the value base of any given organization may reflect the values of the small elite group that has managed to take control. It may be the management, a political party or other groups. It is important to distinguish the source of the values when analyzing values statements.

The above is a framework to explore the underlying values of co-operation. The intent is not to provide a definitive analysis or to rank the values in importance. Rather, I wish to identify values that have been seen in the past as basic to co-operation in order to focus on the underlying values of co-operation in terms of the present co-operative movements.

Co-operation is a social process that occurs in many situations in society. Co-operatives are organizational structures that have evolved from the social philosophy of co-operation. They are an attempt to apply co-operation to everyday activities, particularly in the economic sector of society. The philosophical values and rules apply both to segmental or service co-operatives and to comprehensive co-operative communities. Yet the rationale used in decision-making and dynamics of these two types are very different in practice and lead to different outcomes. Also, the values and principles of co-operation are accepted in situations where both conceptual and directed co-operation dominate. In most cases, directed co-operation is seen as a preliminary stage. The voluntary aspect is temporarily suspended, and the democratic principle is interpreted slightly differently.

As in the 1930s, the assessment of co-operative philosophy carried out by the ICA in the 1960s focused solely on principles. There was no detailed analysis of the workings of co-operative organizations, and the crucial question of the goals of the movement or the goals of particular types of co-operatives was neither studied nor debated. No significant effort was made to come to terms with the discrepancy between the promise of co-operation and its practice. New converts to the movement read about the promises and goals from the last century and attempted to apply them to twentieth-century conditions. Again, the development of co-operative theory lagged.[60]

The 1970s did not realize the promises of a new world order, in which countries with modern economies based on co-operation are linked with strong co-operative sectors in the industrialized nations. Studies of co-operative movements in developing countries have identified massive failures; and even where co-operatives have succeeded economically, often social progress has not followed. In the developed countries, the huge agricultural marketing co-operatives, which leaders promised in the 1930s would be the salvation of the farmers, are now often viewed as just another agribusiness.

Disillusionment with co-operative endeavour is not confined to developing countries and the Western industrialized nations. The promises of Marxism in the nineteenth century were the revolution of the proletariat, the destruction of capitalism, the establishment of the dictatorship of the proletariat, then the withering of the State and a new prosperity of workers who controlled their own jobs and shared in its surplus value. These goals, too, have remained unattainable. The State of the U.S.S.R. and other east-block countries have withered, but not the way Marx predicted. Planned economies have failed and are now discredited. Marxist-Leninist socialism ridiculed co-operative socialism as being utopian, reformist in nature and, with other forms of democratic socialism, doomed to failure. But, as the twenty-first century approaches, democracy is winning the day. Even the last bastion of authoritarianism, the bureaucracies of government and big business are being challenged as workers and the populations in general look for more economic democracy. The Marxist-Leninist governments in the U.S.S.R., Poland, Czechoslovakia, the Democratic Republic of Germany, Hungary, Bulgaria, Rumania, Yugoslavia, Albania and Cuba have all professed to implement Marxian socialism, but the promise of economic democracy and the elimination of worker alienation never occurred. Since the events of late 1989, communism has collapsed; all bureaucracies are moving away from totalitarian socialism, and it is unclear how they will evolve. The co-operatives once dominated by the State are struggling to become and to be seen as member-owned. Whether they can make this transition and survive is unclear.

For the co-operative movement, the growth of voluntary service co-operatives in the developed countries has been dramatic. Voluntary, comprehensive, co-operative communities have proven viable, and considerable growth has occurred. Co-operatives have shown, in practical ways, that they can modify the excesses of capitalism. Yet the promise of a new world order has been abandoned by many co-operators who once held this ideal. Co-operative theory and an analysis of the dynamics of co-operation in practice should shed some light on this situation.

CO-OPERATION AND IDEOLOGY

The above discussion has outlined how ideas in co-operation have evolved. There is, however, more to be said in explaining the existence of such organizations. The underlying social philosophy of co-operation also provides the basis for a co-operative ideology; and ideology is an important factor in understanding why people and organizations behave in the way they do. So we can rightfully still ask:

Where does all this co-operative activity lead? What is the goal for which co-operators are aiming? Is it merely a more efficient economic system? It is that; but it is something more. Is it a more satisfying economic system because it is more moral and because it solves most of the present day problems of industry and commerce? It is that; but it is something more, for co-operation has other aims than economic ones. The earnest co-operator seeks to apply co-operative methods to all purposes of social life, and does so because he believes that in working with others for the common good, man's highest qualities are enlisted and developed; and in the employment and development of these qualities the man himself becomes a better man, and the quality of the human race is improved.[61]

It seems that co-operativism as a social movement is attempting to change not only society, but the human race as well.[62] As we have seen, it is centred on the value sets of equality, equity and self-help through mutual aid. These values constitute the foundation of co-operative ideology. Ideology, it will be recalled, represents an image of the good society and the means of achieving it. This conceptualization does not, however, occur in a pure or isolated setting:

> Every ideology — however great the originality of its creators — arises in the midst of an ongoing culture. However passionate its reaction against that culture, it cannot entirely divest itself of important elements of that culture. Ideologies are responses to insufficient regard for some particular element in the dominant outlook and are attempts to place that neglected element in a more central position and to bring it into fulfilment. There are, therefore, always marked substantive affinities between the moral and cognitive orientations of any particular ideology and those ... which prevail in the environing society.[63]

Social movements that persist over many years and become transplanted into new cultural settings frequently experience modifications in their ideology. The central values remain unchanged, but the nature and scope of the movement's goals may be altered, along with the recommended methods of reaching these objectives. Co-operativism is no exception. Over time, its ideology has evolved in new directions, so that five distinct schools of thought can be identified. These focus variously upon: the goal of a co-operative commonwealth; the idea of a co-operative economic sector; the relationship of co-operativism to Marxist-Leninist socialism; the concept of modified capitalism; and what we might call new age co-operativism. Each of these schools of thought or ideological orientations will be discussed in relation to other dominant social, political and economic theories of the time; for the latter have had a direct influence upon the evolutionary process. Ideology also has an impact upon the rationale for decision-making in organizations. This is explored at the end of the chapter.

The Co-operative Commonwealth

The co-operative movement arose in an era of *laissez-faire* government and highly exploitive capitalism. It opposed the domination of individuals with capital, the profit motive and the inequitable distribution of wealth and income (inequitable because it does not correspond to effort, merit or need). Differences in wealth resulted in differences in power and influence in economic, social and political life in the nineteenth-century Europe.

The argument for the profit motive is that, although capitalism may not result in an equitable distribution of wealth, it is still justified because it so increases wealth that everyone is better off. It is suggested that the poorest people are better off with a small slice of a big economic pie than with a big slice of a small pie. In the nineteenth century, the profit motive was heralded as the spur of economic progress. It reflected social needs and preferences, and induced productive resources to flow in the right proportions (in the long term) into various channels of production corresponding with those needs and preferences.

Against this it may be argued that capitalism generates many restrictive practices which keep the pie smaller than it might be. There is a great deal of unearned income which permits idleness, and owing to the unequal distribution of income neither the price nor the profit index are a true measure of social needs.[64] Neither is there the mobility of resources necessary to enable them to flow easily and quickly to correspond with social needs.[65]

Over time, unrestrained competition leads to monopoly capitalism and centralization, which further negate the alleged relationship between the profit index and social needs. In the process, wage labourers are exploited as well as consumers.

Perhaps the most serious evil of the profit motive, according to co-operators in the co-operative commonwealth tradition and others, is the effect on human character: loss of human dignity and of a sense of personal responsibility — Arnold Bonner summarizes the effects as follows:

> The artist or scientist engaged in lucrative yet anti-social activities may consider he has no responsibility for them, that such responsibility rests with his employers.[66] The typical shareholder in a joint stock company may also feel that he has no responsibility for the way in which the company conducts the business and makes the profits in which he shares. As the company's board of directors may also consider that their prime duty is to make profits for the shareholders, and cannot allow any twinges of individual

conscience to interfere with it, nobody feels morally responsible for the way in which the business is conducted.[67] Moreover they are subject to the dictates of competition. If competitors gain an advantage by malpractice, then they must adopt it to remain in business.... This lack of a sense of responsibility, of indifference to consequence, of assessing the worth of anything by its profitability is partly due to and partly cause of a loss of sense of values.[68]

Co-operators reason that these various ills arise from economic activity being directed to the wrong ends. Different motives for economic behaviour are required for true and lasting social improvement. Co-operativism eliminates the profit motive by applying the principles of fixed interest on capital (which discourages capitalists from investing) and the division of the surplus income (profits) in proportion to participation;[69] and instead of profit, it emphasizes the satisfaction of human needs. Democratic ownership, whereby all members have an equal right to participate, keeps control in the hands of the people the organization serves and keeps the organization responsive to the changing needs of its members.

Co-operatives must accumulate capital in order to serve economic needs, but they may do so without themselves adopting the profit motive. In the co-operative movement, capital accumulation results from the labour of producers and the spending of consumers. It does not come from the exploitation of workers or from the unequal distribution of returns. Capital accumulation permits organizational growth, and with growth there arises the opportunity to form co-operative federations.[70] These federations which exist at the local, national and international levels, allow co-operative organizations to satisfy a very wide range of needs by establishing jointly owned industrial plants, economic infrastructures and educational services. The concept of co-operative organization can, indeed, be extended further to embrace a world-wide co-operative commonwealth, in which free people would engage in economic trade for the benefit of all participants, rather than for the enrichment of a few.

The establishment of a co-operative commonwealth was the goal of British co-operators in nineteenth century. It will be remembered that the vision of Robert Owen and the Rochdale Pioneers was not only to eliminate the profit motive, but also to improve human character. The creation of service co-operatives, such as stores, would provide a capital base to develop comprehensive communities and a new moral order. With free competition in the market place and the absence of State intervention, the idea seemed to be feasible.

The concept of the co-operative commonwealth was also supported in continental Europe, but not as universally as it was in Great Britain. Charles Gide, in his analysis of consumer co-operatives societies, saw a gradual evolution towards the concept of the co-operative commonwealth. He believed that it would become a reality as a result of economic forces, and without the need for a socialist revolution or intervention by the State.[71] Other French co-operative theorists, although sharing the same goal, attributed a more important role to the State. Philippe Buchez and later Louis Blanc outlined plans for self-governing worker co-operatives. Their plans were not inflexible, like those of Owen and Fourier, and they also took into account the power of the State in shaping the economic order. Blanc advocated that the State draw up statutes and provide loan capital to start these social workshops. "Through a successful competition, the social workshops, supported by the State, would progressively engulf capitalist enterprise; the former owners would be paid interest on their contribution."[72] The State would also assume responsibility for managing the economic infrastructure: railways, mines, banks and insurance.

A follower of Gide, Ernest Poisson, published his main work in 1920.[73] He also proclaimed the supremacy of consumer co-operatives, arguing that they could lead to social evolution. His formulation of the "Organic Laws of Co-operation" (the co-operative principles) was the basis of the new order, and the "Law of Indefinite Extendibility" proposed that the concept of consumer co-operation has within it the possibility of limitless extension, to which it is driven by natural impulses. Consumer co-operatives in a competitive situation would grow vertically and horizontally until they swamped capitalism.

> Nothing, therefore, stays the extension of co-operation; no sphere is closed to it; nothing indicates that it will not ultimately succeed. It obeys a law that impels it at all times and in all latitudes. Drawn into all kinds of enterprise, its law, its destiny, is to extend without limit in all economic spheres. Its driving power is its principle of progress and this principle itself springs from its organic laws.[74]

Thus, the natural drive of people joining together to provide themselves with goods and services would produce a completely new economic society, which he called the Co-operative Republic. He acknowledged that the Co-operative Republic would be socialistic, but the methods of attaining it would differ from those of political socialism. Co-operative socialism:

...claims to be establishing itself from now onwards, day by day, and lends no credence to the notion of a great upheaval which would mean no more than the seizure of political power. The Co-operative Republic starts from society as it now is....It revolutionises other social relations. It begins as private property and ends as public property. It substitutes the administration of affairs for the government of men because it tends to deprive the State of its compulsory attributes and abolishes class divisions. It practices the ethics of solidarity and brings to the front once more the national ethics of antiquity, the pursuit of happiness and the love of life, because its basis is the satisfaction of wants.

In a sentence, the Co-operative Republic is shown to be self-sufficient in its own field of action, and to contain in rudimentary form the solution of the social problem which it will accomplish by its own natural and complete development.[75]

Poisson's work was that of a conciliator. He tried to bring the socialism of Gide closer to that of Marxism and other types of socialism. One of his speeches shows how he saw his views fitting with Marxist thought, and how the new co-operative commonwealth could be complimentary. He is quoted by Lambert:

To those who believe only in the political struggle to achieve power, he says in substance: Does co-operation hinder your activities? If you succeed, you will help us triumph over our opponents; we, on the other hand, will have established for you within the old order, the organizations and the officers that you will badly need at that time....

If the Co-operative Republic depends on the organization of production through the consumers needs, if with it the class struggle disappears, if we pass from a regime of restraint to a regime of liberty, there is nothing that can contradict Marxism....Co-operation as a complement to Marxism no longer showing the necessity for the capitalist regime to disappear, but the conditions under which the New Society, the Co-operative Republic, will come into being and develop.[76]

Marx had not been clear on the relationship between his scientific socialism and the co-operative movement.[77] With the Soviet revolution, however, Lenin specified the relationship between Marx-ist-Leninist socialism and co-operativism. The link has been further explained by co-operative theorists in the U.S.S.R., Poland and other centralist socialist States.

The consumer supremacy doctrine was challenged in England by E.V. Neale and T. Hughes in the 1880s.[78] They saw the evolution of a co-operative commonwealth as a combination of consumer co-operatives, controlled by consumers, and production co-operatives, controlled by workers. This concept led to considerable debate and controversy in the British movement, but the goal of a co-operative commonwealth remained one of its central themes well into the twentieth century.

T.W. Mercer further specified this ideal in a book entitled *Towards the Co-operative Commonwealth*.[79] But world events were rapidly over-taking this vision of the good society, and other schools of thought were developing from the writings of other co-operative theorists. In France, Scandinavia and Canada, the idea of a co-operative sector was becoming accepted. In the agricultural sector of the United States, a school of though labelled as "modified capitalism" was being developed.[80]

The co-operative commonwealth ideal was shaped by conditions in England in the nineteenth century — specifically, by the rapid growth of and the existence of a laissez-faire State that allowed com-petition. In these circumstances, the concept of a co-operative com-monwealth was not utopian, but achievable. With the success of the welfare State in Europe, Marxism in the Soviet Union and corporate capitalism in the United States in America, the dominant ideologies had a profound effect on co-operativism. The definition of the good society, to which co-operators aspired, changed. Nevertheless, there was still agreement on the means of attaining it: through co-opera-tive organizations based on co-operative principles.

The Co-operative Sector

In 1935, Dr. G. Fauquet published a small book called *The Co-operative Sector*.[81] In the preface, he states:

> Confronted by the new forms of capitalism and by the in-creasing intervention of the state in economic life, co-operative thought cannot remain wedded to nineteenth-century conceptions, which have ceased to guide and direct the practical activities of the movement...
>
> No doctrine claiming to guide and inspire the co-operative movement can find its moral basis outside the

body of motives and standards of value which within the co-operative institutions themselves direct the wills of co-operators and determine their behaviour. These motives and standards are at once the condition and the product of co-operative activities. Theory records them as facts and does its best to record them. The role of doctrine is to formulate them clearly so that they may be better understood and appreciated in practical application and as a moral influence.[82]

Fauquet argues that economies of most countries consist of four sectors. First, there is the public sector, which is made up of all the enterprises that are run by the State at it various levels (from municipalities to the national government). Second, there is the capitalist sector, comprising all the enterprises dominated by private capital interests, which incur the risks and take the profits. Third, there is the private sector proper (or pre-capitalist sector), which is comprised of the innumerable non-capitalist units and activities of family economy and of peasant and handicraft economy. The fourth is the co-operative sector, which embraces all forms of co-operation already linked or tending to be linked socially and economically.

There are differences between countries in the degree to which each of these four sectors is developed and represented, but Fauquet argues that they are present in all countries. The co-operative sector and the private sector are closely intertwined, as the development of co-operatives tends to associate these small basic units for their common good without impairing their autonomy. The relations of the co-operative sector, it competes and conflicts, though it also engages in business relations within national economies or on international markets. Relations with the public sector are complex, varying with the degree of development of co-operative institutions and the political and economic outlook of the State.

Fauquet's theory represents the co-operative sector as being quite different from the other sectors and capable of performing some functions more effectively, efficiently and humanely than the others. At the same time, the co-operative sector does not have all the answers for economic activity at every point in time and place. Depending upon a host of political, cultural and economic circumstances, there may be activities that are better done by the other three sectors. The goal of co-operatives, then, is to grow, develop and serve the needs of people, so that they can have a fulfilled life. They will be a counter-force to prevent the capitalistic sector from being exploitive and the public sector from becoming overburdened with red tape. Both the capitalist and public sectors tend towards the concentration of power into fewer and fewer hands (those of capitalists and politicians). Co-operatives, on the other hand, have a decentralizing tendency, which enables disadvantaged groups and people in various regions in a country to become masters of their own destinies, instead of being dominated by large and powerful interest groups.

Fauquet's perspective was consistent with the developments of the time, both within the co-operative movement and in the dominant ideologies of liberalism, democratic socialism and the welfare State. The Antigonish movement in Canada, spearheaded by Moses Coady and Father Tompkins, was advocating the development of a co-operative sector through adult education.[83] This approach focused on educating people to identify problems in their communities and then working together to resolve these problems through co-operative action. The development of a strong co-operative sector in Scandinavia, described by Childs and later by Johansson and Böök also is consistent with Fauquet's analysis.[84] The theories did not reject the co-operative commonwealth as an ultimate ideal, but rather envisioned the co-operative sector as achievable and a desirable end for which to strive.

Centralized (Marxist-Leninist) Socialism

Marx and Engels were not explicit about the role of co-operatives. In the communist manifesto they dismissed them as utopian. Later followers saw them as organizations to capture and use to press the class struggle to a political revolution. But Lenin specifically addressed the role of co-operatives, following the Soviet revolution:[85]

> Why were the plans of the old co-operators, from Robert Owen onwards, fantastic? Because they dreamed of peacefully remodelling contemporary society into socialism without taking account of such fundamental questions as the class struggle, the capture of political power by the working class, the overthrow of the rule of the exploiting class. That is why we are right in regarding as entirely fantastic this 'co-operative' socialism, and as romantic, and even banal, the dream of transforming class enemies into class collaborators and class war into class peace (so-called class truce) by merely organizing the population of co-operative societies.
>
> Undoubtedly we were right from the point of view of the fundamental task of the present day, for socialism can-

not be established without a class struggle for political power in the State.

But see how things have changed now that political power is in the hands of the working class, now that the political power of the exploiters is overthrown and all the means of production (except those which the workers' State voluntarily abandons on specified terms and for a certain time to the exploiters in the form of concessions) are owned by the working class.

Now we are entitled to say that for us the mere growth of co-operation (with the 'slight' exception mentioned above) is identical with the growth of socialism, and at the same time we have to admit that there has been a radical modification in our whole outlook on socialism. The radical modification is this; formerly we placed, and had to place, the main emphasis on the political struggle, on revolution, on winning political power, etc. Now the emphasis is changing and shifting to peaceful, organizational, 'cultural' work. I should say that emphasis is shifting to education work, were it not for our international reactions, were it not for the fact that we have to fight for our position on a world scale. If we leave that aside, however, and confine ourselves to internal economic relations, the emphasis in our work is certainly shifting to education.

Two main tasks confront us, which constitute the epoch — to reorganize our machinery of State, which is utterly useless, and which we took over in its entirety from the preceding epoch; during the past five years of struggle we did not, and could not, drastically reorganize it. Our second task is educational work among the peasants. And the economic object of this educational work among the peasants is to organize the latter in co-operative societies. If the whole of the peasantry had been organized in co-operatives, we would by now have been standing with both feet on the soil of socialism. But the organization of the entire peasantry in co-operative societies presupposes a standard of culture among the peasants (precisely among the peasants as the overwhelming mass) that cannot, in fact, be achieved without a cultural revolution.[86]

The educational self-help characteristics were seen as good, but development and the operations of the co-operatives were to be closely co-ordinated with the State plans. State socialization is seen as a superior form to group socialization within co-operatives. In most communist countries, however, co-operatives have been given a role. Cholaj points out that the development of co-operatives in Marxist-Leninist societies is not just a phase in developing the socialist State:

> The co-operative system from the social point of view, fits better such branches in which economic activity is basically decentralized and the concentration and centralization of means of production is not particularly strong....
> Where the economic objective is to meet the needs of a small circle of population, the organization and development of activity through a union of the group of people interested in it, that is that co-operative form, is the most expedient....
> Some branches of economy show greater predisposition to the co-operative form. This applies in particular to agriculture with agricultural processing and turnover, to handicrafts, to retail trade in the countryside and partly in towns, to services and housing construction....
> The co-operative system of economy contains a specific stimulating function. The co-operative form of ownership of enterprises has economic incentives that fulfil useful functions.... They are an expression of the fact that the co-operative enterprise constitutes not only a production unit but also a determined social group, a community that is based not only on technical specialization and hierarchical subordination but also on complex social ties. The interpretation of these ties can contain various accents...The unions of co-operatives can in socialism, and not only in capitalism, look after the interests of the consumers or producers.[87]

Co-operatives within communist countries endorse the idea of voluntary membership, but many of the agricultural co-operatives were introduced by the power of State. Consumer co-operatives were defined as best suited to rural areas. Capitalist stores were nonexistent, and State stores were limited. Citizens often had no other services available except those provided by co-operatives; but as they are not required to become members, there is an element of voluntarism in their participation.

The co-operative principles reformulated in 1966 were accepted and applied in co-operatives in many communist countries, although the image of the good society is quite different from that understood by co-operators elsewhere. Thus, the underlying philosophical values are universal, but the ideology of co-operativism may vary in different socio-political environments.

Communism is not completely monolithic, other views prevail. For some socialist theorists co-operatives and worker self-management are seen as a superior form of socialization to State bureaucratic control. This was the ideology behind worker self-management initiatives in Yugoslavia and the reforms since 1978 in China. To some, co-operatives are seen as an inferior form of socialization to State nationalization and to others they are a superior form. This school of thought have a number of sub-schools.

Modified Capitalism

In England, Scandinavia, France, Belgium and Italy the stimulus to develop co-operatives came from the workers; in North America, it came mainly from the farmers. In some cases, organizers had prior knowledge of European co-operatives, and the North American movement at times reflected this influence. For example, the large marketing co-operatives were aimed at pooling producers' goods as a means of modifying existing capitalist structures and developing a new marketing system controlled by the farmers. The social philosophy was similar to that of credit and consumer co-operatives in Europe, but the social setting was different.

In the agricultural communities of Europe in the early twentieth century, there were often sharp class divisions between landowners, farmers and farm workers. On the North American prairies, however, farmers were themselves landowners, and they and their families did much of the work as well.[88] These farmers were acutely aware that they were exploited, not by landowners, but by a marketing system that was monopolistic and controlled in cities hundreds of miles away.

Until World War II, the ideology of the movement in North America emphasized the uniqueness of co-operatives as compared with capitalist or Marxian socialist organizations. A number of populist political parties — the CCF with left leanings, and Social Credit leaning right — were launched in the prairie region. They were not formally connected with co-operatives, but they grew out of the same discontent and were sympathetic to them. Both types of organization shared many supporters.[89]

The 1930s were a period of poverty for prairie farmers as well as most other farmers in North America. They turned more and more to co-operative organizations. Thus, the movement continued to grow and gradually became institutionalized. The mechanization of agriculture, which began in the 1920s, gained momentum after World

War II. Farms grew in size, and production per farmer increased dramatically. Farms became a business, rather than a way of life for the family.

McCarthyism and the cold war forced the leaders and many members of American farm co-operatives to rethink their ideology. They saw themselves as small capitalists and loyal Americans.[90] At the same time, they were critical of the excesses of capitalism and wished to modify the economy by extending the ownership of agricultural products beyond the farm gate. Market forces worked against farmers, and co-operation was a viable way to influence the market to their benefit. Raymond Miller describes this ideology as follows:

> Capitalistic enterprises develop along various lines: profit and loss corporations, nonprofit co-operative corporations, individual enterprises and partnerships....
>
> Canada and the United States have developed this same general type of co-operative-service capitalism and have largely put the old exploitative type in legal strait jackets....Co-operative-service capitalism has not led to State ownership of all the means of production, Karl Marx advocated. It has not caused the individual to regress into a mere pawn of the State, as is the case in all of the communist countries today. But it has marvellously succeeded in accomplishing all and more than was valuable in Marx's programme.
>
> Our North American system of capitalism centers in the profit motive. It permits the individual citizen to own land and property, productive equipment and resources, to work at a job of his own choosing, to take risks, to compete in the market place—and to keep as his own a fair share of what he earns.[91]

The school of modified capitalism suggests that co-operatives provide a decentralizing influence that counteracts the centralizing tendencies of corporate capitalism. They enable little people with limited means to pool their resources and compete effectively in the market place. By their collective efforts, individuals can improve their income and achieve a higher degree of personal freedom and individualism than they would otherwise enjoy. They argued that co-operatives are not socialist in nature, or a separate sector. Rather they are the epitome of the capitalist ideal. They enable people to become capitalists and lead the way to service-oriented capitalism. This school of thought is strongest in the United States; but, like the co-operative movement itself, this ideology is by no means confined to one country or one continent.

New Age Co-operativism

A new ideological orientation is emerging in Europe and North America. It has grown out of the protest movements of the 1960s and the resource crises dramatized by oil embargoes in the 1970s, and the more recent ecology movement of the 1980s and 90s. This perspective tends to see liberal capitalism, Marxism and the welfare State as leading to intense frustration among people who are confronted with uncaring monolithic organizations. The core problem with present societies is the sheer scale of social organization. Smaller, humanistic organizations are regarded as the ideal.[92]

The good society envisaged by new age co-operativism would replace monolithic organizations with small life-oriented organizations that are community based and understandable by those who use them. This perspective goes further, however, as a cultural shift also must occur. The new culture must be concerned with the process of living, emphasizing self-development, helping others and developing satisfying lifestyles that conserve resources. Co-operatives are seen as an important means of achieving this end.

The co-operative organizations of the new age theorists must be predominately comprehensive, providing support to people so that they can shape and reshape their communities. Service co-operatives are viewed as important as long as they operate in federations. Huge centralized co-operatives are considered to be as undesirable as large capitalist corporations and government bureaucracies, for they too tend to be unwieldy, impersonal and self-serving.

This perspective is not a reactionary one, harking back to the days when life was slower. It advocates using current technologies to reduce the drudgery in life and directing them for the benefit of ordinary individuals. Mark Satin summarizes this point as follows:

> The politics we need in North America today will not and cannot come from liberalism or Marxism, or even from 'just muddling through'. The situation we're in is so new — so unprecedented — that we need a whole new way of looking at the world.... The new politics is arising out of the work and ideas of many of the people in many of the social movements of the 1970s: the spiritual, environmental, feminist, and mens' liberation movements; the human potential, simple living, appropriate-technology, and business-for-

learning and pleasure movements; the humanistic-transfor-
mational education movement and the new nonviolent-ac-
tion movement... Each of these movements and each of
these writers has something to add to the new politics.[93]

The social value of equality, equity and mutual self-help are consistent with this evolving ideology. Co-operatives are seen as one of
the few organizational forms that are consistent with their ideology.
The new age perspective is not yet fully articulated, but it is clearly
evolving through a number of writers.[94] Several recent theorists
elaborate this decentralist ideology with a host of examples of how it
is growing. Co-operatives play a central role in this process of
grassroots change to alter the dominant centralizing pressures in the
world.[95]

IDEOLOGY AND THE RATIONALE FOR DECISION-MAKING

Co-operators and leaders within the movement are typically
preoccupied with the task of resolving pragmatic economic problems
that confront the members of the co-operative organizations. They
do not spend a great deal of time attempting to reconcile their
ideological differences. These differences generally reflect influences
in the larger social environment in which particular organizations
operate. The impact of other ideologies upon co-operativism —
notably, in Third-World countries — will be discussed further in
Chapter 4.

Various ideological orientations affect the rationale used in
making decisions in co-operative organizations; and the decision-
making rationale in turn has an effect upon the dynamics of co-
operation in practice. We shall briefly examine the relationship
between ideology and rationale.

What are good decisions in organizations? How do people in organizations and social movements know which decisions are good
and which are bad? The organization itself must establish criteria by
which to judge both collective and individual decisions. These
criteria are derived from the values and belief systems that are built
into the day-to-day habits of individuals. The values and belief systems may vary considerably between organizations and within organizations. The criteria for judging decisions are rarely discussed
explicitly. They are usually expected to be understood and accepted
by those involved in decision-making, and discussions focus directly
on the matter to be decided. In the process of making any decisions,
participants become aware of the criteria that are being applied.

The criteria for decision-making are of particular interest in the present context: profit, service and meaning. These represent three types of rationale (but there are more) that may be adopted by organizations engaged in activities for an economic purpose. The profit rationale is typically found in capitalistic organizations. Capitalism has a very simple logic, which may be summarized as follows. Individuals have the freedom to pursue their self-interest. When all individuals in a society are pursuing their individual self-interest, they should weigh good and bad decisions in terms of personal profit. Thus, the owner or manager and all the workers in an organization know that the greater the profits attributed to a decision, the better the decision. In corporate capitalism, however, the clear-cut single criterion has been blurred. Many observers of corporations argue that within corporate capitalism the criterion for decision-making has shifted from maximizing profits to growth. Accordingly, when an organization is already extremely profitable, management will seek growth for its own sake, as well as continuing to maximize profits for shareholders. This argument has an intuitive appeal but is not well supported by empirical research.[96] There is evidence that, although the growth criterion has become a factor in decision-making, the profit motive is still the predominant influence.

The logic of this rationale is that if all individuals pursue private profit and their own self-interest, then a decentralized society will be created. When people are pursuing their self-interest, essential tasks are carried out because they have a monetary value. It is assumed that the laws of supply and demand will make the necessary adjustments to society as conditions change, so that the invisible hand of the market place can continue to regulate economic activity. It is further assumed that through this process, an economic system will emerge that will be the best system, and that the decisions of organizations will be the best for a large number of people. Thus, any rules that are imposed by a central authority which reduce growth and personal profits are harmful to the fabric of society. This rationale is contrasted to the rationales in co-operative thought.

There are two rationales that seem to flow logically out of the philosophy and theory of contractual co-operation. Both are consistent with the various schools of co-operative thought that we have reviewed in this chapter. One is the service rationale. This rationale holds that organizations exist to provide services to meet individual needs. Democratic participatory structures are present to enable individuals to define their needs and to translate these needs into tangible services provided by the organizations that they control. Thus, it follows that good decisions made in such organizations are those that meet the service needs of the largest number of individual members over the longest period.

This rationale or belief system also holds that profits, after a reasonable rent on capital is paid, represent a surplus exploited from others. Thus, any profits or surplus in the organization should be returned in monetary or service form to those people who have generated it. In accordance with the belief system of mutual self-help, growth is seen to be of secondary importance to the organization, and assistance to other groups on a non-paternalistic basic is an important value.[97]

All of the various co-operative ideologies accept that the central criterion for decision-making is the provision of the services to the people who use the organization. Co-operative organizations are not ends in themselves, but a means to an end. They exist to serve the members.[98]

The other rationale that is implicit in contractual co-operation is that of involvement in co-operative activities — or, more simply, the meaning of participation. Since co-operative organizations exist to serve people's needs, it follows that participation and dialogue are necessary to enable individuals to specify these needs and to translate them into action. If the participation process is followed to its fullest extent, then the best possible decision for the group at a particular point in time is the one that emerges from this process. Thus, the actual decisions are less important than the manner by which they are reached. In this setting, individuals gain meaning in their lives and a fulfilment of their belief systems through the simple act of co-operating.

Pateman outlines the theory of participation. In her analysis, she draws heavily from the works of Rousseau, Mills and Cole. Rousseau claimed that the ideal situation for decision-making was one in which there were no organized groups but only individuals. He recognized that the coalitions would form, but that the common interest would be uppermost, rather than the support for any particular associations within the group. As a result of participating in decision-making, the individual is educated to distinguish between his/her own impulses and desires. S/he learns to be a public person as well as a private citizen. Thus, the more an individual participates, the more s/he learns about how to participate and the better the public decisions that come out of this process. Rousseau also felt that the human results that accrue through the participatory process provide an important justification for the participatory system.[99]

When importance is placed on the process rather than on the ultimate decisions, a number of integrating functions emerge. First, participation means control over the forces that infringe on one's life. This increasing control results in increased individual freedom. The individual is most free when s/he participates with equals in making the rules and laws that are collectively made. Third, the participatory process increases the feeling among individuals that they belong to their community and that decisions that affect their lives are made in their best interests as individuals.

Involvement in participatory processes results in personal development and personal growth for individuals. The long-term effect is a moral transformation of people. Meaning is generated only through participation, and people can learn to participate only when they are involved in the democratic process of resolving their own problems.

This rationale suggests that concentrated power cannot be trusted. People must define their own needs and must keep control over the means used to meet them. It also holds that, even if our great bureaucracies were run by saints, the needs of the people would go unmet, since a centralized organization must base its policies and its evaluations of those policies upon mathematical demographic generalizations — generalizations that may have but little relevance to the incredibly complex needs of real people.[100] Thus, good and bad decisions cannot be determined by outsiders or by those who are not familiar with the complex needs of the people who are affected by those decisions. With this kind of reasoning, it follows that criteria for good and bad decisions in organizations can be made only by the people involved in a continual, participatory decision-making process.

The three rationales outlined here are not exhaustive or exclusive. There may well be many other rationales that are used in organizational contexts to distinguish between good and bad decisions. The point, however, is that the service and meaning rationales flow clearly out of the philosophy and various ideologies of contractual co-operation. Thus, adherents to co-operativism may use a service rationale in some organizations and a meaning rationale in others in order to judge the quality of decisions. Also, there may be individuals in each organization who employ different rationales. As a result, there may be considerable argument and discussion as to what decisions should be made. For example, a small food co-operative may very well be started by people who hold a meaning rationale. They may meet as a group every few weeks in order to place a collective order with a wholesaler for food. When the order arrives, they then meet and divide up the food into individual orders. This process of working with neighbours and people whom they like and respect

Figure 2:5

IDEOLOGIES AND RATIONALE FOR DECISIONS

Ideologies		Predominant Rational for decisions
Images of a good society	means	
A. Co-operative Commonwealth		
B. Co-operative Sector		
		Segmental co-operation → Service co-ops → Service Rationale
C. Co-operative Socialism		
D. Modified Capitalism		
		Comprehensive co-operation → Co-operative Communities → Meaning Rational
E. New Age Co-operativism		

may be made very meaningful in the lives of participating members. The co-operative may also involve people who have rejected the supermarket mentality and feel that they are gaining a major benefit for their families by obtaining higher-quality food without considerable amounts of added chemicals. This continual process of obtaining food collectively and spending time actually working with others in dividing it may be very meaningful. The decisions made in the organization are concerned not only with providing food services, but also with maintaining the fellowship of participation. However, "success" will threaten these kinds of organizations. If individuals in such buying clubs are saving a good deal of money by co-ordinating their purchasing power, they may attract many other individuals who espouse a service rationale. These people will be interested in obtaining a steady supply of foodstuffs and perhaps opening a regular store. But the act of hiring full-time employees may deprive the original members of some of the meaning of involvement; thus, they may well view the formalization of operations as a negative decision.

The service rational and the meaning rationale are related to many intricate values within the individual's belief system. Thus, their interpretation into day-to-day activity is more complex and less clear-cut than that of the profit rationale. The result is that decision-making is more complicated, although it also may be argued that the quality of the decisions is much superior. To outside observers, it is sometimes difficult to understand why certain decisions are made and others are rejected. The explanation lies in the values and belief systems that are represented in these organizations, through their many individual members. Observers will also find considerable differences between co-operative organizations in their particular mix of the two rationales as a basis for decision-making. The example of the food co-operative clearly shows that the emphasis may change over time, with changes in membership.

In conclusion, the strength and ability of co-operative ideology to capture the imagination of millions of people has, within it, a weakness which enables it to be dominated, reshaped and reworked by other ideologies. The goals of co-operative organizations are limited by the need for decentralization in the interest of democratic decision-making. Decentralization slows decision-making and makes management more complex than in the centralized businesses with which co-operatives compete. The aim of helping the little person may result in an emphasis on maximizing patronage refunds or expanding services. The organization may then maximize refunds or expand services beyond its means, draining its capital reserves; in times of economic difficulties, it may be destroyed completely.

Finally, the rationales that are used in decision-making are decentralist in practice and without the benefit of a centralized authority to specify clearly which are good and bad decisions. The simplistic criteria of greed, self-interest and maximization of profits are easily understood, but are incompatible with co-operative ideologies. Organizations following co-operative principles must sift out for themselves, within their own particular circumstances, which decisions are the most appropriate using a service and/or meaning rationale. These are more complex to understand and provide an added dimension to the organizational dynamics.

NOTES

1. Nisbet, Robert A. 1968. "Co-operation." *International Encyclopedia of the Social Sciences*. 1: 384.
2. Nisbet, 1968: 385-386.
3. Automatic co-operation has been well studied by people interested in crowd behaviour and collective action. For examples of such studies see: Smelser, Neil J. 1962. *Theory of Collective Behavior*. London: Routledge & Kegan Paul; or Olson, Mancur. 1965. *The Logic of Collective Action*. Cambridge: Harvard University Press.
4. This area has been the traditional concern of anthropologists. For example, see Margaret Mead's (1961) pioneering work in the South Pacific. Mead, Margaret. 1961. *Co-operation and Competition Among Primitive Peoples*. Boston: Beacon Press: (c1937).
5. Brooke, Marcus. 1977. "The Real Bali." *Thai International Magazine*, Nov.: 31-34.
6. Stephenson, T.E. 1971. "Conflict in the co-operative retail society." *Annals of Public and Cooperative Economy*, 42 (July-Sept.): 203-217. The author discusses the nature of organizational conflict in general, and conflict in the co-operative society in particular.
7. Nisbet, 1968: 387.
8. Coser, Lewis A. 1968. "Conflict: social aspects." *International Encyclopedia of the Social Sciences*. 3: 232-236.
9. Bromberger, Norman. 1973. *Conflict and Co-operation*. Regina: Saskatchewan Co-operative Credit Society.
10. Kohn, Alfie. 1986. *No Contest: The Case Against Competition*. New York: Houghton Mifflin.
11. Kohn, 1986: 5-9.
12. It cannot be assumed that all members have a commonly held set of beliefs, differentiating them from non-participants. This may be the case for the main activities, but the motivations for the others may be very different. For example see Stallings, Robert A. 1973. "Patterns of belief in social movements: clarifications from an analysis of environmental groups." *Sociological Quarterly*, 14: 465-480.
13. Downs, Anthony. 1957. *An Economic Theory of Democracy*. New York: Harper & Row: 96.
14. A number of typologies of social movements have been developed. For example, see Curtis, Russell L. Jr. and Louis A. Zuncher, Jr. 1974. "Social movements: an analytical exploration of organizational forms." *Social Problems*, 21 (3): 356-370.
15. For an example of the effect that environments may have, see Nelson, Harold A. 1974. "Social movement transformation and pre-movement factor-effect: a preliminary inquiry." *The Sociological Quarterly*, 15 (Winter): 127-142.
16. Banks, J.A. 1972. *The Sociology of Social Movements*. London: Macmillan: 37-39.
17. See Zald, M. and R. Ash. 1966. "Social movement organizational: growth, decay and change." *Social Forces*, 44 (March): 327-341, for a series of propositions regarding the growth, decay and change of social movements.
18. Lambert, Paul. 1963. *Studies in the Social Philosophy of Co-operation*. Manchester: The Co-operative Union: 28.
19. Nisbet, 1968: 384.
20. Robert Owen's life, aspirations and attempts to create co-operative communities have been well documented. For example, see Garnett, R.G. 1972. *Co-operation and Owenite Socialist Communities in Britain 1825-45*. Manchester: Manchester University Press. Morton, A. 1969. *The Life and Ideas of Robert Owen*. New York: International Publishers; and Gattrell, V.A.C. ed., 1969. *Robert Owen: Report to the County of Lanark and A New View of Society*. New York: Penguin. There are also many Robert Owens Associations and Foundations around the

world. The Japanese association recently published an edited volume of research on co-operatives to celebrate the first ICA Congress being held in Asia. See; Tsuzuki, C. 1992. *Robert Owen and the World of Co-operation.* Tokyo: Robert Owen Association of Japan.

21. Infield, Henrik F. 1956b. *The Sociological Study of Co-operation: An Outline.* Loughborough: Co-op College Paper No. 3: 21-22.
22. Podmore, Frank. 1924. *Robert Owen: A Bibliography.* London: 277.
23. Infield. 1956b: 22.
24. Lambert. 1963: 44-45.
25. Hirschfeld, Andre. 1973. "Charles Fourier and the co-operative movement." *Journal of Rural Co-operation,* 1: 11.
26. King's writings, including all the issues of *The Co-operator* and a number of letters, are reprinted in Mercer, T.W. 1947. *Co-operation's Prophet and the Co-operator,* 1828-1830. Manchester: Co-operative Union Ltd.
27. Infield. 1956b: 24-25.
28. Lambert. 1963: 49.
29. See, for example Lambert. 1963, Bonner, Arnold. 1970. *British Co-operation: The History, Principles and Organization of The British Co-operative Movement.* Manchester: Co-operative Union; Carr-Saunders, A.M., P. Sargant, Florence and Robert Peers. 1938. *Consumers' Cooperation in Great Britain.* London: George Allan & Unwin; or Cole, G.D.H. 1944. *A Century of Co-operation.* Manchester: Cooperative Union.
30. Lambert, 1963: 292.
31. Infield. 1956b: 27.
32. Infield. 1956b: 30-31.
33. MacPherson, Ian. 1979. *Each for All: A History of the Co-operative Movement in English Canada,* 1900-1945. Toronto: MacClelland & Stewart (Carlton Library Series).
34. MacPherson. 1979.
35. International Cooperative Alliance. 1967. *Report of ICA on Cooperative Principles.* London: ICA: 2.
36. Fauquet, G. 1951. *The Co-operative Sector.* Manchester: Co-operative Union. (4th edition).
37. The United Nations' first resolution 2459 (XXIII) in 1968 recommended the promotion of co-operatives as "one of the important instruments for the full economic, social and cultural development of all members of society."
38. Craig, J.G. 1976. *Multinational Co-operatives: An Alternative for World Development.* Saskatoon: Western Producer Prairie Books.
39. Fals-Borda, Orlando. 1976. "The crisis of rural cooperatives: problems in Africa, Asia, and Latin American," June Nash et. al., eds., *Popular Participation in Social Change.* The Hague: Mouton: 439-56.
40. The United Nations Research Institute for Social Development (UNRISD) study resulted in seven publications in the early 1970s. A major conclusion was that rural co-operatives in developing countries "today bring little benefits to the masses of poorer inhabitants and cannot be generally regarded as agents of change and development for such groups." Verhagen, Koenraad. 1984. *Co-operation for Survival.* Amsterdam: Cebemo/Royal Tropical Institute. The studies were flawed in many ways but the conclusion about directed co-operation is widely shared by other observers.
41. Laidlaw, Alexander F. 1980. *Co-operatives in the year 2000.* Ottawa: Co-operative Union of Canada.
42. Laidlaw, 1980: 66.
43. Bottomley, Trevor. 1989. *Farmer-Centred Enterprise for Agricultural Development.* Oxford: Plunkett Foundation for Co-operative Studies.

44. Pestoff, Victor A. 1989. *Swedish Consumer Policy as a Welfare Service: Organizations in an Negotiated Economy.* Stockholm: University of Stockholm, Department of Business, Studies in Action and Enterprise.
45. Quarter, Jack and George Melnyk. 1989. *Partners in Enterprise: The Worker Ownership Phenomenon.* Montreal: Black Rose; Whyte, William Foote and Kathleen King Whyte. 1988. *Making Mondragon: The Growth and Dynamics of the Worker Cooperative Complex.* Ithaca New York: ILR Press.
46. Levy, Lair and H. Litwin eds., 1986. *Community and Co-operatives in Participatory Development.* London: Gower.
47. Jordan, John. 1989. "The Multi-stakeholder Concept of Organization," J. Quarter and G. Melnyk, *Partners in Enterprise: The Worker Ownership Phenomenon.* Montreal: Black Rose: 113-31.
48. Holloway, Richard ed. 1989. *Doing Development: Governments, NGOs and the Rural Poor.* London: Earthscan Publications.
49. Laurinkari, Juhani. 1986. *Co-operatives Today: Selected essays from selected fields of co-operative activities.* Geneva: International Co-operative Alliance: 309.
50. Craig and Saxena, 1986: 67.
51. See Kagawa, Toyohiko. 1936. *Brotherhood Economics.* New York: Harper and Brothers. Coady, M.M., 1939 *Masters of Their Own Destiny.* New York: Harpers. p. 165. and Mercer, 1947: 143-146.
52. See Saxena Suren K. 1985. *Co-operatives and Peace.* Markham Ontario Canada: Saxena and Associates, for a discussion of this issue at the international level.
53. Marcus, Lars. 1988. "Co-operatives and Basic Values," in ICA *Report of the ICA Congress,* Stockholm. Geneva: ICA.:100.
54. Marcus, 1988: 99.
55. 1986. *Co-operative Principles: Today and Tomorrow.* Manchester: Holyoake Books, Co-operative Union Ltd: 56.
56. Watkins, 1986: 92.
57. Watkins, 1986: 91.
58. Mercer, 1947: 93.
59. For example see Coady's speech to the United Nations, 1949 in Laidlaw, 1971: 43-49.
60. This is not to degrade the contributions made by Gide, Charles. 1922. *Consumer's Co-operative Societies.* New York: Alfred A. Knopf; or Poisson, Ernest. 1923. *The Co-operative Republic.* Manchester: The Co-operative Union and Fauquet (1951). Their writings remained primarily within academic and international leadership circles during the 1920s and 1930s. By and large, they were not a source of inspiration to the great bulk of practioners. Their contributions remained isolated, rather than triggering debate and follow-up research to further the development of co-operative theory. This process lagged until after World War II.
61. Hall and Watkins, 1934, cited in Bonner. 1970: 472.
62. The term co-operativism is used here to refer to the ideological component of co-operative action. For a discussion on the use of this term, see Saxena, Krishna Kumar. 1974. *Evolution of Co-operative Thought.* New Delhi: Somaiya Publications: 35-37).
63. Shils, 1968: 67.
64. This is evident in the range of consumer goods produced today in North America. The largest and most profitable market is the urban upper-middle-classes. When the needs of the poorer classes are recognized as being different, the corporate response is usually to attempt to reshape their needs by advertising, rather than to reshape the products offered for sale.
65. Bonner. 1970: 473.
66. An example was operation "Camelot" where U.S. social scientists were co-opted into being involved in CIA activities in Latin America.

67. This point is supported by the practice of large multinational corporations of paying bribes to government authorities in return for favours. The extensiveness of this activity has been periodically brought out by U.S. Congressional hearings. For example of this practice in the grain trade, see Morgan, Dan. 1980. *Merchants of Grain.* New York: Penguin.

68. Bonner. 1970: 475.

69. In the case of consumer co-operatives, the division of surplus represents a reduction in the price paid for consumer goods; in the case of farm marketing co-operatives, it represents a higher return for produce. This may appear to be the same as making a profit, but it is different. Any surplus remaining after the payment of employee wages is a fair earning for members of the co-operative, since it is allocated on the basis of participation. Each member is benefitting, not from someone else's labour, but only from their own efforts. The nature of the return is fundamentally different from profits received by investors.

70. For examples at the international level, see Craig, J.G. 1976.

71. Charles Gide's most extensive writings were published in 1922, but his ideas were developed in lectures and speeches starting in 1880 in France. They had considerable influence among co-operative thinkers of that period. Gide, Charles. 1922. *Consumer's Co-operative Societies.* New York: Alfred A. Knopf.

72. Lambert 1963: 58.

73. It was published in English in 1923.

74. Poisson, 1923.

75. Cited in Bonner 1970: 480-482.

76. Lambert. 1963: 121-122.

77. Scholars' interpretations of Marx's writings are in conflict. In some writings, the co-operative movement was lumped with utopian socialism and discounted. However, in a careful analysis of Marx, Shirley Telford (1973) claims that scientific socialism leads to a decentralized network of worker co-operatives with economic exchange based on a market.

78. The concept of consumer supremacy was also rejected by Sydney and Beatrice Webb (1968) in their vision of the co-operative commonwealth. Webb S. and B. Webb. 1968. "Democracies of Producers." Coates Ken, and Anthony Topham, eds., *Industrial Democracy in Great Britain.* London: MacGibbon and Kee.

79. For other writings that convey the ideology of co-operative commonwealth from slightly different perspectives see Grenlund, Laurence. 1886. *The Co-operative Commonwealth.* London: Swan Sonnenschein, LeBas & Lowrey. Lloyd, Henry Demarest. 1963. *Wealth Against Commonwealth.* Englewood Cliffs, N.J.: Prentice Hall (originally published in 1894).

80. These terms have been used by Casselman, P.M. 1952. *Cooperative Movement and Some of its Problems.* New York: Philosophical Library, and more recently by Laidlaw A. 1974. "The Cooperative Sector," paper presented in Columbia Mo. to the Graduate Institute of Cooperative Leadership, University of Missouri. Knapp, Joseph G. 1979. *Edwin G. Nourse: Economist for the People.* Dansville II: Interstate Printers and Publishers.: 91. Nourse saw co-operatives as the "balance wheel" in the economy.

81. It was promptly translated into English and seven other European Languages. The fourth edition (1951) is still in print and available.

82. Fauquet, 1951: 7.

83. See Coady, M.M. 1939. *Masters of Their Own Destiny.* New York: Harpers and Fowler; Bertram B. 1938. *The Lord Helps Those...How the People of Nova Scotia are Solving their Problems through Cooperation.* New York: Vanguard Press.

84. Childs, Marquis William. 1947. *Sweden the Middle Way.* New Haven: Yale University Press (revised and enlarged edition); and Johansson, Tore & Sven Ake Book. 1988. *The Co-operative Movement in Sweden.* Stockholm: The Swedish Society for Co-operative Studies.

85. Immediately after the revolution, the leaders of existing co-operatives were removed and replaced by State appointees.
86. Lenin, V.I. 1923. "On cooperation," in *Collected Works*. Moscow: Progress Publishers, Vol. 33: 467-475.
87. Cholaj, Henryk. 1969. "The changing functions of co-operatives in socialist countries." *Proceedings of the sixth International Conference on Co-operative Science*: 35-38.
88. The exception was at harvest time, when large numbers of unemployed urban labourers would work on the farms for one or two months, then return to the cities.
89. Lipset, S.M. 1968. *Agrarian Socialism*. Garden City, N.Y. Doubleday.
90. The sharpest conflict occurred in the United States, but some arose in Canada as well.
91. Miller, Raymond W. 1964. *A Conservative Looks at Cooperatives*. Athens, Ohio: Ohio University Press.
92. For example, see; Satin, Mark. 1978. *New Age Politics: Healing Self & Society. The Emerging New Alternative to Marxism and Liberalism*. Vancouver: White Cap Books. Also Schumacher, Ernst. 1973. *Small is Beautiful*. New York: Harper and Row. And Kumar, Satish, ed., 1984. *The Schumacher Lectures*. London: Abacus.
93. Mark Satin. 1978: 5.
94. These writers include; Satin. 1978; Illich. 1971; Schumaker. 1973; and McRobie. 1981.
95. Ekin, Paul. 1992. *A New World Order: Grassroots Movements for Global Change*. New York: Routledge. Ostrom, Elinor. 1990. *Governing the Commons: The Evolution of Institutions for Collective Action*. Cambridge University Press, and Melnyk, George. 1985. *The Search For Community: From Utopia to a Co-operative Society*. Montreal: Black Rose Books. Melnyk traces the shift in ideology of co-operatives in western Canada. He demonstrates how ideologies can evolve over time in the same movement.
96. For example see Galbraith, John K. 1967 *The New Industrial State*. New York: Signet Books. or Steiner, G. 1975. *Business and Society*. New York: Random House. or Davis, K. and R.L. Blomstrom. 1975. *Business and Society: Environment and Responsibility* (3rd ed.). New York: McGraw-Hill. All argue that capitalist businesses are less profit-oriented and more concerned with social responsibility in their decision-making. Keim, Gerald D. 1978. "Managerial behavior and the social responsibility debate: goals versus constraints." *Academy of Management Journal*, 21 (Mar.): 57-68. Argues that the evidence concerning corporate philanthropy in the United States does not support this position. He suggests that the social constraints on businesses have changed to some degree, but that the goal of making profits as the main rationale has not. In other words, the rules of the game have changed, but the object of the game remains the same.
97. Once a service co-operative reaches a certain size, growth drives are reduced. Foreign investment and extensive diversification into non-related activities are not rational with a service framework. The logic of self-help produces an attitude that others who need co-operatives should start their own. Any assistance given is directed at helping another group in overcoming some specific problems, rather than controlling them as a subsidiary firm.
98. There are times when this fact is overlooked by co-operative enthusiasts.
99. Pateman, Carol. 1970. *Participation and Democratic Theory*. Cambridge: Cambridge University Press.
100. Abel, I.W., 1976 *Collective Bargaining: Labour Relations in Steel, Then and Now*. Pittsburgh: Carnegie Mellon University Press.

Chapter 3

CO-OPERATIVES IN THE WORLD TODAY

You can have public ownership of the means of production without State ownership. You can have free enterprise without capitalism. Answer: co-operative ownership. But does it work? The *Economist's* Spain correspondent reports from a place where it does.[1]

Once people are actually engaged in practising co-operation in co-operatives a new set of circumstances arises. Co-operation becomes dynamic and gets complimented by organizational dynamics. The more static conditions that explain the origins of co-operative action are no longer useful guides for predicting behaviour. Like other organizations, co-operatives are more than the sum of the individuals involved. They are dynamic social entities that take on a life of their own. If they are successful, they are not dependent upon one individual or a small group of people, and over time they are reshaped and changed by many factors and conditions. Most function in a market economy and must successfully compete in order to survive, yet they are caught in a dilemma, they must reconcile the tensions between being a social organization responding to the needs of members and the reality of the market place.[2] This dilemma is not negative as it is the dynamic that gives them a distinction and a social relevance. But it is a dilemma, and cannot be reconciled by denying its existence.

SERVICE CO-OPERATIVES IN INDUSTRIALIZED COUNTRIES

Co-operatives are located around the world. Not all the co-operatives belong to the International Co-operative Alliance but of those that do there are over 666 million members. Figure 3.1 shows the number of individual members by type of organization. About 10% of the individual members belong to agricultural co-operatives, 21% belong to consumer co-operatives and another 30% of the 666 million belong to credit co-operatives.

In 1985 these numbers increased dramatically when the 132 million members belonging to Chinese agricultural co-operatives became affiliated with the International Co-operative Alliance (see Chapter 4). Affiliation requires that the co-operative principles be applied. Numerous co-operative movements are so closely controlled by government officials that the principle of democratic control is seriously violated. This had been the case in China, but an international study team found that with the economic reforms, party control in the working of the organizations had declined and membership was granted. Their are now 194 national organizations from eighty-two countries members of the ICA. These include fifteen countries from Africa, fourteen in the Americas, twenty-four in Asia, and twenty-nine in Europe.

In Europe, 45,000 agricultural co-operative organizations market more than half the value of total farm production within the European Economic Community. They also provide a substantial share of the inputs used in agricultural production. Figures 3.2 and 3.3 summarized market share in Canada and the U.S.A. The statistics give some indication of the present importance of co-operatives in various agricultural sectors. In most of the industrialized countries, co-operatives are important in agricultural marketing and providing the major farm inputs of fuel, feed and fertilizer.

In Canada, the gross business volume of Canadian co-operatives was $14.6 billion in 1988, showing a steady increase during the 1980s. In terms of market shares, co-operatives in 1989 marketed 72% of the grains and seeds sold, and 57% of the dairy products. The share of the fertilizer and chemical market is 32%. The co-operative market share of farm marketing was 44% and co-operative supplied 23% of all farm inputs.

Agricultural co-operatives are important in the marketing of agricultural products beyond the farm gate. North America is one of the largest food-producing area in the world and farmers market 26% of their produce in the United States and 44% in Canada (see Figure 3.2). In the United States the dairy sector is dominated by co-operatives which account for nearly 80% of the market share, and in Canada the dominant sector is grain marketing. Co-operatives also supply about one-third of the farm supplies in Canada and one-quarter in the U.S.A. (see Figure 3.3). In fresh vegetables, seventy-three associations in the U.S.A. served about 8,000 members mostly in the West and South. They account for only 4% of the market share, but for a sales volume of $218 million. Bargaining co-operatives are important in the fruits and vegetables sector.

U.S. agricultural co-operatives have had the National Bank for Co-operatives organized on a regional basis to provide a source of

Figure 3.1

STATISTICAL SUMMARY OF THE NUMBER OF SOCIETIES AND INDIVIDUAL MEMBER AFFILIATED WITH THE INTERNATIONAL CO-OPERATIVE ALLIANCE

Type	No. of societies	%	No. of individual members	%
Agricultural	251,080	33.9%	66,628.3	10.0%
Consumer	51,845	7.0%	141,252.0	21.2%
Credit	204,400	27.6%	196,534.2	29.5%
Fishery	17,775	2.4%	3,314.4	0.5%
Housing	82,952	11.2%	15,907.8	2.4%
Industrial	39,951	5.4%	3,314.4	0.5%
Insurance	14,072	1.9%	45,307.2	6.8%
Multipurpose	58,511	7.9	155,243.9	23.3%
Other	22,219	3.0%	37,311.8	5.6%
TOTAL	740,650	100.0%	666,282.8	100.0%

Source: McLanahan, Jack & Connie, eds., 1990 Co-operative/Credit Union DICTIONARY and Reference: United States, Canada, World. Richmond Kentucky: The Co-operative Alumni: 387-388.

Figure 3.2

CO-OPERATIVE SHARE OF AGRICULTURAL MARKETING ACTIVITY

Year	USA			CANADA		
	1982	1986	1989	1982	1986	1989
ALL FARM PRODUCTS	30%	26%	26%		44%	
DAIRY	77%	78%	80%	51%	57%	56%
GRAIN	36%	27%	36%	76%	73%	75%
COTTON	36%	35%	43%			
VEGETABLES	20%	4%		9%	10%	11%
FRUIT		18%	18%	17%	22%	17%
HONEY & MAPLE				25%	20%	26%
LIVESTOCK	11%	8%	7%			
hogs				13%	13%	12%
beef				17%	15%	19%
poultry	7%	8%		35%	34%	35%
EGGS				3%	3%	4%

Source: Market share statistics come from several published sources and are estimates only. For Canada Co-operation Canada, 1986, Ottawa: Co-operative Secretariat, Government of Canada; Statistics Canada. For the United States, Farmers Cooperatives, Washington: US Department of Agriculture/Agric. Co-operative Services. (Jan. 1990 and Feb. 1989:8).

Figure 3.3

CO-OPERATIVE SHARE OF AGRICULTURAL SUPPLY ACTIVITY

Year	USA			CANADA		
	1982	1986	1989	1982	1986	1989
ALL FARM SUPPLIES	28%	26%	24%	33%	33%	31%
FEED STUFF	18%	18%	18%	30%	28%	26%
FERTILIZER	42%	46%	42%	32%	32%	36%
CHEMICALS	30%	31%	24%			
SEED	17%	17%	15%	25%	25%	20%
MACHINERY				17%	15%	12%
FARM FUEL	36%	38%	39%	42%	47%	52%

Market share statistics come from several published sources and are estimates only. For Canada, Co-operation Canada, 1986, Ottawa: Co-operative Secretariat, Government of Canada; Statistics Canada. For the United States, Farmers Cooperatives, Washington: US Department of Agriculture/Agric. Cooperative Services. (Jan. 1990 and Feb. 1989:8).

Figure 3.4

CO-OPERATIVES BY TYPE & MEMBERS IN USA AND CANADA

Type	United States #	members (000)	Canada #	members (000)
Agriculture	6,009	4,190.3	1,260	683.4
Consumer goods	6,897	1,700.0	615	1,728.3
Daycare/nursery	1,700	70.0	347	20.0
Finance				
Credit unions	15,109	60,300.0	2,649	8,744.8
Insurance *	1,800	20,000.0	13	10,059.9
Farm Credit	267	600.0		
Other	100	1,500.0		
Fishery	102	10.0	50	9.6
Handicraft	400	50.0	37	
Housing	10,000	1,500.0	1,147	60.0
Health Care	13	1,000.0	8	229.7
Memorial Society	150	350.0		
Rural electric	986	10,077.0	191	55.0
Rural telephones	252	1,575.0	26	
Student housing credit, retail	220	210.0	8	1.6
Worker	800	55.0	147	8.0
Other	1,197	624.0	207	307.4
TOTAL	46,002	103,811.3	6,705	11,910.8

Policy holders of insurance co-operatives are usually not included in Canadian statistics in order to reduce double counting of total members. Source of data: USA, McLanahan, 1990: 384. Canada, Sullivan, 1990: 29-31 and Co-operative Secretariat, 1990.

Figure 3.5

STATISTICS ON AGRICULTURAL CO-OPERATIVES

(combined marketing and supply)

	E.E.C 1983	USA 1988	Canada 1988
No. of Co-operatives	40,000	6,200	3,000
No. of members (million)	10.m	5.3m	1.3m
Full-time employees	550,000	204,000	40,000
Net business (x US$ 1B)	120b	102b	9.5b

credit. The national system ran into difficulties in the recession of the early 1980s. Most regional banks were merged into one national bank called CoBank in 1988. It has assets of $12 billion (1989) its loan portfolio included 39% to marketing co-operatives, 25% to rural utility co-operatives, 7% to farm supply co-operatives and 23% to finance products exported to international customers.

Animal feed is a major expense in livestock production. In 1987, almost 3,000 U.S.A. co-operatives provided feed valued at nearly $3 billion to their members. The number of co-operative feed mills grew 18% to 1,913. Expansion of mill capacity and feed production increased proportionally. The trend is toward larger capacity mills to gain greater economies of scale. However, market share in both countries has declined by 2% during the 1980s, and the market share of all farm supplies has remained constant at about one-quarter in the United States and one-third in Canada.

Australia's rural exports accounted for over 50% of the total export earnings, and co-operatives marketed a major proportion of them. In western Australia, the grain pool handles most of the wheat and course grains marketed. Rice processing and marketing is wholly handled by co-operatives; 50% of the sugar, and 85% of the tobacco, is processed by co-operatives. About 70% of the cotton is handled, up to the milling stage; about 40% of the vegetables; about 50% of the milk; 25% of the bulk honey and 40% of the jar pre-packed honey. One-third of the world's wool is supplied by Australia and of this, 20% is marketed co-operatively.[3]

The growth of consumer co-operatives started in the United Kingdom and quickly spread to other countries in western Europe, where these organizations account for about 10% of the food trade in western Europe and about 6% of total retail sales. The highest shares are achieved in Scandinavia (Finland, 38%; Iceland, 32%; Sweden, 23%; Denmark, 20%; Norway, 15%). In the United Kingdom the co-operatives share of food trade exceeded 12% in the 1950s. This has declined to about 5% by the end of the 1980s.[4]

Although consumer co-operatives have a very small market share in North America over 3.4 million consumers are members. Canadian consumer co-operatives have developed in the western provinces, and the maritimes, particularly in rural areas. In rural and many isolated areas they are important suppliers of food and household supplies. In some regions, notably Atlantic Canada, they are located in most cities and currently have 20% of the food market share. The Calgary Consumers Co-operative is the largest consumer co-operative in North America with 14 stores, membership of over 250,000, and annual sales in excess of $440 million for about 35% of the food market share in its trading area. There have been some innovative success stories in Canada plus some rather stunning failures.[5]

The large consumer co-operatives with food stores in Berkeley, Palo Alto, and Washington D.C. have gone out of business or discontinued food operations.[6] The exception is the Hyde Park Co-operative which markets food in the Chicago area. The over 7,000 consumer co-operatives are mainly small organizations serving a particular niche in the market place.[7]

Co-operative credit societies trace their origins to Germany, in the same period that saw the rise of consumer co-operatives in Great Britain. The urban credit societies initiated by Herman Schulze-Delitzsch and the rural societies of the Raiffeisen movement (named after Fredrich Wilhelm Raiffeisen) have formed well-integrated organizational structures and become major banking institutions in Germany.[8] The idea of co-operative credit quickly spread to other countries in Europe, and by 1991 the 11,000 co-operative banks in Europe had 57,000 banking points with 33 million members, employing 400,000 and assets of ECU 1.1 trillion accounting for 17% of the savings in the European Community.[9] Alphonse Desjardins, a Canadian legislative reporter, studied the movements in Germany and Italy; and, in 1901, he organized a *"caisse populaire"* (people's bank) at Levis, Québec. Under the laws of the time, he was personally responsible for all liabilities incurred by the organization. Nevertheless, several were organized and considerable pressure had to be exerted on the Québec government before *caisses populaires* could obtain limited liability. The organization proved highly successful. Within a few years, a social movement emerged, and parish-based *caisse populaires* were organized throughout Québec. The idea was also picked up and adapted in the United States, and credit unions in North America have since developed into a strong financial movement, which has considerable impact on consumer credit. (Combined assets of credit union in the United States in 1990 were nearly $200 billion, and in Canada were $60 billion.) These organizations differ considerably in structure from the European co-operative banks.[10]

These aggregate statistics are impressive, but they convey the impression that co-operatives are huge monolithic organizations, growing rapidly and extending their activities into all facets of people's lives. A closer look shows that the structure is anything but monolithic. Various federations of organizations have emerged at different times and places, some in opposition to existing co-operatives and in fierce competition with each other.[11] In almost all the industrialized countries, there are several factions within the co-operative movement, and the competition and collaboration between them varies considerably. Sometimes they are divided in terms of their perceived co-operativeness, for example when a new group emerges to challenge an existing co-operative, and each generates a core of supporters and competes aggressively in the market place.[12] In other instances, some co-operative organizations may be closely identified with a particular political party and differ with other co-operators on political grounds.[13]

Using an analogy, the seeds of co-operation that are planted are similar, but the soil conditions and environment have varied considerably. In some cases, co-operatives have grown slowly, suffering from severe competition; in other places, they have taken root and grown to maturity quickly; elsewhere, they have struggled with recurring drought and frequent failures, but finally they have experienced favourable conditions to blossom and mature. In other cases they have been started and quickly failed. Those that develop features that respond to local members needs tend to flourish and over time take on many unique characteristics.

As individuals, we are all products of our own history and are socialized to fit our surrounding social milieu. A similar process occurs with organizations as they attempt to serve the needs of people in different social and cultural settings. But reading the histories and studies relating to particular segments of the co-operative movement, one is struck by the similarities in their development. The next section of the chapter identifies some of the common elements in the emergence and growth of co-operatives in the industrialized countries of western Europe, North America and Japan. A few examples are included to illustrate general points. But first we will explore the dynamics of service co-operatives. The section begins with a review of the present state of development of such organizations in industrialized countries throughout the world, then it focuses on their emergence and growth in western Europe and North America. Service co-operatives have had a substantial impact on the economies within which they operate. They have, in fact, effected changes that have brought other organizations closer to the values of the co-operative movement. The nature and extent of their influence are described in later sections of the chapter.

THE DYNAMICS OF DEVELOPMENT

The co-operative movement in all industrialized countries has its roots in severe social discontent and popular protest against the existing order. Protest movements are not a new phenomenon. The slaves in ancient Rome revolted from time to time, and peasant revolts and rebellions have occurred periodically throughout European history. With the notable exception of the religious reformation period, these protests rarely emerged as social movements.[14] The domination of church and State over people's lives left little room for change. But during the time of the Crusades, Europeans came into contact with other cultures on the way to the Holy Land. The burgeoning of a merchant class gave rise to a money economy and created the commercial revolution that eroded the foundations of feudal society. The industrial revolution opened the door to a greater degree of freedom of thought and expression, making fertile ground for the growth of social movements. It is not surprising that England, with the more advanced industrial revolution, was also a centre for critical thought, social protest and social movements during the eighteenth and nineteenth centuries.

Living conditions at this time were extremely harsh for the masses. Many people shared frustration with their circumstances and initiated random acts of rebellion. Alcoholism was a problem, as men attempted to escape temporarily by getting drunk. But the drinking halls also provided a place to talk, where people could express their visions of how the state of affairs could be changed. Slowly, various ideologies emerged and gained supporters. Historians usually credit the ideas of a social movement to its main orators and writers. This practice may be justified, but few of these individuals developed their ideas in isolation. They, too, were a part of the social milieu which also included bright articulate women. Their ideas crystallized from their own observations and were refined through discussion with others. In any event, regardless of the process by which the original vision of a changed society emerged, the social milieu enabled the ideas to spread.[15] People who shared the same values could be motivated to positive action in either the political or the economic sphere.[16]

Social movements usually encounter setbacks when their first attempts fail to build organizations consistent with the movement's goals. Repeated failures destroy the movement, whereas even limited successes will provide a spark for development. The failure of the Owenites resulted in a search for the weaknesses in their approach, rather than a rejection of their ideals. King's union shops in the 1830s were a startling success for four years; and although they eventually collapsed, they provided a stimulus to further experimentation with co-operatives. Subsequently, the success of the Rochdale Pioneers provided a successful example for other co-operative organizations. Perhaps more important, "the disillusion of many chartists by the fiasco of 1848, removed the enmity of some of them to what they regarded as a rival movement."[17] Similarly, violent opposition by the State to the political initiatives of the labour movement resulted in recourse to co-operatives for immediate self-help. As the movement grew, it encompassed supporters of other movements, and with success the co-operative movement in England became a major part of the larger labour movement in the nineteenth century. The ideology of consumer co-operation was partly shaped by, and also helped to shape, the ideology of the labour movement, including the Labour Party.[18]

The flexibility that existed in the retail economy of English villages and cities was not present within the agricultural system. Landowners lived on their holdings and often provided credit to their tenant farmers. Thus, the farmers were "not in a position to dare to promote or adopt developments disagreeable to their landlords."[19] Because of these unfavourable conditions agricultural co-operatives did not develop to any great extent in nineteenth-century England.

The environment was considerably different in Germany. The leadership of the German labour movement was opposed to consumer co-operative societies "not on the grounds of experience, but as a result of the iron law of wages." Lassalee, one of the labour leaders, explained this reasoning in a pamphlet published in 1863:

In this pamphlet, Lassalee expounded the theory that consumers' co-operative societies are completely incapable of bringing about an improvement of the situation of the working class.... The wage rate could never rise above the average in the long run, for any slight improvement in the situation of workers would bring about an increase in the hands offered, which would depress the wage to its former level.[20]

Thus, they reasoned, if only a few workers joined consumer co-operatives, their standard of living would improve; but as soon as the co-operatives included most of the workers, wages would drop in direct proportion to the reduction in consumption expense. With the active opposition of the labour movement, consumer co-operatives did not develop in urban areas until the late 1800s.

However, the agricultural conditions in Germany were different from those in England. Landlords did not supply credit to their tenant peasants, and the degree of poverty among farmers was much worse. Raiffeisen led a movement to establish co-operative credit societies in rural areas, so that all local residents would have access to savings and loan services. These associations were successful and quickly expanded their activities to include volume buying of seed, fertilizer and other agricultural inputs. Credit was also needed by the urban middle class. Starting in 1849, Schulze-Delitzsch spearheaded another movement to organize shopkeepers, small merchants and artisans into credit societies.[21] Although both the Raiffeisen and the Schulze-Delitzsch organizations varied in the rules they followed, they both claimed to be part of the co-operative movement, but contact was slight and in some cases they actively competed.[22] The Raiffeisen associations were clearly a dynamic agricultural movement, and the Schulze-Delitzsch was an urban movement.[23]

Consumer co-operatives emerged as part of the Schulze-Delitzsch movement; but until the 1890s, they were supported more by the middle class than by workers. Hesselbach points out:

In Germany, the consumer's co-operative movement was predominantly a middle-class affair up to the time when it broke loose from the general middle-class movement. The rejection of the consumers' co-operatives by the early theoreticians of the workers movement inhibited their development among the working class and contributed to the fact that they were discovered late by organized labour.[24]

As close contact developed between the consumer co-operatives and the workers' movement in the 1890s, disagreement flared up. As a result, the groups separated. Consumer co-operatives were expelled from the General Association (Schulze-Delitzsch) at its Congress in 1902 because of their close association with the Social Democratic Party. In 1894, forty-seven autonomous consumer co-operatives founded the Wholesale Society of German Consumers' Co-operatives. Some consumer co-operatives even began to accept savings from their members. This practice gave rise to a full-blooded conflict between consumer co-operatives on one side and traders and credit co-operatives on the other. As both kinds of co-operatives, from a sociological point of view, had their origin in different social classes, they exhibited contrasting developmental inclinations.

In France, social movements of workers and peasants emerged in the mid-nineteenth century; but circumstances differed from those in Britain and Germany, and the co-operative movement took a slightly different form. The revolution in 1848 provided the opportunity for workers to establish worker-owned producer co-operatives. These had been tried before in the 1830s under the guidance of Buchez, but most failed. In 1848, conditions were more favourable. The workers gained initial success, and co-operatives were organized and developed close contact with the movement in Britain. The success of the German agricultural co-operatives influenced French agricultural leaders, and rural co-operatives emerged in the latter part of the nineteenth century.

The earliest development of the co-operative movement occurred in the most industrialized countries of western Europe: the United Kingdom, Germany and France. In the United Kingdom and France, it was mainly a workers' movement, but in Germany it was middle-class and agricultural. Agricultural and economic crises during the 1880s led to the development of agricultural co-operatives in Switzerland, Denmark, Iceland and Ireland.

In Switzerland, co-operatives were started in order to combine the purchasing of artificial fertilizers, seeds, feed and implements.[25] In 1886, the Union of Agricultural Co-operatives of East Switzerland was formed as the first central organization. This was followed by the development of large marketing organizations for milk and livestock producers as well as rural credit co-operatives based on the Raiffeisen model.

When the co-operative movement was started in Denmark, conditions were highly conducive to its development. There had been more than sixty years of free compulsory education. Folk High

Schools had been established for thirty years; local councils had been publicly elected for forty years; and for almost fifteen years, the farmers had their own political party.

From 1866 onwards there was a constant struggle for a more liberal constitution and the farmers organized themselves in a political party, the Liberal Democrats, in opposition to the estate owners; behind the farmers followed the small holders and the industrial workers with their own political parties. The allegiance of the three democratic parties gave them a majority in the lower house from 1872 onwards.[26]

The farmers party achieved considerable reforms, but economic depression in the 1880s brought forth the need for more positive action. Dairy co-operatives, starting in 1882, developed quickly and within fifty years the agricultural sector was transformed from a capitalistic to a co-operative economic structure.

Different, but also favourable, conditions were present in Ireland during the 1880s:

It was a country of small peasants, bound together by common grievances against absentee landlords, and a strong desire for Irish national independence....Landlordism, however, was only one of the evils afflicting the Irish peasant; he was heavily in debt, exploited by merchant moneylenders, and suffered from the lack of an efficient marketing system and the inefficiency of his own farming methods. The only means of improving his condition was co-operation.[27]

In 1888, the Irish Co-operative Aid Association was formed.

The 1880s were also times of difficulty for Scandinavian workers, and the successful consumer co-operatives in the United Kingdom drew their interest. Childs points out that

Sweden followed the English co-operative plan. Individual societies, most of them at the outset in towns and cities, and especially in industrial areas, enroled members who each subscribed a fixed amount of share capital in order to establish the retail store of the society. These struggling societies finally united, in 1899, to form the Ko-operativa Forbundet.[28]

Today the co-operative is both a wholesale society and a co-operative union for educational and promotional work.

By the turn of the century, Germany, Switzerland, Denmark, Ireland and Iceland had a co-operative movement spearheaded by farmers. Industrial workers were the force behind the movement in the United Kingdom, France, Sweden, Finland, Norway, Belgium and Italy. The various organizations exhibited considerable differences but many similarities as well. They had all emerged out of difficult times with high social unrest. Co-operatives were seen as a way to improve the lot of both workers and farmers. The failure rate in early years was high, but enough local societies developed and prospered that federation of co-ops were formed to assist in refining operations, as well as to strengthen management and co-ordinate resources for further extension at the local level. The strongest organizations were the consumer co-operatives, which expanded both horizontally and vertically. The dynamics of growth crisis and member involvement is summarized in Figure 3.6.

In the early phases of development, participation was high, and many meetings were organized and conducted by volunteers. The co-operatives organized adult education classes and seminars; social events, such as football matches, picnics and summer camps for young people; and a host of activities not normally associated with business organizations. Both their social and economic aspects were apparent. However, increased effectiveness and efficiency were also desired. Economic rationalization and growth resulted in an increase in bureaucratization. Employees were hired to promote co-operatives to organize meetings; and at the same time, there was marked decline in the energies expended by volunteers.[29] The emphasis on effectiveness and efficiency brought forth more members. More facilities, more employees and more bureaucratization were required in order to co-ordinate and control the burgeoning organizations. There was usually a marked expansion of services, then a period of consolidation as management gained a hold on all the diverse activities created.

Many writers have documented the decline in member participation as co-operative organizations have matured.[30] This decline is not particularly problematic, as long as organizations are in tune with local thinking and the change is gradual. But the participation of members is an important factor in ensuring that co-operatives remain locally responsive. When members' needs and expectations change over time, organizations that lack a participatory base face a crisis.[31]

If democratic structures have withered and the co-operative is non-responsive, member support will decline and members may become cynical. Dissatisfaction may lead to new protest movements,

Figure 3.6

DYNAMIC OF SERVICE CO-OPERATIVES

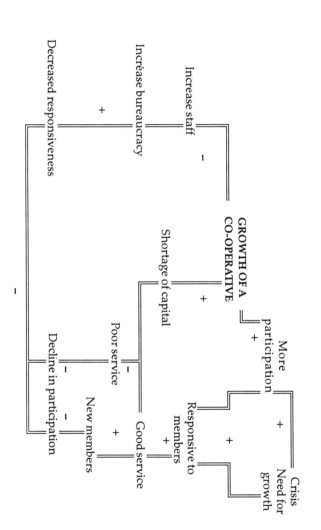

and rival co-operatives may develop. Alternatively, disenchanted members may turn to other kinds of organizations to meet their needs, so that co-operatives eventually decline and die out.[32]

On the other hand, the crisis may precipitate reorganization and development of a new participatory base. Such responsiveness may produce a surge of energy that rekindles the movement, introducing an era of new growth and organizational vigour. Bureaucratization will be reduced and a more flexible and imaginative leadership will emerge. Changes will be made to take account of the new reality, but over time, rationalization will once again occur. The fat will be cut to increase efficiency. The surge of participation will slowly decline. Once again, this decline in participation will not be crucial until changing conditions result in another crisis of local responsiveness. It is a general organizational problem and one not exclusive to co-operatives. The internal contradictions of trying to achieve goals effectively, make efficient use of all resources, yet remain responsive to the needs of local people are difficult to resolve. But failure to satisfy all three requirements to a minimum degree results in the decline and collapse of the organization.

Many service co-operatives have grown to be effective, efficient organizations; and, as we have seen, they have captured a substantial share of the market. They exercise sufficient influence that they may produce structural changes and a new order in some sectors of the economy. It is difficult to measure precisely the market share that is required to effect change. If the economic sector consists largely of a vertically integrated oligopoly (few firms), co-operative control of a relatively small share of the market (10-15%) will create sufficient leverage to break cartels. But if vertical integration has not occurred within the co-operative network, local organizations must obtain supplies from the oligopoly with which they compete; and in this case, a much larger share of the market is necessary to effect significant change in economic structures and practices.[33]

The growth and development of service co-operatives in western Europe and North America have followed a similar dynamic pattern. When growth occurs, organizations can become well developed. Under these conditions, co-operation between co-operatives can result in basic changes to the economic sector. Sometimes these changes occur quickly and dramatically, but most take place slowly and go unnoticed by most of the population. The remainder of this chapter will deal briefly with the basic changes that have resulted from the dynamics of co-operative development.

These dynamics have played an important role, but certainly not an exclusive role in reshaping the economies in Europe and North

America. I am not suggesting that co-operatives are the only forces at work. Rather they are one force among many others. They are discussed as points and each point is illustrated by one or two examples. The forces are in fact much more extensive than is indicated by the few selected examples from the past.

CONTRIBUTIONS TO THE ECONOMY

Breaking Monopolies and International Cartels

The Rochdale Society was successful because it was able to resolve a major problem for consumers which arose out of local retail practices. Merchants cheated customers on weight, adulterated good by adding cheap impurities and used credit to prevent their clientele from shopping elsewhere. The introduction of honest practices into the market place in the 1840s brought an immediate change to the retail industry and substantially altered the habits of retailers. During the late nineteenth and early twentieth centuries, problems for consumers existed not only at the retail level, but also further up the chain at the manufacturing level. Huge international cartels controlled the output of many plants and regulated both quality and prices for European consumers. Co-operatives were as dependent upon these cartels as any of the other retailers. However, if they had a sufficient volume of sales to take a major proportion of the output of a factory, they could integrate vertically and break the cartel. The Scandinavian co-operatives did just this in the 1920s. They effectively broke cartels in the production of light bulbs, margarine, cash registers and fertilizers.[34]

Agricultural co-operatives also have broken cartels, particularly in marketing. Elevator monopolies granted by the railroads when the Canadian prairies were settled were effectively nullified by the formation of the United Grain Growers in 1902.[35] Similarly, the growth of the prairie wheat pools in the 1920s and the pressure they exerted for orderly marketing of Canadian wheat and other cereals forced a reluctant government to curtail the monopoly of commodity speculators.[36]

A vertically integrated co-operative network, using a service rationale, provides competition with a different orientation towards producers and consumers, and the possibility of exploitation by cartels is eliminated.[37] Critics may argue that the domination of any industrial sector by co-operatives means that, in effect, the co-operatives form a cartel. What they overlook is that these organizations are fundamentally different from capitalist cartels and have a different impact on both economic and social structures.

Elimination of Windfall Profits

On February 11th, 1978, the Utah Development Company in Australia announced dividend profits of $141.13 million.[38] This amount may seem large; but companies are large these days, and profits are only to be expected since (as we are told) these companies take huge risks. On closer inspection, the figures are quite revealing. The 1976 dividends were a $2.71 per share. The 1977 dividends were A$3.14 per share. Interestingly, the value of the shares in 1970 was A$1.85 each, and by 1977 they had risen to A$3.22 (value on February 10, the day before the announcement). The owners, it appears, are receiving nearly 100% return on their equity investment each year.[39] Is this reasonable with the risks? Or is it a windfall profit? The owners, Utah International Inc., in the United States, received $126 million during 1977 for their 89% interest in the Australian company.

There are no co-operatives in the mining industry in Australia. In sectors where co-operative development has taken place, these windfall profits are automatically eliminated in a few years, by the mere fact of the presence and operations of these organizations. By returning the surplus back to users of the business rather than to owners of the capital, co-operatives lower prices and keep them lower than they would otherwise be. The history of dairy co-operatives in Europe and North America shows how this sector of production was reshaped by the activities of co-operatives, and how it is now dominated by co-operatives. At the turn of the century, the profits from operating dairies was substantial. When co-operative dairies were organized, the prices paid to producers went up considerably. Private dairies had to increase payments to farmers in order to get milk, and their return on investment decline. Over a period of years, capitalists began to lose interest in these operations and to invest their money into sectors where the return was higher. Many dairies were offered for sale to the co-operatives, and farmers now find that their co-operatives have a substantial share of the market. (see Figure 3.2)

A similar situation exists in most of the agricultural marketing sectors and in the major commodities needed by farmers (for example fuel, animal feed and chemical fertilizers). Over time, these sectors become noted for thin margins and a lower return on investment. This is not an historical accident but rather an evolutionary change brought about by the activities of co-operatives.

Elimination of Middlemen

Several economic sectors include a long string of middlemen, each making a profit as a commodity moves from producer to consumer. Some of these middlemen perform important functions while others gain a high return for playing a minor role. Although few or none of them make windfall profits, the spread between what the producer is paid and what the consumer pays is considerable. In 1918, the Scandinavian co-operative wholesales formed an international purchasing organization called Nordisk Andelsforbund or NAF.[40] This organization was set up to buy fresh fruits and vegetables for the consumer co-operatives in Scandinavia. They have been highly successful for a number of reasons, and a major one is the fact that they have eliminated several middlemen who substantially increased the price of imported foodstuffs. This exclusion has meant lower prices for members of consumer co-operatives. Other retailers have also had to lower prices in order to remain competitive.

The process of vertical integration that reduces the need for middlemen. This is not unique to co-operatives. Capitalist and State corporations also may eliminate the middlemen by vertically integrating and rationalizing an economic sector. What is unique for co-operatives is that the rationalization results in direct benefits for consumers and/or producers. This may or may not occur with other organizational types.

Decentralized Decision-Making

We have noted that democratic involvement by the membership decreases in large service co-operatives, and this decline represents a major problem. But when large co-operatives are compared with capitalist corporations of the same economic sector, they are found to be relatively highly decentralized. The decentralization of decision-making is an important process within the economy of large countries. For example KF is a highly integrated retailing system in Sweden, accounting for about 20% of retail sales. They regularly hold national Consumer Congresses which involve about 10,000 members, ordinary consumers from across Sweden, who discuss and develop consumer policies for consideration by the elected officials.

Corporate capitalism centralizes more and more head offices into fewer and larger cities.[41] This distribution can create severe regional disparities within a country, as the hinterland becomes increasingly dependent upon decisions from the metropolitan areas. The higher-paid employees are located in these head offices, as well as the innovative and entrepreneurial functions of the organization. The higher-paying jobs also shift to the metropolitan areas, and the other regions are faced with a shrinking tax base. The spiral of an over-developed metropolitan area and large underdeveloped hinterlands is set up. The day-to-day functioning of co-operatives is one of the few economic processes that reverses this spiral, which is so evident in industrialized countries. Activities in which co-operatives are dominant are among the few economic sectors in industrialized countries that are not controlled in large metropolitan centres.[42]

More Equitable Distribution of Wealth

At the local level, service co-operatives do not redistribute income by taking money from the rich and giving it to the poor. They may in fact increase the income disparity in a particular community if, for example, members of the co-operative receive a higher price for their products than do other producers in the same area.[43] For a variety of reasons, individuals may choose not to deal with the co-operatives, realizing a lower price for their products or paying a much higher price for money borrowed.[44] In many cases, the difference in prices at the co-operatives is slight; but over time, these small variations may become rather substantial, so that members of co-operatives eventually accumulate more wealth than their non-co-operating neighbours.

Despite this possible local effect, in a broader context co-operatives do achieve a more equitable distribution of wealth. A simple example illustrates the point. In Canada in 1983, the value of farm products marketed and farm supplies sold amounted to over $13.9 billion.[45] Out of this volume, a surplus of C$222.9 million was reported by various co-operatives.[46] A substantial portion of this sum was returned to members in cash, and the remainder allocated to members' equity accounts and paid back over a period of years. If these businesses were owned by capitalist corporations, the entire surplus would flow to investors. In Canada, about 2% of the population owns a sizeable amount of corporate stocks, and only 10% own any stock at all. A large majority of these investors live in or near the three largest Canadian cities Montréal, Toronto and Vancouver. The bulk of the $223 million was generated from business done in rural Canada; very little involved people living in these urban centres. In accordance with co-operative rules regarding distribution of surplus, most of the money was returned to people in the rural hinterland, in proportion to the business that they did with their local co-operatives. Thus, the earnings from commercial activity are spread more widely through Canadian co-operatives than through large private enterprise. Similar effects are found in the United States, Japan and western Europe. The co-operative movement has slowed and at times reversed the trend of monopoly capitalism in these industrialized countries, particularly in the agricultural sector, and has helped to redistribute some of the wealth.

Figure 3.7

STATISTICS ON CONSUMER CO-OPERATIVES

	W. EUROPE 1983	E. EUROPE 1983	JAPAN 1988
No. of Co-operatives	2,924	1,097	654
No. of members (million)	19.5m	9.4m	11.8m
Full-time employees	177,150		48,000
Net business (x US$ 1B)	32.4	8.2	16.4b

Source: INTERCOOP Information, No. 4, August 1984.

Market Manipulation

During the 1970s and 1980s, developing countries have been clamouring for a new economic order for world trade. Part of the problem results from multinational corporations, which are vertically integrated and use transfer pricing to decrease earnings in some areas and artificially increase the wealth elsewhere.[47] A multinational corporation is not a legal entity, but rather a grouping of separately incorporated companies. However, when one company completely owns all the others in the group, the ability to move profits around greatly increases. For example, if one firm owns both the wholesale and retail outlets, it can reduce or augment the profits at either point.

The exercising of this prerogative is known as Transfer Pricing, a hypothetical example of which is outlined in Figure 3.8. In both situations, A and B of this example, the price to the consumer is $12.00 per unit. The profit per unit at the retail is $1.00 in situation A. By increasing the price that the wholesale store charges by 5% (that is, from $10.00 to $10.50) and leaving the retail price the same (situation B), the profit per unit at the retail level can be lowered from $1.00 to 50 cents per unit (a drop of 50%). This procedure is quite legal. Furthermore it can be good business practice if the goal is to maximize profits. In this hypothetical situation, the firm's total profits are left unchanged, as both retail and wholesale outlets are owned by the same company. Suppose the retail stores are in a country or State where corporation taxes are high, and the wholesale can be located in a country where taxes are lower. Profits can be reduced in the high-tax area and increased in the low-tax area, so that bigger after-tax profits can be realized.

Figure 3.8

HYPOTHETICAL EXAMPLE OF TRANSFER PRICING

	Situation A	Situation B
Wholesale price/unit	$10.00	$10.50
Cost of marketing	1.00	1.00
Total Cost	11.00	11.50
Retail Price	12.00	12.00
PROFIT/UNIT	1.00	.50

Figure 3.9

THE STEPS TO MOVE CRUDE OIL TO CONSUMERS

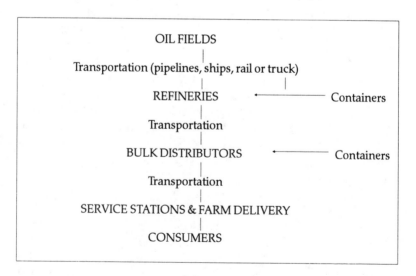

Figure 3.9 illustrates the steps involved in moving crude oil to consumers. When a corporation is completely integrated vertically, the movement of oil involves a series of transfer prices. By changing the prices paid at each step, the organization can leave gross profits of the group unchanged. But the mind boggles at the types of options that are available to shrewd managers. For example, in recent years governments have closely regulated the prices at the oil fields. However, the price charged between the refinery and bulk distributors may reflect either: 1) the market price (the one charged by other companies operating at arms' length); 2) a calculated market price (one that falls between the market price and the marginal cost of the product; 3) an economic optimum price (that is one that falls between the market; price and the marginal cost of the product); 4) a price calculated on the marginal cost; 5) a price based on variable cost (fluctuations on labour, overheads, and similar factors); 6) a price based on full costs; or 7) a fixed optimum price (one determined by the corporate head office to achieve a corporate objective).[48]

All of these are standard ways to arrive at a transfer price. Now assume that the refinery has very little competition and that the other refineries will follow the price setter. By establishing the refinery price on the basis of 1), 2) or 3) above, the corporation can keep the price of its product high. If methods 4), 5) or 6) are used, a lower transfer price will be realized. By using one of methods 1) to 3) over a period of years and keeping the consumer price stable, a vertically integrated corporation can reduce the operating profits of some of its competition specifically those who do not own refineries and are limited to bulk distribution or operation of service stations. This practice lowers the return on investment, and suddenly small businesses are up for sale. Once the independent retailers are bought out, independent refiners also may be disciplined. When techniques 4), 5) or 6) are used, the profits at the refineries are lowered and passed on to bulk distributors and service station operators. Over a period of years, the return on investment drops at the refinery level, the less efficient lose money and they sell their refineries to the vertically integrated companies. The industry become concentrated.

There are other possibilities too. Suppose that the oil is carried in company-owned supertankers that are registered in a country where no public disclosure of financial operations is required, taxes are low and very few restrictions apply to the movement of capital.[49] By paying the highest possible price for shipping and requiring all subsidiary companies to use the shipping company, the corporation can redirect much of the profit to this chosen haven.

If all the steps in the chain of a product have an open market for the commodity, the extent of manipulation of transfer prices is reduced. However, by owning suppliers of containers and other products, the corporation may transfer considerable profits out of one industrial sector into another. If a company has a near-monopoly in the supplying of containers, such a move may make corporate sense and be used to maximize total corporate profits, yet make competition extremely difficult for small, less integrated businesses.

Hypothetical situations such as these could be spun out for many pages. The point is that transfer pricing is used at times to manipulate markets for a host of reasons. Many of these manipulations are detrimental to primary producers and consumers. Government regulations against such practices are difficult to enforce, as the pricing is buried in a sea of accounting techniques. But such practices quickly come to light when an equally integrated co-operative organization develops. In short it provides a window into an industry.

For example, in the 1930s, the major oil companies refused to sell gasoline and kerosene to agricultural supply co-operatives in Saskatchewan, Canada.[50] The farmer-owned co-operatives had either to go out of business or integrate vertically by building a refinery. They chose the latter; and to their surprise, they found that the profits were great enough at the refinery level to pay completely for the plant in its first year of operation. Until then, they had no idea that profits were so high at the refinery level.

In 1973, the increased cost of energy and shortages of manufactured fertilizer sent the prices of fertilizer rapidly upward. CF Industries and Farmlands (two American co-operatives) did not increase their prices to the world level because they were aware that this was not justified by increased costs. As a result, the United States price lagged behind prices in western Europe. Windfall profits were being made at the raw material and manufacturing level. Co-operatives in North America could influence the market to prevent its manipulation only because they were vertically integrated. Since European farm-supply co-operatives own few fertilizer manufacturing plants, they were dependent upon the manufactures who were manipulating the market. The high profits went to the oligopoly, not to the farmers.

Information is needed within an economic sector to prevent market manipulation from being detrimental to producers or consumers. One of the few ways these groups can obtain such information is to have a share of the industry at each step in the processing chain.[51] Once this distribution has been achieved, a given economic sector is much less vulnerable to manipulation.

New Economic Power Relations

A major criticism of multinational corporations is that their day-to-day operations are biased towards wealthy metropolitan countries where the corporate owners and managers live. In other words, they concentrate economic power in the centre. Considerable autonomy may be delegated to management in less wealthy countries, but veto power is still retained. Furthermore, the dominant corporate values are usually those of the metropolitan areas.[52]

Multinational corporate linkages do provide enormous benefits. They enable the quick and easy transfer of technology, management know-how and capital. All three are usually in critically short supply. But foreign ownership which brings these advantages also brings problems. The nationalization of industry which is frequently attempted as a solution to this problem becomes counterproductive because it reduces access to an international network. The industry is cut off from markets and information, and it may thus be severely hampered. Multinational organizations provide a basis for industrialization. If they are co-operatively owned, they can supply benefits without incurring the disadvantages referred to in the preceding pages.[53]

The logic of the subsidiary structure of capitalist multinationals is that the power of ownership and control is vested in the international head office, and peripheral units are subordinate to the centre. The logic of a consortium structure is that the peripheral organizations own and control the international head office; thus, no single organization dominates and decisions are made in the best interest of the autonomous members. It is the structure of ownership and control that is important in this case. Federations of co-operatives provide this structure, but other corporate types may also organize in a similar way with similar effects.

One problem of the present international economic relations is the concentration of power at the centre, so that peripheral organizational units are strictly controlled. As co-operative organizational networks emerge they can reverse this process. They enable new economic relations to develop that can transform the dynamics of world trade. To date, only a few have developed, but the potential for substantial change is present.

WHY IS THE POTENTIAL NOT REALIZED?

Because of their operating dynamics, co-operatives are an important force in reshaping economics. But because of these dynamics, they are not a cure-all. They also have negative consequences.

The structural changes that can result from the development of service co-operatives require large and highly integrated organizations. The process of vertical integration within the industrial sector is important. Considerable responsibility must be delegated to technicians, decisions become complex, and it is difficult for ordinary people to keep informed and understand the developments. Democratic participation becomes extremely difficult. The pressures exerted on management to be effective and efficient increase, as members rely on the bottom line of the financial statement to judge whether or not the organization is well run. Profitability becomes an increasingly important criterion in evaluating how well various units are performing. Senior management and directors may still be service oriented, but middle management is grouped into cost centres (or profit centres) and evaluated on economic criteria. (This dynamic is explored further in Chapter 7.)

Many members may rightly feel that they have created a monster, rather than fundamentally changing an economic sector for the better. This feeling among the membership is widespread in countries where service co-operatives have been highly successful in economic terms.[54] It has been referred to as a crisis of affluence and one that could destroy the efforts of the past 150 years.[55] Organizations have been effective and grown efficient, but at the expense of remaining responsive to the needs and want of many ordinary co-operative members. Service co-operatives can easily take on the characteristics of a bureaucracy and the goals become distorted, and lost in the day-to-day business. Numerous critics argue that face-to-face co-operation is vital in order to realize the co-operative ideals. Comprehensive co-operatives provide this form of co-operation.

NOTES

1. *The Economist*, 1976. "Worker-capitalist dragon seed." *The Economist* (Dec.11): 86-87.
2. Fulton, Murray E., ed., 1990. *Co-operative Organizations and Canadian Society: Popular Institutions and the Dilemmas of Change.* Toronto: University of Toronto Press.
3. *Co-operatives in Australia,* Australian Information Service.
4. Lundberg, W.T. 1978. *Consumer Owned: Sweden's Cooperative Democracy.* Palo Alto: Consumer Cooperative Publishing Association; Roy, Ewell Paul. 1976. *Co-operatives: Development, Principles and Management.* Danville, Ill: Interstate Printers and Publishers, Inc.
5. Friedrich, D. 1984. *Direct Charge: The Common Sense Approach.* Saskatoon: Co-operative College of Canada, Working Papers, Vol. 2, No. 1; Bariteau, Claude. 1983. *Lessons from a Failure.* Saskatoon: Co-operative College of Canada Working Papers Vol.1, No. 6.

6. Cooper, Donald and Paul O. Mohn. 1992. *The Greenbelt Cooperative.* Berkley: University of California Press. This was the U.S.A.'s second-largest consumer co-op, but failed in the 1970s. Fullerton, Michael, ed., 1992. *What happened to the Berkley Co-op?* Berkley: University of California Press. A collection of articles introduced by Ralph Nader. No supermarket in America had as much impact as the Berkley Co-op. It was a leader in consumer protection, the environment Kiddies Korral, Home Economist, social justice, the Vietnam War protests, etc., but it failed in the late 1980s.

7. Cotterill, Ronald. 1982. *Consumer Food Cooperatives.* Danville Ill.: The Interstate Printers & Publishers.

8. Credit was developed first, but the movements quickly developed marketing and trading facilities.

9. Ravoet, Guido. 1992. "Capital Formation and Co-operative Values—The European Experience." *International Co-operative Banking Association* . 4: 26.

10. In Québec, the local *caisses* were parish-based. The early credit unions in the United States were usually located in factories, and membership was restricted to factory workers.

11. For example, there were two consumer co-operative retailing systems in Finland until the late 1980s. In Belgium, there were three — the socialist, the Christian Democrats and the neutral — all in competition until the mid 1970s and co-operating very little with each other. For an interesting analysis see Ilmonen, Kaj. 1992. *The End of Cooperative Movement? Sociological Affiliation and Morality.* Helsinki: Labour Institute for Economic Research.

12. This is the situation in Canada where the United Grain Growers compete with the Wheat Pools for delivery of grain by farmers. See: Wright, James F.C. 1956. *Prairie Progress.* Saskatoon: Modern Press; Colquette, R.D., 1957 *The First Fifty Years: A History of United Grain Growers Limited.* Winnipeg: Public Press; Nesbitt, Leonard D. 1964. *Tides in the West.* Saskatoon: Modern Press; Fairbairn, Garry L. 1984. *From Prairie Roots: The Remarkable Story of Saskatchewan Wheat Pool.* Saskatoon: Western Producer Prairie Books.

13. See the case of Austria, Korp, A. 1967a. "Structural reform in the co-operative system." *Annals of Public and Co-operative Economy,* 38 (Jan-Mar): 17-24. and 1967b. "Co-operative self-help in Austria." *Madras Journal of Cooperation,* 58: 420-427. Where the Raiffeisen and consumer co-operatives support different political parties and collaboration is minimal.

14. The work of such men as Luther and Calvin shows the incredible difficulties encountered by social movements in this era of European history.

15. For example, the development of the folkschools in Denmark was important in enabling farmers to analyze their social conditions and develop both political and co-operative movements to resolve problems. See Webster, F.H. 1973. *Agricultural Co-operation in Denmark.* London: Plunkett Foundation for Co-operative Studies.

16. An example of an early political movement in England is the Chartist see; Thompson, Dorothy. 1971. *The Early Chartists.* London: Macmillan. When their actions in the political arena failed, many supporters turned to co-operative economic action.

17. Bonner, Arnold. 1970. *British Co-operation: The History, Principles and Organization of The British Co-operative Movement.* Manchester: Co-operative Union: 50.

18. Co-operators have consistently elected M.P.s in the United Kingdom. They have actively supported the labour and have been responsible for pressing the case for co-operatives within the parliamentary caucus and party conventions.

19. Bonner, 1970: 409.

20. Hesselbach, Walter. 1976. *Public, Trade Union and Co-operative Enterprise in Germany: The Commonwealth Idea.* London: Frank Cass: 34-35.

21. Lambert questions whether such organizations of craftsmen and shopkeeper were true co-operatives as their object was to make profits from consumers, in

Lambert, Paul. 1963. *Studies in the Social Philosophy of Co-operation*. Manchester: The Co-operative Union: 2, pp. 95-97.

22. Davidovic, George. 1966. *Reformulation of the Co-operative Principles*. Ottawa: Co-operative Union of Canada: 5. The author points out that the basic principles of the Schulze-Delitzsch societies, the Raiffeisen associations and the Rochdale Pioneers were essentially similar. The three sets of organizations differed mainly in emphasis and in the translation of principles into action.

23. These two sets of organizations merged in 1971. Schiffgen, Werner. 1975. "Mobilization and co-ordination of co-operative self-help in rural and urban credit services," pp. 12-24 in *Report of 1975 Australian Co-operatives National Convention*. Canberra: The Cooperative Federation of Australia.

24. Hesselbach, 1976: 46.

25. Jaggi, E. 1974. *Agricultural Co-operatives and Associations in Switzerland*. Oxford: The Plunkett Foundation for Cooperative Studies. Occasional Papers No. 40: 5.

26. Webster, F.H. 1973. *Agricultural Co-operation in Denmark*. London: Plunkett Foundation for Co-operative Studies: 17.

27. Bonner, 1970: 409-410.

28. Childs, Marquis William. 1947. *Sweden the Middle Way*. New Haven: Yale University Press, (revised and enlarged edition): 1-2.

29. One cannot assume a causal relationship between the decline in voluntary activity and the hiring of employees. Voluntary activity may in fact decrease because of "organizational exhaustion" or "burn-out" of those shouldering the heaviest loads.

30. Furstenberg, Friedrich. 1985. "Problems of Member Participation at Different Stages of Co-operative Development," E. Dufler and W. Hamm, eds., *Co-operatives: In a Clash between Member Participation, Organizational Development and Bureaucratic Tendencies.*: London: Quiller Press: 103-117.

31. The participatory base of co-operatives in the United Kingdom had withered by the 1950s and is well documented in Ostergaard, G.N. & A.H. Halsey. 1965. *Power in Co-operatives: A study of Democratic Control in British Retail Societies*. Oxford: Basil Blackwell. Consumers needs changed quickly with prosperity; Watkins, W.P. 1977. *The International Co-operative Movement: Its Growth, Structure and Future Possibilities*. Manchester: Holyoake Books, Co-operative Union Ltd. Page 96 reads: "In the course of the 1950s consumer co-operatives became aware that some of the long standing assumptions would not hold, for they were inconsistent with observable facts. For most elements in the population the pressure of poverty had been relaxed, perhaps entirely removed. Where consumer co-operatives had been accepted for generations as setting the fair price of staple articles of consumption they were losing custom to competitors whose armoury of price cutting techniques were destroying the very concept of market price for any given commodity. Member's loyalty was undermined. Nor could they be lured back to the Co-operative store by the traditional rallying-cries and slogans. Rising labour costs, consequent upon full employment, led to narrower trading margins and made dividends on purchases at the accustomed rates difficult or impossible to earn. Then it was discovered that the older stores, which had been sited conveniently near to people's homes, were less remunerative than the newer ones placed on traffic arteries or adjacent to important road junctions. Moreover, the married women, who in increasing numbers found employment outside the home, found that self-service saved time and was better suited to their daily routines. Finally, the goods assortments carried by Co-operative stores, mainly restricted to foodstuff and household articles, would not stand comparison with those of the private supermarkets, emporiums and specialized shops which acquired a rapidly expanding share of the national retail markets of Western countries, with the possible exception of some bordering on the Mediterranean Sea."

32. This happened in the Netherlands in 1974, when the consumer co-operative wholesale and many locals went into liquidation. In Belgium, the Socialist co-operatives (FEBECOOP) had 170,000 families as members in 1914. Membership increased to only 320,000 in 1973 and shrunk to 150,00 by 1976. On a worldwide basis, the movement has not declined, but many national failures have occurred.

33. Ward, Michael; Robert Briscoe and Mary Lineham. 1982. *Co-operation Between Co-operatives: A Case Study of Agricultural Co-operatives in the N.E of the Republic of Ireland.* Cork: University of Cork.

34. Child, 1947.

35. When the railroads were built across the prairies in the 1800s, much of the land was not yet under cultivation. Railroad companies granted monopolies to capitalists in order to encourage them to build grain storage facilities. They also refused to let farmers load grain directly into rail cars, forcing them to sell to grain merchants at a price decided by the merchant. Organized farmer opposition was successful in 1902. Wright, 1956.

36. The change took a long time, from 1920 when the first pool was discontinued, until 1935. The fifteen years of frustration, however, were also the era of rapid co-operative development in the prairies.

37. Cartels are used to inflate artificially the price of a commodity. When the profits go to the people who use the services, cartels are pointless.

38. The information on the Utah Development Company was obtained from the *Sydney Morning Herald,* Saturday, February 11, 1978 page 31.

39. It is impossible to calculate exact returns from the limited information published.

40. Odhe, Thorsten. 1960. *Iceland: The Co-operative Island.* Chicago: Co-operative League of the U.S.A.

41. Hymer, Stephen. 1971. "Partners in Development." *NEWSTATEment,* Vol. 1: 4-15.

42. Sectors dominated by small entrepreneurs and cottage industries also are decentralized.

43. Marketing co-operatives that practise pooling often pay 50 to 60% of the expected market price when the product is delivered and the remainder when the pooling period is closed and the total income known. Private traders may pay 70-80% in cash at the time of delivery. Thus, producers who deal with private traders may receive 20% more than co-operative members when the product is delivered but, in the long term 20% less.

44. The convenience of automobile dealers' finance plans at the point of sale or credit cards induces many North American consumers to pay 20% + interest on loans, rather than half that rate through dealing with a credit union or a chartered bank.

45. This figure includes the sales volume of consumer co-operatives through purchases of both farmers and workers in cities such as Calgary, Edmonton, Saskatoon, Regina, Moncton and Winnipeg.

46. See Co-operative Secretariat, Agriculture Canada (1991). The surplus earnings were not reported as such. The figure is called undistributed surplus which is the usual category used by Canadian co-operatives to report yearly earnings prior to allocating patronage refunds.

47. Slater, A.G. 1978. "International transfer pricing," *Management Decision,* Vol. 15 (6): 551, defines a transfer price as "a mechanism for allocating costs and profits for a product or service between two separate units of a company in a manner agreed by both parties. This internal transfer is artificial because no revenue or profit is obtained for the company as a whole, since the sales of one division becomes the raw materials of another and the figures cancel out when the accounts are consolidated. International transfers are between different legal

entities...and may be defined as...the establishment of an artificial price for a product or service from one legal entity to another."

48. Slater, A.G. 1978. "International transfer pricing." *Management Decision*, 15 (6): 550-560.

49. Such countries exist (eg., Panama and Liberia), and many companies register their ships there to obtain such advantages.

50. Wright, 1956.

51. The presence of co-operatives enables the information to be available. However management may not reveal it for a variety of reasons. If members have lost control of the co-operative this benefit may be lost. Thus, the generalization is true only when democratic processes are working.

52. Perlmutter, Howard V. 1969. "The Tortuous Evolution of the Multinational Corporation," *Columbia Journal of World Business* (Jan-Feb).

53. For a fuller discussion of the benefits of multinational co-operatives, see Craig, J.G. 1976. *Multinational Co-operatives: An Alternative for World Development*. Saskatoon: Western Producer Prairie Books.

54. See the following sources for examples of this frustration: in Germany, Carpenter, Susan M. 1977. "Some problems arising from the structure of the West German agricultural co-operative organization," *Research Report, Second Co-operative Research Seminar*. Oxford: The Plunkett Foundation for Co-operative Studies. In France; Louis R. 1977. "A United Nations general assembly resolution and the future of co-operatives," *Co-operative Information*, 77 (1) 1-21.

55. Watkins, 1977: 95-104.

Chapter 4

COMPREHENSIVE CO-OPERATIVES

Comprehensive co-operation involves people co-operating with each other on a day-to-day basis. They participate in common decisions, and from this process a sense of community can emerge. As a result, co-operation may become a way of life. In the most comprehensive co-operative communities, members work together, live together and spend much of their leisure time together.[1] The *kvutza* and *kibbutzim* in Israel are the best known examples of this kind of arrangement. Similar groupings, such as the co-operative farms of North America and Europe and the *moshavim* in Israel, may lack communal living arrangements, but they still have high levels of face-to-face co-operation. Members work together and, because of close proximity, may spend leisure time together, but they also have considerable privacy and develop outside relationships. A similar situation exists in some types of housing co-operatives and in other co-operative households, where a number of people pool their resources to rent or buy a house. They live as a family, spending leisure time together, but working hours are spent apart.

Most worker-productive co-operatives involve daily, face-to-face interaction on the job, but workers then go to individual homes and most do not interact with each other during leisure time. This form of co-operation often confines member relations to economic transactions, leaving other matters outside the formal structure of the organization. Consequently, although comprehensive co-operation could occur in these settings, it is also very easy for individuals to view their involvement in the co-operative as means of obtaining income for private consumption. In these cases, the practice of co-operation will be segmental. If members develop social relationships as well as economic ones, they may become friends and acquire a sense of community.[2] It is this sense of community, and the practice of the values of co-operation in everyday life, that transforms segmental or service co-operatives into the comprehensive co-operative communities.

In 1975, there were 44,000 worker-productive societies affiliated with member organizations of the International Co-operative Alliance. These societies had a total membership of 6 million, or an average of about 130 members in each society. By 1983 there were 91,000 co-operatives with more than 23 million members. In the 10 EEC countries in Europe, workers in worker-owned co-operatives increased from 261,000 in 8,000 societies 1976 to 771,000 workers in over 22,000 organizations in 1983.[3]

These co-operatives are increasing in number in both Canada and the U.S.A.,[4] but the main places where workers' co-operatives exist are India; France, Spain, Denmark and Italy in western Europe; and Israel, where the *kibbutzim* are a major part of the economy. They are growing rapidly in other countries like England and Sweden but they are still fragile.[5]

We shall first examine the emergence and development of these co-operatives, their common characteristics and the significance of such forms of co-operation.

WORKER-PRODUCTIVE CO-OPERATIVES IN WESTERN EUROPE

The idea of worker-productive co-operatives was a part of socialist theory long before Marx. The Owenite and Fourier settlements were agricultural, but other necessities of life also were to be manufactured and traded between settlements. As the Industrial Revolution continued to develop, and skilled artisans were reduced to unskilled factory workers, the concept of worker-productive co-operatives became attractive to workers. Such organizations were conceived within the framework of a larger socialist strategy for collectivization of capital and the emancipation of entire trades from the wage system. These plans were explicitly articulated by Philippe Buchez in the 1830s, and later by Louis Blanc.[6] They were very much a part of socialist thought in France in the mid-nineteenth century. But while the early utopian socialists made elaborate plans, it was a group of Parisian printers who launched one of the first workers' societies in 1830.[7] The writings of Buchez and Blanc were inspired, not only by ideas from the workers, but by actual attempts to create such societies.

The years 1830 to 1848 were a period of great industrial growth in France, and most Parisian trades were confronted with stagnating wages and recurring crises of unemployment. By 1848 the vast majority of Parisian workers were employed in small- or medium-sized shops with little mechanization. They were skilled craftsmen, and were conscious of the deskilling that was taking place with mechanization.[8]

The overthrow of the French monarchy in the 1848 revolution brought forth a period of intense activity for workers to help themselves. The *Société des Corporations Unies* sought to end the exploitation through the creation of associated workshops.[9] It began with contributions from 50,000 workers, in order to establish a social workshop in a vital industry. It planned to gradually expand production to other trades, until all trades were included in a complete circuit of collective production and exchange. The repression following the uprising virtually eliminated political and trade unionist activity although it hardly interrupted the workers association movement.

Interestingly, the Lunetiers Society of Spectacle Markers, which was formed in 1848, has survived all the difficulties and is still in existence.[10] The initiatives of the workers in 1848 were spontaneous and lacked co-ordination. After several abortive efforts, the workers reorganized in 1849. Moss points out that the plans and actions were elaborate. The union proposed to reorganize mutual credit and exchange among associations until all trades had acquired their own means of production. They had 104 member trade associations organized by early 1850 and the union was prepared to issue its own labour bonds to fund the co-operatives when the Government, fearing the resurgence of Republican Socialism, invaded its headquarters, arrested its leaders and dissolved the organization. The worker co-operatives survived for a time. Nearly 300 associations involving 120 trades with perhaps 50,000 member workers were created in Paris during the second Republic.

These new organizations were fragile, and within a few years most had failed because of the hostile environment in which they found themselves, and because of internal problems. They lacked an immediate source of credit and customers. Also, many were beset with administrative problems. Elected managers did not always possess the requisite managerial and commercial skills. Internal disputes over managerial authority and the distribution of earnings often led to the dismissal of managers and the exclusion or resignation of members. But the urge to organize associations was strong. As Moss points out:

> Contrary to the views of most historians, the experience of the commune did little to alter traditional faith in the association strategy. When Parisian syndicates recovered from the repression of 1872, they immediately resumed efforts to build associations.[11]

By 1884, the number of societies had risen to sixty. In 1893, consistent with the pattern of development for other kinds of co-operatives, they established their own central bank. With this organization to provide advice and support, the movement grew to 476 co-operatives by 1913 with a membership of 20,000 workers.

In 1983, there were 1,269 worker-owned co-operatives affiliated with the central organization in France, and together they employed 40,000 workers or about 0.15% of the total labour force. Most of these are basically small organizations; 554 (44%) have less than 10 members, another 560 (44%) have between 10 and 50 members.[12] The largest was the Precision Instrument Society with 1,500 workers. Established in 1915, this organization is the fifth-largest producer of telephone equipment in France, and manufactures many other kinds of precision instruments as well. The Society runs its own apprenticeship school, and all of the employees are paid equal wages, whether they are directors or ordinary mechanics.[13] Under French law, only a limited interest can be paid on capital and reserves. All surpluses are divided between all the working people, members and non-members. Thus, older members have no personal interest in restricting membership or in exploiting casual labourers.[14]

It is unclear how many worker-productive societies in France have achieved a strong sense of community and practice comprehensive co-operation to its fullest extent. Experiments have, however, been attempted with other co-operatives having a community focus. For example, in 1940 Marcel Barbu, a watchmaker, succeeded in interesting a group of workers in establishing a watch-case factory as a community of work.[15] They started production in a town in southeast France and successfully developed a factory following World War II. When it was studied in the early 1950s, 273 persons belonged, including eighty children and fifteen teenagers. The organization federated with the *Entente Communautaire* (Communities of Work) in Paris, which listed eighty-three communitarian projects in different stages of development in 1950. By 1957, only twenty-seven were in existence, and by the 1970s the movement had disappeared.[16]

The struggle to develop successful worker co-operatives in France was long and slow. Since the turn of the century, however, such organizations have been firmly established in a number of enclaves in Europe. With the development of the *kibbutz*, the period from World War I to 1950 was an era when comprehensive co-operative communities became a reality rather than a utopian dream.

In the Basque country in northern Spain, the Mondragon co-operative started industrial production in 1956. By the mid-1980s, this had grown to about 100 industrial organizations and 160 organizations in all with about 20,000 workers. These organizations produce industrial goods, including electronic components, dishwashers, washing machines and other household items, as well as car parts and equipment for steel mills and refineries. They have also contracted to provide the equipment for entire factories in Mexico, Libya and the Ukraine. Industrial sales by the mondragon group rose from $47 million in 1966 to $336 million in 1975, earning nearly $82 million in foreign exchange for Spain. By 1990 sales were $2.9 billion Cdn with exports of $544 million.[17]

Besides the industrial co-operatives, the federation also includes a co-operative bank, with 70 branch offices in the area, five agricultural co-operatives, eight housing co-ops, and a regional consumer co-op, and nine co-ops concerned with education and services which run schools and evening classes in technical and social subjects.[18]

The Italian workers co-operative movement is the biggest in western Europe, and the most diverse.[19] The Lega co-operative federation had 2,129 affiliates with 122,300 workers in 1983. The three federations total about 215,000 workers besides the many working in unfederated co-ops.[20] In 1975, Mehta reported there were a hundred societies of specialized woodwork; fifty societies making dental equipment, elevators, metal tools and similar products; and about thirty societies in the printing trades.

As noted earlier, worker-productive co-operatives did not achieve significant success in the United Kingdom during the nineteenth century; but by 1965, there were 120 producer societies, mostly involved in small shops.[21] Some of these were co-partnerships, one of the most famous being the John Lewis Partnership, established in 1914 and engaged in retail trade.[22]

In the early 1970s, there were a number of plant closures in Britain, followed by "work-ins"; and in three major concerns, workers bought and reorganized the factories as worker co-operatives.[23] Of these three, the *Scottish Daily News* never got off the ground, and collapsed after a brief flutter. The Triumph Meridien Co-operative, makers of Triumph motorcycles, managed to overcome a number of growing pains; and by 1977, it employed 800 workers with a production level of 24,000 machines a year. It lasted until the summer of 1983 when it went into receivership. The Kirby Manufacturing and Engineering Co-operative "provides sobering lessons for all those people who hoped that worker co-operatives would demonstrate an easy route to industrial socialism."[24] After a difficult start it operated until 1980 when it dissolved.

In all three cases, large corporate capitalism had failed. The workers were convinced that the failures were due to incompetent management and felt they could overcome the problems and retain their jobs. In the three cases cited above the attempts ended in failure. But with the world recession in the 1980s many more worker buyouts have taken place. Many are still operating, but long-term viability is still not shown. It is unclear whether attempts to develop worker productive co-operatives have created a sense of community. The studies carried out to date have focused on economic performance, and they have not reported on the extent to which a community identity has emerged. The large attempts that have failed have been well publicized, but many small-scale co-operatives have been incorporated, and by 1984 over 1,000 were in operation, employing about 10,000 workers.[25]

WORKER CO-OPS IN EASTERN EUROPE (BEFORE 1989)

Before the collapse of the communist governments in 1989 and 1990 the eastern European countries of Bulgaria, Czechoslovakia, Hungary, Poland and Rumania had 5,080 worker co-operative societies comprised of 1,460,000 workers. Poland had the greatest number with 2,406 societies. All these countries had centralized socialist economies, and the co-operatives were generally small, employing up to about 200 workers. A few were larger, with up to 500 workers. In the case of Poland, the societies supplied 10% of the entire socialized output. They produced 30% of the clothing, 23% of the leather and footwear, 22% of the food processing and 27% of the printing industry. "They distributed half of their surplus to worker-members, 45% is allotted for reserves and 5% to social purposes."[26] Since the dramatic political changes that occurred in 1989 these co-operatives have grown and flourished and will be competing with privatized State companies. Their future at this point is unclear.

The U.S.S.R. only permitted consumer co-operatives in rural areas to operate. With the Gorbachev economic reforms, worker-owned co-operatives were made legal. Tens of thousands were organized the first year to provide goods and services. They quickly made money and many individuals became very wealthy. Consumers have become angry about the price increases and the co-operatives have been blamed. How they will evolve in the liberalized economic environment remains to be seen.

WORKER-PRODUCTIVE CO-OPERATIVES IN INDIA

There are 20,000 active worker co-operatives in India. Most are small factories and cottage industries, but they represent a livelihood for 2,000,000 workers. Many of these co-operatives had their origins in pre-independence days, when Ghandi advocated the establishment of cottage industries as a means of breaking India's dependence on British manufacturers. Following independence, the government promoted worker co-operatives, realizing that the cost of starting them was low: the rural areas of the country have an abundance of unemployed and under-employed workers, and most consumer goods can be marketed locally. Government departments were created to help establish societies, and funds were made available to invest in shares. In recent years, the drive to develop heavy industry in India has meant less assistance to small business in general.

Mehta points out that an average worker co-operatives in India has sixty-three members and share capital of RS 3,791 ($455 Cdn), of which only RS 645 ($77 Cdn) has been contributed by the government. This is a healthy ratio of worker financial involvement as compared with that of co-operatives in other countries. He also points out that:

> We must remember that the society developed almost single-handed from a shoestring budget and consists of people who are short of finance, talent and training. Even in our socialist economy, there is a built-in bias in favour of individual units as against co-operative business. Co-operatives, in fact, expressed in a blunt phrase 'are doomed to receive merely the scrapings of the barrel, in the field of supplies, finance, technical help and research'.[27]

Co-operative experience in India is important, as there have been many successes and many failures. A number of studies enable us to get a feel for the reasons for these results.

COMPREHENSIVE CO-OPERATIVE COMMUNITIES IN ISRAEL

The 230 *kibbutzim* in Israel, with their 90,000 members, have accomplished what the Rochdale Pioneers defined as their ultimate goals: "to arrange the powers of production, distribution, education, and government, or in other words to establish a self-supporting home colony of united interests or assist other societies in establishing such colonies."[28] The *kibbutzim* are groups with similar economic and social purposes, which have established integrated co-operative communities.[29] There are no wages except in kind and services. The *kibbutzim* combine co-operative ownership of all property (except personal belongings), purchasing, production, marketing, consumption (including housing), rearing and education of children, and cultural, recreational and other services. Everyone in the *kibbutz* enjoys the same rights and assumes the same obligations. Hired labour is taboo, in principle, but has been and still is used by a number of *kibbutzim* in workshops and to a smaller extent in agriculture.[30]

An elaborate system of committees for decision-making and the host of functions performed mean that a significant part of the adult population has some sort of community responsibility. Approximately 30-40% of the adults take part in the everyday running of *kibbutz* affairs. Because of the deliberate policy of rotating office holders, most adults are involved over a period of a few years.

The *moshavim* movement, which involves co-operative small holders and agricultural settlements, has a lesser extent of collective effort than the *kibbutzim*. The *moshav ovdim* form was first established in 1921, and the *moshav shittufim* was first organized in 1935 by immigrants from Bulgaria.[31] The *moshavim* all lease their land from the Jewish National Fund.[32]

> Every member has his own house. Except for the *moshvim shittufim* in which there is all inclusive co-operative joint production, every member in each of the other three types of the *moshav* has a lease for and cultivates and equal area of land. With few exceptions there is no joint farming in the *moshavim* other than in the *moshavim shittufim*.[33] But co-operative marketing and purchasing, the joint development of/water supply, use of agricultural machinery, educational and other communal services are obligatory basic principles in all four types of *moshavim*.... Generally speaking, there is one multipurpose co-operative in every *moshav*, which does all the marketing, purchasing, etc.[34]

Besides the *kibbutz* and *moshaves* there are three main types of worker-productive co-operatives in Israel: factories and workshops; transportation in the form of bus and trucking: and worker-owned enterprises that provide consumer services, such as hotels, restaurants, theatres and laundries. Each member has one vote and is required to put up the same amount of share capital as all others. When a member leaves, becomes incapacitated or dies, a special committee estimates the value of the member's participation in the share capital in terms of the purchasing or replacement price at the time.

The transportation co-operatives which run the largest bus line in the country pay the same basic wage rate including fringe benefits, allowances for work clothes and education, etc., to all members irrespective of the type of work. There is also a graduated allowances for seniority and dependents. Most of the other two types of societies grade the basic wages according to skill and seniority.[35] The combined economic activity of both the co-operative and institutional sector accounted for 21% of the Israeli GNP at the beginning of 1981 and it employed 22% of the active labour force.[36]

It is a mistake to evaluate these comprehensive co-operatives in terms of monetary criteria alone. Certainly they must be economically viable, but their importance to members goes far beyond material gain. The Mondragon annual report observes that, "Civilization is a matter not of improving machines but of giving people a chance to improve themselves."[37] Similarly, a *kibbutz* statement of principle says, "The strength of the *kibbutz* lies in the essential social nature which strives for the complete harmony of the individual and the group in every sphere of life, for the maximum development of each individual...and for the constant deepening of human ethical relations."[38] While service co-operatives use their potential to change the economic order, the dynamics of involvement in comprehensive co-operatives also has an impact on the individuals, both in terms of personal growth, and also in a broader moral sense. This point is difficult for many social scientists to grasp. It is hard for people who have experienced this to describe it clearly. Social scientists may try to observe, but to understand they must experience the co-operative way of life within comprehensive co-operation.

ANALYSIS

Internal Dynamics

Comprehensive co-operative communities are a reality in many countries. They are a delicate social organization whose will to develop must come from within the membership. They cannot be simply ordered into existence by an outside authority. For this reason, each tends to become a closed system isolated from the outside world to some degree, and over time, some may drop out of the mainstream of economic activity. They may in fact come to be regarded as curiosities, rather than as a readily available alternative of working and living.[39]

The organizations discussed in this chapter become communities by combining co-operative work relations with, to some degree, social relations. The loss of community, in the early phases of the industrial revolution, inspired reformers and has been a constant theme of writers since then.[40] The advantages of community are much easier to expound than to practice. The growth of a community is a complex and subtle process, which depends as much upon spontaneity as upon planning. And how does one plan for spontaneity? Infield, a lifelong student of co-operative communities, points out that:

A community is a blend of contradictory traits. It must be anchored in the minds, attitudes and emotions, and depends on the full participation of all concerned. Such participation must not be forced, but remain free and voluntary. The vitality of a community depends mainly on the intensity of the we-feeling it engenders. Yet it cannot thrive on an unsound economy. To avoid the pitfalls of isolation, a community must keep in step with the world around it; to preserve its identity, it must know how to shield itself against adverse influences. In short, it must succeed in being at the same time a world within itself and a part of the world as a whole.[41]

The conditions for the successful development of comprehensive co-operatives communities appear to be similar as those for service co-operatives. The difference is not in kind, but in degree. In the case of co-operative communities, conditions must remain favourable and constant. Comprehensive co-operation tends to be more vulnerable to adverse change than segmental forms.

Superordinate Goal

Commitment of a superordinate goal is necessary for the emergence of segmental co-operation; but once service organizations have become established, they can take on a life of their own, independent of the collective goal or commitment of their members. In co-operative communities, this is not the case: commitment is a central ingredient in enabling a community to persist. Provided that the economic basis for co-operation is sound, the community "can afford to experience crises of one sort of another, so long as there always remains at the end of the day a nucleus of people whose commitment to the idea and practice is unshaken."[42]

The most successful comprehensive co-operative communities in the past, excluding the *kibbutzim,* have been those founded on religious commitment. In an extensive study of commitment and community, Rosabeth Kanter asserts that:

The problem of commitment is crucial. Since the commune represents an attempt to establish an ideal social order within the larger society, it must vie with the outside for the members' loyalties. It must ensure high member involvement despite external competition without sacrificing its distinctiveness or ideals. It must often contravene the earlier socialization of its members in securing obedience to new demands. It must claim internal unison in order to present a united front to the world.[43]

Yet in egalitarian communities, participation and disagreements cannot be stifled for the sake of maintaining a united front. Wide disagreement must be tolerated, as well as experimentation with different means of achieving goals. But commitment to a clear superordinate goal must be present in all members, or the sense of community can evaporate.

The experience of the *kibbutzim* is instructive in this regard. Although some are religious communities, the movement itself is not based on a commitment to Zionism; rather it reflects the principle "that each should labour for the community according to his ability, and share according to his needs."[44] People migrating to Palestine and later to Israel were not forced to join a *kibbutz* or to remain once they joined. When their commitment waned, many left. Studies on *moshavim* in Israel show that many members formerly lived in a *kibbutz,* and either the husband or the wife lacked a commitment to its more communal aspects.[45]

The community of work that Marcel Barbu organized in France in the 1940s succeeded in developing a set of rules for the organization. These shared beliefs were sufficient to sustain the commitment of the founders for three decades, but they did not attract sufficient new members to sustain the organization. The communities of work were unsuccessful in finding a common system of transcendent beliefs that could legitimate their rules. In the absence of a shared belief-system and a strong superordinate goal, they were unable to survive.[46]

It appears that the superordinate goal must be very desirable and one that is completely unattainable through individual effort. If it is not, individualistic tendencies will predominate, and the existence of the community will be short.

Commitment to Non-exploitation of Others

Co-operative ideology is clearly a reaction against the exploitation of human by human. In a co-operative community, the shared labour of members is essential for a co-operative way of life. Studies of many worker-productive co-operatives show that, although they were based originally on members' labour, other workers were eventually hired for a variety of reasons. This hired labour, when denied membership, destroyed the co-operativeness of the enterprise over time.[47]

Daniel analyzes the problem in terms of the economic development of a *kibbutz.* Typically in agriculture, there is a seasonal fluctuation in the demand for labour. The *kibbutz* has tried to diversify its economic operations to balance the work load during the year; but these attempts, as well as the mechanization of harvesting methods, have only partially solved the problem. Economic fluctuations in domestic and world markets also necessitate flexibility in the supply of labour.[48]

Kibbutzim became industrialized partly in order to accommodate changes in labour needs and partly in order to adjust to food surpluses during the 1960s. Industrialization was successful, and the growth of *kibbutz* manufacturing has been even more rapid than that of the general rate of industrialization in Israel. The number of persons employed in *kibbutz* industrial enterprises doubled between 1960 and 1968. They have made important contributions not only to the *kibbutz,* but also to Israeli society in general. What should the *kibbutzim* do when labour needs peak in both agricultural and manufacturing enterprises: close down a factory, or hire temporary workers?

Moshavim ideology also is explicitly non-exploitative of others. Farms are designed to make hired labour unnecessary, while at the same time supplying the farmer a satisfactory living. Abarbanel clearly identifies the relationship between the family cycle and the availability and amount of labour required to meet labour needs. In the *moshav* he studied, the problem was partially resolved by collaboration and informal partnerships with neighbours who had different labour requirements.[49]

The practice of paying equal wages and bestowing benefits, described earlier in this chapter, is one way of avoiding exploitation of members. But many very successful co-operative communities have found that this rule must be adjusted in certain circumstances. For example, members who work hard may be exploited by those who do not. What seems to be crucial is that members should perceive the situation to be non-exploitive. In some cases, it may be expedient to hire an outside manager, at a higher rate of pay, to undertake a job that members cannot perform by themselves. In other instances, members who carry out tasks that many consider to be distasteful may be paid at a premium for their work, as a reward for getting the job done. In Kantor's study, the successful communities adopted a more egalitarian approach to labour and engaged in more community sharing than those that failed.[50]

The use of members' labour alone to avoid exploitation of others is easiest to apply in agricultural settings. It is more difficult in an industrial setting as changes in technology occur. Even in the *kibbutzim,* which have a strong commitment to members' labour, the pressure to hire additional workers is present.[51] Members are experimenting with ways to resolve the problem without creating a superior-subordinate relationship.[52]

Commitment to Democratic Decision-Making

Participation is a central aspect of comprehensive co-operative communities. The only people who can define what decisions are needed and what are good decisions are the members of the communities themselves. Research into the success and failure of co-operative communities makes this fact abundantly clear.[53]

Virtually all the successful communities have developed a format of regular (usually weekly) general meetings that are open to all members and where any aspect of community life can be discussed.[54] They have institutionalized mechanisms of self-criticism, and mutual criticism which are legitimate and dealt with routinely. In small communities, criticism may take place in small group sessions. In larger ones, it involves a regular, routine assessment of activities, as well as norms for confronting problems and speaking one's mind.

Pressures to bureaucratize and to centralize power are always present in organizations. It requires a strong, widely shared commitment to resist these tendencies and to keep a participatory format for decision-making.

Commitment to Mutual Self-Help

Mutual self-help is a condition that seems clearly necessary, yet its absence is a major cause of failure in many comprehensive co-operative communities. Obviously, if competitive or selfish attitudes are present, there is little hope for a community to survive. What seems less obvious is the power-dependency relationship between those who start the community and the members. Marcel Barbu, the French watch-maker discussed earlier, wanted to form a community of work. He had the knowledge and skills to make and market watch cases. He established a successful enterprise, but searched for years before he found a group of workers who wanted to form a community of work rather than be just wage labourers.

Vaillancourt studied worker-productive co-operatives in the province of Québec, Canada. Intensive case studies of twenty-five co-operatives showed that success was closely related to *esprit de corps*: "If co-operatives lacked an *esprit de corps* there was a general absence of discipline resulting in unmotivated workers. Materials were wasted; tools and supplies sometimes disappeared from the workshop."[55]

Mutual self-help often requires sacrifice and involves individuals in intense personal relationships as they jointly try to work out problems. It may accentuate personality problems and point out those members who are not prepared to help the total group. In almost all cases studied by Vaillancourt, there came a point where some members left or were asked to leave. This existence of such conflict emphasizes the importance of voluntary membership.

Voluntarism

Voluntary membership is one of the essential principles of cooperative organizations. It is also the source of a fundamental dilemma in democratic theory: the balance between equality and personal liberty. Both are highly valued; but when a choice must be made between them it is difficult to decide which should dominate. Should the wants of the group (equality) come first or those of the individual (personal liberty)?

Regardless of how this dilemma is resolved in specific situations, it is clear that voluntary involvement and withdrawal are important in co-operative communities. The development of a community is complex, and occurs only where there are smooth interpersonal relations. When personality conflicts interrupt a group's development, they must be resolved. Working these conflicts through can build a community; but failure to eliminate them means that a member will have to leave, or be asked to leave. Forcing dissident members to remain is harmful to the development of a co-operative way of life. The *kibbutzim* failure rate is low, but member turnover is often high. People cannot know whether they want to be in a particular co-operative community without experiencing it. But along with the opportunity to become involved, they must have the right to withdraw voluntarily. In a study of co-operative communities in Israel, Weintraub found that disputes erupted between the members of one *kibbutz* twice in the course of five years (1921-1926) concerning the orientation of the community. The solution in both cases was similar; the protagonists could no longer live together, and one of the groups was compelled to leave.[56] This is not an uncommon pattern. Splitting proceeds in dividing the land or the economic foundation of the organization may cause the community to fail completely, for the unit of production may be destroyed. If the unit remains intact, new members can be admitted, and the community can continue and develop stable relationships.

The founders of the community are likely to see it as a social experiment; a "right" social order, with rules and an ideology that have fostered success and which, having been proven, should not be changed. Cohen and Rosner point out that members of the second generation usually perceive the world differently. To them, the community is not a social experiment but a home, an emotional experience rather than a right social order.

The second generation do not necessarily deviate by not accepting the orthodox interpretation of the *kibbutz*. The situation is more complex.... The second generation, less constrained by the experiences and obligations of the past, feel free to reinterpret and, by so doing, reformulate the ideology and actually recreate *kibbutz* life.[57]

A dynamic community must continually redefine and recreate itself with successive generations in order to build membership commitment and satisfaction. The changes from the experience of one generation to those of the next may be vastly different, and the ways in which values are translated into rules of behaviour for one generation may make little sense to its successors.[58] Unless the community adjusts to these differences, second and third generations may feel that they are being forced into a rigid and incompatible lifestyle. Their only recourse may be to leave the community and create their own social environment elsewhere.

Organizational Skills and Economic Factors

Any comprehensive co-operative community must be able to organize itself, and must quickly become economically viable in order to survive. If it does not it will fail, regardless of its social desirability.[59] In addition to the sheer difficulty of raising capital and getting organized (problems that face all new organizations), co-operative communities must overcome the hurdle of their ideology, which severely limits the means available to succeed.

Capitalist and State-owned productive units can exploit cheap labour, employ profits generated elsewhere to establish the new plant and use central power to initiate activities. These options are not available to co-operative communities. Moreover, most western industrialized countries are prepared to subsidize large capitalist ventures in the form of credit, tax holidays, subsidized infrastructures and similar benefits. These are rarely available to co-operative communities. Even in the case of the *kibbutzim*, which were recognized at an early stage of the Zionist movement as a desirable way for Jews to settle in Palestine, the outside assistance offered to communities was severely limited.

The *kibbutz, Ein Harod*, was created in 1921 and did not become economically viable until 1931. Settlement authorities were doubtful that large *kibbutzim* could be successful and exerted considerable pressure, even to the point of threatening to cut off funds, to have *Ein Harod* develop in the form they prescribed, rather than according to the aspirations of the members.[60]

All organizational forms require some assistance and subsidization in order to become established, but supporting agencies must protect their funds. Thus, they often prescribe the organizational form that must be established and, by withholding funds, prevent the members from evolving a community which fits their needs and aspirations. For co-operative communities, such external influence is fundamentally in conflict with their ideology.

Co-operatives may require outside assistance even when the necessary organizational skills and resources are present within the group. But in many cases, the aspiring group lacks these skills and resources. In worker-productive co-operatives, the workers may have the skills to produce the goods but lack the skills for co-ordinating work processes. In addition, they are often cut off from markets and supplies.[61] In industrial sectors that are highly interdependent, a radical new form that has no established marketing and supply network is extremely vulnerable. Co-operatives then have two choices: to try to evolve a self-contained economy, or to develop secondary organizations to handle the credit, supply and marketing functions.

It is frequently assumed that worker-controlled enterprises are inherently less efficient and more poorly organized than capitalist corporations, and that this fact accounts for their failures or limited success. It may be true that many fail for this reason, but there is also ample evidence to show that it is not an inherent weakness. Research by Jones and Backus on worker-productive co-operatives in the United Kingdom shows that the "failure to pay a scarcity-reflecting remuneration for the use of collectively owned capital is responsible for the frequently short life span." These co-operatives operate on a minimum of reserves, and the limited amount of collectively owned capital is inadequate in times of economic crisis.[62]

Seymour Melman studied industrial efficiency under both managerial and co-operative decision-making, comparing enterprises in *kibbutzim* with other Israeli enterprises. He found that:

> The co-operative enterprises showed higher productivity of labour (26%), higher productivity of capital (67% and 33%), larger net profit per production worker (115%), and lower administrative cost (13%)...The data assembled here bear upon three widespread assumptions: (1) that there is no workable alternative to the managerial form of control

for operating modern industry; (2) that even if there were alternative, the managerial mode or organization is inherently most efficient; and (3) that technology itself sets the requirement for managerialism. Whatever constraints maybe assigned to the data of this paper, it is evident that they do not support these familiar themes. Evidently, there is a co-operative mode of organization that is a workable alternative to managerialism for industrial operations, and the use of machine technology does not itself exclude the use of co-operative decision making.[63]

Although nothing inherent seems to limit worker co-operatives, they are difficult to develop because of the number of favourable internal and external conditions that must be present.

External Environment

Just as the right internal conditions are very important for the emergence and development of comprehensive co-operative communities, the correct external conditions also are critical. It is sometimes assumed that only specific industries are suitable to be operated by comprehensive worker co-operatives, and that this explains the concentration of these societies in such areas. Research certainly casts doubt on this assumption. Weintraub observers that:

> The functional fit of the *kibbutz* to national requirements and conditions was neither easily accepted nor in fact inevitable. Indeed, the collective fought a hard up-hill battle for recognition both within and without the workers movement. Nor was it for a long time the clear choice from the point of view of numerical strength.... The dominance of the *kibbutz* was by no means historically pre-determined.... It was the growth of the power of Hakibbutz Hameuchad[64] (and of other collective movements) that affected, to no small degree, the actual pattern of rural development, which might have taken another path.[65]

The strong central organizations were able to influence the political-economic environment so that the needs of local co-operatives could be heard and acted upon. It was not enough to gain a sympathetic response from the central authority. This sympathy had to be translated into workable policies and resources, which the grassroots members could use. The co-operatives themselves also had to develop the capacity to absorb and employ the resources that were made available. Berman's study of plywood co-operatives in the Pacific Northwest of the United States concludes that:

> The establishment of the unusual cluster of co-operatives in the plywood industry...[is] to be explained in terms of a combination of historical-accidental factors with favourable industry-characteristics and not in terms of an industry uniquely predisposed to co-operative operations.... The conclusion of the viability of worker owned co-operatives does not need to be abandoned, or limited to the plywood industry.[66]

In the case of the plywood industry, there was sufficient economic flexibility to enable the co-operatives to obtain supplies for the factory, as well as to sell the plywood they produced. In many economic sectors, this is not so. As explained earlier, where large vertically integrated firms exist as competitors, co-operatives may not be able to obtain supplies or market their products. A commission of inquiry into the problems of worker-productive co-operatives in India listed the following problems in order of importance: 1) a lack of purchase orders, 2) a shortage of working capital, and 3) onerous labour and factory laws.[67] Although these organizations face hundreds of problems, the most pressing are related to marketing and supplies.

The history of co-operative communities in Mexico shows how vulnerable they are to environmental conditions established by the government. The earliest communities (*ejidos*) emerged as a result of and reforms initiated in 1915. Until 1934, however, they were controlled primarily by an administrative committee, and few of them worked co-operatively. Land reform was a major part of the Cardena government, which came into power in 1934. By 1940, 15,000 *ejidos* had been organized. A study carried out in 1939 estimated that one-third of 5,000 were operating as collective co-operative communities.[68] By 1960, there were 18,699 *ejidos* and, of these, 431 were collectives. The disintegration of the collectives had occurred in almost all areas, despite continued policies by the Mexican government to continue large-scale productive farms. Like the Israeli migrants, *ejido* members were formerly labourers who owned neither land or capital. Unlike the *kibbutzim* the collective ejidos were designed to produce a single market commodity — cotton or sugar cane — for a capitalist-controlled plant. The only way for the peasants to diversify agricultural production in order to improve their own nutrition was to divide up the *ejidos* into plots. Ronfeldt's 1973 study of an *ejido* shows how diverse means were used to deprive the *ejido* of its co-operative content and to turn it into a conventional tool (controlled by the sugar factory and government bureaucracy) for exploiting the peasants.[69]

The interest of the State and that of the sugar factory was to maintain the maximum cropping of sugarcane, but the interest of the peasants was to develop a multicrop farm that would enable the farmers not only to improve their diet, but also to increase their disposable income and reduce their dependence upon the sugar factory. The interests of more recent Mexican governments and the peasants in the *ejidos* also differed. The outcome, as Ronfeldt states, "gives dramatic testimony to the power and stability of the governments system of control." With unsympathetic governments, as successive Mexican governments have been since Cardena, it was difficult to develop comprehensive co-operatives.[70]

Clearly the external environment is crucial to the development of co-operative communities. If there is scope for democratic processes to be practised at the local level, local societies may emerge, particularly ones with self-contained economies.[71] If the industrial sector in which they emerge is characterized by many firms that are not vertically integrated, it may be possible to establish an economic niche, as in the case of the building trades in France and Italy. Most important of all is the State's response. Such organizations require early support, particularly if they are founded with little start-up capital by people who have limited financial resources. But if they have initial success, decentralized control and internal autonomy enable members to become highly conscious of the roadblocks they face. Any mistakes by government and it will have a severe critic. In a historical context, the opposition of co-operatives to government may be understandable; but it is often thought that these organizations are ungraciously biting the hand that feeds them. In order to deal with confrontations with governments, co-operatives need a strong federation of local organizations. This structure is seldom present in the early stages of development. In the absence of strong and articulate spokespersons, co-operatives may be subject to a shift in government policy, so that they are ignored or attempts are made to discredit and control them.

In conclusion, there are many organizational forms through which people co-operate on a day-to-day basis. The realization of a co-operative community or a sense of communal purpose is a psychological outcome of the process of co-operation. Thus, typologies based on distinctive structural differences between co-operatives tend to hide as much as they reveal. Some worker co-operatives, in which production is communal but consumption is private, may attain a stronger sense of community than a commune where production and consumption are technically communal, if there are numerous internal conflicts and a changing membership. French notes that:

> In communal work groups, people gradually come to think of themselves as "family," a relationship that embraces work, play, loving, learning indeed the whole range of life activities for those involved. For each person, of course, the pursuit of these things will not be restricted to the communal group alone. But it will be centred there, and there people will find the greatest latitude for experimenting with their own possibilities.... In addition to all the other things they offer, communal work places present us the opportunity to be fully ourselves.[72]

Through commitment and full interdependence within a group, individuals have a greater opportunity to fulfil their own potential and to take initiatives than is possible in situations where interaction is based on self-interest. Self-interest and individual action encourage people to conform rather than experiment. The comprehensive co-operative community that achieves communalism allows members wide scope to realize their individuality. As French concludes from the studies of the *kibbutzim,* "it seems almost too good to be true: strong individuals co-operating fully within a supportive and productive environment."[73]

It is the self-governing aspect of co-operative communities that enables people to work towards their image of the good society. In order to direct communal and community resource, the group engages in a continual process of reassessment and redefinition of purposes.

Involvement in this process develops members' skill of analysis, discussion, debate and group decision-making. They learn about leadership and democracy, not by reading about them, but through daily experience and practice. The development of these skills can have a spillover effect upon the broader society. For example, in 1965, when the *kibbutz* population was less than 4% of that of Israel as a whole, 14% of representatives to the Israeli parliament were from *kibbutzim.* According to Dan Leon they play a role quite out of proportion to their numbers in every military action which requires special initiative, staying-power and the readiness to make quick and independent decisions.[74]

David and Elena French argue that only fully communal work processes are sufficiently strong to prevent the domination of individualism and materialism which is characteristic of North American and western European culture. They correctly point out that the that the new wave of co-operative activity that followed the student protests of the 1960s did not fundamentally change economic and social structures in America. Most of the co-operatives have developed a sense of community around only one aspect of a person's life. In common households, work hours are spent apart; and in the case of worker co-operatives, labour is a co-operative activity, but consumption and leisure time involve other interest groups. These 1960s co-operatives may have had a strong communal sense when they were first started, but they have gradually come to be regarded as performing a service function. Members seek greater efficiency and refrain from being committed. This lack of member commitment forces the co-operatives to imitate capitalist competitors, and they are then unable to effect fundamental changes in social values and relationships.

Despite the French's arguments, it is reasonable to suggest that many types of comprehensive co-operatives can effect basic changes in social values and enable members to co-operate as a way of life. Many organizations that have failed have generally been attempted in socio-economic settings that were hostile to highly participatory, decentralized activities. It is quite conceivable that in a more supportive environment, co-operative communities which are not communal in all aspects may be able to emerge, maintain commitment and have a significant impact on people's lives.

NOTES

1. The definition of a co-operative is important. In this book, we have used one stated in behavioural terms; thus, many communes may be co-operative communities, even though they are not incorporated as such. A co-operative community is one in which the members attempt to practise the essence of co-operation and the values of equity, equality and mutual self-help by developing rules that allow each person to have an equal say, do not exploit others in the community and do not force members to remain against their will.
2. Isolation can be an important factor. The Inuit communities in Canada have organized consumer, marketing and fishing co-operatives. Because of a lack of other community organizations, these have become the focal point of the community, facilitating comprehensive co-operation within the entire community.
    Arbess, Saul E. 1966. *Social Change and the Eskimo Co-operative at George River, Québec.* Ottawa: Northern Co-ordination and Research Centre, Deptartment of Northern Affairs and Natural Resources. Describes the case in George River. For an overview, see Boyd, Leslie S. 1991. *Co-operatives, Communities and Culture: An Assessment of the Arctic Co-operative Development Program.* Toronto: York University, Unpublished Masters thesis in Faculty of Environmental Studies.

Sprudzs, Aleksandrs. 1975. *Co-operatives in Native Communities*. Iglauer, Edith. 1979. *Inuit Journey*. Vancouver: Douglas and McIntyre. Stager, J.K. 1982. *An Evaluation Study of the Federated Co-operatives in Nouveau Québec and the Northwest Territories after the Co-operative Development Programs*. Report for the Program Evaluation Branch Department of Indian Affairs and Northern Development. Ottawa: Indian and Northern Affairs.

3. Catalano, Bruno. 1984. "Work Co-operatives: What will be their evolution?" Paper presented to the General Assembly of CICOPA—Hamburg, Germany: 2.

4. Quarter, Jack. 1993. *Canada's Social Economy*. Toronto: James Lorimer and Company: 27-32. Also see articles in Quarter, Jack and George Melnyk, eds., 1989. *Partners in Enterprise: The Worker Ownership Phenomenon*. Montreal: Black Rose Books. For the U.S.A. see Woodward, Warner. 1986. "Participatory Research and Economic Democracy in the 80s: Experience from the U.S.," *Community and Co-operatives in Participatory Development*. Yair Levi and H. Litwin, eds., London: Gower.

5. Holmstrom, Mark. 1989. *Industrial Democracy in Italy*. Aldershot, UK: Avebury. Lindkvist, Lars G. and Claes Svensson. 1982. "Worker-Owned Factories in Sweden." *Economic Analysis and Workers' Management*. Vol. XVI: 387-400.

6. The difference between Blanc and Buchez was in the matter of scale. Buchez favoured small co-operative industries. Blanc conceived co-operative activity on a large scale, to blossom ultimately into a complete collectivist society. According to Blanc, one-third of the profits were to go to the workers, one-third were to support the old, sick and infirm, and the rest would enable new members to purchase needed tools and start more industries. Mehta, S.C. 1975. *Industrial Co-operatives in India*. Delhi: Atma Ram: 18.

7. Moss, B. 1974. "Parisian producers' association in the nineteenth century: the socialism of skilled workers."International Archives of Sociology of Co-operation and Development, 36 (July-Dec.): 107-127.

8. Strikes were illegal under the Napoleonic Code. They occurred in 1830, 1933 and 1840, and troops were used in each case to break them up. Moss, 1974: 114.

9. Moss, 1974: 115.

10. Mehta, 1975: 19.

11. Moss, 1974: 123.

12. Axworthy, Christopher. 1985. *Worker Co-operatives in Mondragon, the U.K. and France; Some Reflections*. Saskatoon: Centre for the Study of Co-operatives: 57.

13. Mehta, 1975: 21.

14. Antoni, Antoine. 1968. "Workers' control in the French co-operative societies." *Review of International Co-operation*, 61: 228-234.

15. This attempt was documented by Claire Bishop and reported by Infield 1956a: 188-203.

16. French, David and Elena French. 1975. *Working Communally: Patterns and Possibilities*. New York: Russell Sage: 121.

17. Giddard. 1991. "Mondragon Update." *Worker Co-op* Vol. 4: 15.

18. Whyte, William Foote and Kathleen King Whyte. 1988. *Making Mondragon: The Growth and Dynamics of the Worker Co-operative Complex*. Ithaca New York: ILR Press.

19. Earle, John. 1986. *The Italian Co-operative Movement: A Portrait of the Lega Nazionale della Co-operative e Mutue*. London: Allen and Unwin.

20. Holmstrom, Mark. 1989. *Industrial Democracy in Italy*. Aldershot, UK: Avebury: 21.

21. An exception is Equity Shoes. It was originally owned by the Co-operative Wholesale Society (CWS). In the 1880s CWS ran into economic problems and decided to close the shoe factory. It was purchased by the workers and is still operating successfully.

22. Thornley, Jenny. 1980. *The Product Dilemma for Workers Co-operatives in Britain, France and Italy*. Co-operative Research Unit of the Open University; and 1981.

Workers' Co-operatives: Jobs and Dreams. London: Heinemann Educational Books.
23. Coates, Ken. 1976. *The New Worker Co-operatives.* Nottingham: Published for the Institute for Worker's Control by Spokesman Books.
24. Eccles, Tony. 1976. "Kirby manufacturing and engineering," *The New Worker Co-operatives,* Ken Coates, ed., Nottingham: Published for the Institute for Workers Control by Spokesman Books: 141-169.
25. Holmstrom, Mark. 1989: 22.
26. Mehta, 1975: 24-25.
27. Mehta, 1975: 5.
28. Lambert, Paul. 1963. *Studies in the Social Philosophy of Co-operation.* Manchester: The Co-operative Union: 292.
29. Various types of communities are grouped within the broad category *kibbutzim.* Kvutza were originally small collectives with a maximum of about 12 families in the 1920s. Ein Harod developed a strategy of completely open membership, unlimited size and unlimited growth. It is this type which has been called the *kibbutz.*
30. Viteles, H. 1966. *A History of the Co-operative Movement in Israel.* London: Vallentine, Mitchell Publishers: 31-32.
31. Viteles, 1966: 32-34 defines four types of *moshav.*
32. The *moshav shittufim* is the smallest in number. It provides separate housing for families, but the farm (or industry) work is done collectively, as in the *kibbutzim.*
33. Informal arrangements do develop as the available farm labour fluctuates at different points in the family cycle. Such relationships are on a sharing basis and vary over time. Abarbanel, Jay S. 1974. *The Co-operative Farmer and the Welfare State: Economic Change in an Israeli* Moshav. Manchester: Manchester University Press.
34. Viteles, 1966: 33.
35. Viteles, 1966: 35.
36. Palgi, Michael and Menachem Rosner. 1983. *Industrial Democracy in Israel.* Haifa: Centre for the Study of Industrial Democracy and Self-Management.
37. The Economist. 1976. "Worker-capitalist dragon seed." *The Economist* (Dec.11): 86.
38. Spiro, Melford E. 1975. *Kibbutz: Venture in Utopia.* Cambridge: Harvard University Press (Augmented edition): 10.
39. A problem for communes practising comprehensive co-operation in the United States is a steady stream of visitors. French, 1975: 169.
40. The renewed interest in alternative lifestyles in industrialized countries has generated considerable interest in the development of co-operative communities. For example, see Rigby, Andrew. 1974. *Communes in Britain.* London: Routledge and Kegan Paul; and Kephart, William M. 1976. *Extraordinary Groups: The Sociology of Unconventional Life-Styles.* New York: St. Martin's Press.
41. Infield, 1956: 195.
42. Rigby,1974: 140.
43. Kanter, Rosabeth Moss. 1972. *Commitment and Community.* Cambridge, Mass.: Harvard University Press: 65.
44. This principle is attributed to Abe Morelleto (*Code de la Nature,* published in 1755) quoted by Viteles, 1966: 32.
45. Abarbanel, 1974: 39.
46. French, 1975: 121.
47. For examples, see Mehta, 1975: 147 or Bellas, Carl J. 1972. *Industrial Democracy and the Worker-Owned Firm.* New York: Praeger: 92-94.
48. Daniel, Abraham. 1975 "The Kibbutz movement and hired labor," *Journal of Rural Co-operation,* 3 (1): 31-40.
49. Abarbanel, 1975: 105-178.
50. Kanter, Rosabeth Moss. 1970. "Communes," *Psychology Today,* 4 (July): 53.

51. Daniel, Abraham. 1975 "The Kibbutz movement and hired labor." *Journal of Rural Co-operation*, 3 (1): 35.

52. Kanovsky, Eliyaha. 1966. *The Economy of the Israeli Kibbutz.* Cambridge, Mass: Harvard University Press: 65 reads: "One suggested solution to this dilemma has been the conversion of these industries into co-operatives, jointly owned by the *kibbutz* and the permanent staff of hired workers. One *kibbutz* has, in fact, begun to adopt this method of solving its problem with hired labour. It has a large establishment for the manufacture of doors, in which IL 1.1 million has been invested by the *kibbutz*, with a regular staff of 10 *kibbutz* members and 25 hired workers. The *kibbutz* retains 70% of the shares of the co-operative, and the 25 hired workers are offered shares in the co-op at IL 5,000 per share. The *kibbutz* will arrange to seek the necessary loans to help these workers pay for their shares."

53. For example, see Abarbanel, 1974; Kanter, 1970 and 1972; Kephart, 1976; and Rigby, 1974.

54. Over time, the items raised at the general meetings change. As the members learn more about democratic participation, trivial matters tend to be handled by committees and the meetings are used to debate more crucial matters. Spiro, 1975: 283.

55. Vaillancourt, Pauline Marie. 1975. "Quebec worker production co-operatives." Paper presented to annual meeting of the Canadian Political Science Association in Edmonton.

56. In the terminology of this book, the disputes were over the superordinate goals of the *kibbutz*.

57. Cohen, Erik and Menaham Rosner. 1973. "Problems of generations in the Israeli kibbutz." *Communes.* R.M. Kanter, ed., New York: Harper and Row: 534-44. On page 538, the authors identify five points of difference in the interpretation of *kibbutz* life by the founders and the second generation respectively: 1) The *kibbutz* as a social environment versus a home; 2) Cognitive versus emotional emphasis; 3) Emphasis on values and concepts versus emphasis on persons: 4) Emphasis on institutional form versus emphasis on human content; 5) Emphasis on collective needs versus emphasis on individual needs.

58. Goldberg, Harvey E. 1972. *Cave Dwellers and Citrus Growers: a Jewish Community in Lybia and Israel.* Cambridge: The University Press, describes an old Jewish community in Libya where the members lived in caves. They migrated *en masse* to Israel and formed a *moshav*. Thus, in one generation, they moved from a medieval cave dwellers' setting to the modern Israeli milieu.

59. Communes based on subsistence agriculture must produce sufficient food to feed the members. This may be possible in a few months, but in the meantime they must have resources to buy food and agricultural inputs. For those involves in a more complex economic undertaking, the economic base may take much longer to develop.

60. Weintraub, D., M. Lissak and Y. Azmon. 1969. *Moshava, Kibbutz and Moshav.* Ithica: Cornell University Press: 91.

61. If their emergence is controversial, others may refuse to handle the goods produced. If the economic sector is dominated by an oligopoly and vertically integrated, they may be frozen out of the economy.

62. Jones, Derek C. and David K. Backus. 1977. "British producer co-operatives in the footwear industry: an empirical evaluation of the theory of financing." *The Economic Journal*, 87 (Sept): 488-510.

63. The study involved twelve paired enterprises from a stratified random sample. Melman, Seymour. 1970. "Industrial efficiency under managerial versus co-operative decision-making." *International Development*, 6: 47-58.

64. This is a central federation of the *kibbutzim*.

65. Weintraub et. al. 1969: 306-307.

66. Berman, K. 1967. *Worker-Owned Plywood Companies*. Pullman: Washington State University Press: 213.

67. Mehta, 1975: 210.
68. The others were settlements where the peasants each farmed a small parcel of the land. This arrangement was similar to that of a *moshav*, but it lacked a developed co-operative infrastructure for marketing products and obtaining supplies. Infield, 1947: 77.
69. Ronfeldt, David. 1973. *Antecingo: The Politics of Agrarian Struggle in a Mexican Ejido.* Stanford: Stanford University Press: 220.
70. Ronfeldt, 1973: 239.
71. Greece is an example. See Mariadis, Stavros. 1972. *Groups of Farmers Collaborating on a Non-Statutory Basis.* Athens: Thessaloniki.
72. French, 1975: 132.
73. This statement may seem contradictory, as communal living is often equated with conformity and the opposite of individuality; but empirical observation shows that this does not hold in the *kibbutzim.* Rabin, A.I. 1965. *Growing Up in the Kibbutz.* New York: Springer: 22: "There is full recognition of individual differences in talents and abilities...Every child is encouraged to follow his interests and do the best he can in contributing to the group effort." In such environments, people become comfortable with their own abilities. They do not have to conform to gain acceptance; rather, they can develop their individual talents. Neubauer, Peter B., ed., 1965. *Children in Collectives: Child-Rearing Aims and Practices in the Kibbutz.* Springfield, Ill.: Charles C. Thomas: 204.
74. French, 1975: 131.

Chapter 5

CO-OPERATIVES IN DEVELOPING COUNTRIES

Co-operative activity in the developed countries of western Europe and North America arose during periods of intense dissatisfaction with existing social and economic conditions. Some local organizations were successful and formed secondary or central organizations. Centrals promoted more locals and in this way, the co-operative movement became institutionalized. The years from World War I to 1950 saw considerable organizing activity in countries that were politically independent.

Dissatisfaction also was evident in African and Asian colonies during the same period. In East Africa, co-operatives were organized and peasants reacted against the dominance of both Asian traders, and their own chiefs supported coffee and cotton marketing co-operatives in the 1920s. The success of the local societies threatened colonial planters, and the indigenous movements were carefully watched and controlled. In India, credit co-operatives were organized before World War I, in opposition to the domination of the money-lender-traders. The colonial office did not regard co-operatives as a major threat, and laws were passed in 1904 and 1912 to enable incorporation. Co-operative ideology was compatible with the non-violent, self-help ideology of Mahatma Ghandi; and the 1920s and 1930s, grassroots societies were organized for a host of activities in British India (which now comprises India, Sri Lanka, Pakistan and Bangladesh). These co-operatives did not represent a mass movement to transform economic institutions. They were closely controlled by the colonial administration, and only a small proportion of the population was involved.

By the end of World War II, the successful co-operatives in British India and Africa, as well as in the French and Dutch colonies, provided tangible evidence that native people could manage their own affairs. Co-operation captured the imagination of the leaders of independence movements and was viewed as a main reform mechanism to transform backward agricultural sectors into modern independent economies.

132

A new era for co-operatives began. By the 1950s, the United Nations agencies were promoting co-operatives as major instruments of development. A host of newly independent States, and independence movements in other States, were promoting State sponsorship of co-operatives. It was a widely held belief that the co-operative traditions of the peasants would lend themselves to the development of a modern co-operative economy, as soon as the exploitive colonial structures were swept away.[1] Government employees organized and incorporated thousands of co-operatives in dozens of newly independent States during the 1950s and early 1960s. By the late 1960s and early 1970s, the reports of dramatic failures far outweighed the fewer, seemingly isolated, success stories.

The first decade of co-operative development attempted by the United Nations (the 1960s) was evaluated as a failure. In the second, the 1970s, efforts were directed towards developing fewer but sounder projects. The notion that peasants have a predisposition towards co-operation in its contractual form has proven to be an illusion.[2] In most countries, the wars of liberation were not social revolutions, and co-operatives failed to revolutionize peasant agriculture or bring about massive development. On the other hand, "in almost every country the performance of co-operatives in certain fields of activity or in certain specified geographical areas is quite credible."[3]

This chapter is concerned with identifying the reasons for the massive failures of co-operatives in developing countries and for their success in some enclaves. The usual explanations for failure include poor management, illiterate or ignorant members, lack of trained leadership, complicated rules and regulations, and lack of resources. It is commonly thought that these problems can be remedied by educating members and supplying some resources. There is little doubt that more and better education and resources would improve the situation; however, the accumulated research of the past fifteen years also suggests that there are many more complex and intricate problems, which education and resources alone cannot resolve.

Agricultural development is a case in point. The range of options for economic structures is limited in Third-World countries. It is not realistic to discard co-operatives for other economic organizations, for they too possess inherent weaknesses that are a hindrance to development. Large, highly mechanized capitalist farms or State farms, for example, would remove many peasants from the countryside and would not achieve development objectives.

Agricultural modernization in industrialized countries has been assisted by industrial growth. New industries have been established to develop technological innovations for the farm sector; and the expansion of these and other industries has absorbed the surplus population freed from the countryside by mechanization. In North America, the agricultural sector, which employed 60-70% of the total population at the turn of the twentieth century, today supports less than 3%. Since 80-90% of the population in many developing countries is involved in agriculture and related work, industry could not possible grow rapidly enough to provide employment for the people who would become redundant in a mechanized farm sector.[4] Most Third-World countries must employ the bulk of their population in agriculture, for there is no other alternative. Worsley points out:

> As a model for societies which are going to be predominantly agrarian for the visible future, the U.S.A. is, therefore, unattractive and in any case inimitable. Such conditions are entirely lacking in the non-communist Third World. The U.S.S.R., still hampered by shoots of pain in its Achilles heel, is no more attractive as a model and its example in the field of industrialization is qualified in that it was achieved only at the very dangerous expense of risking class warfare in the countryside. The indications…[seem] to be that China's progress is one of secular improvement, following a disastrous attempt to impose ideology upon agriculture in the heyday of the communes. It cannot be urged too strongly that there is no general optimal way of growing crops there are only differential optima for different crops in different regions…. All in all, agriculture is the area least amenable to radical transformation but most in need of it.[5]

Developing countries do not have a suitable model for development. They must proceed with experiment after experiment and try to learn from the results. Most of the countries in Asia and Africa, and to some extent in Latin America, are seeking innovative ways to modernize their agriculture, which is privately owned and organized in small-scale units of production. Co-operative forms are:

> …singularly attractive to the modernizing State. Rejecting collectivized agriculture, the co-operative offers economies of scale, infrastructural support to innovating farmers and socialization via vertical integration. The State intervenes not only via technical and extensive assistance but also by providing credit, by organizing co-operative marketing in

a way that replaces the private middlemen by State marketing boards or marketing co-operative monopolies, by subsidizing transport and storage facilities. The State also
underwrites subsidies and price stabilization arrangements, and by forward trade agreements seeks to ensure a
guaranteed market so as to protect the small producer from
the vagaries of fluctuating demand and the uncertainties of
nature that still constitute the principle hazard confronting
the farmer.[6]

In order to ensure that State intervention will produce the
desired market change, the planning and establishment of co-operatives are closely controlled by the State, with very little involvement
of the peasant population. Large tea, wheat, sugarcane and coffee estates may be nationalized and run as State farms, but for the most
part peasants are left to their own production, supposedly protected
by their co-operatives from exploitive middlemen and the fluctuations of the market.

The experience of the past twenty years has been marked by
limited success at best. We are faced with several major questions.
Why have these attempts failed? Are these State-sponsored and State-
controlled organizations really co-operatives? Could they be successful if they became autonomous organizations controlled by the
peasants? Hyden observes: "Co-operatives cannot become effective
agents of socio-political change in the direction of more egali-
tarianism unless the right conditions exist. The question is, to what
extent can these conditions be created by political, administrative and
educational measures?"[7]

These questions will be explored later. First a brief overview of attempts to develop co-operative economies in three countries: India,
Tanzania and China. In India, as we have observed in earlier chapters, serious efforts have been made to develop co-operatives since
the nation attained independence in 1947. Tanzania has tried harder
to develop co-operatives than any other African country. It has also
tried to revolutionize the agrarian base with its *ujamaa* villages. China
contains about 25% of the world's population and since the reforms
in 1978 co-operatives have been developing rapidly.

THREE EXAMPLES

India
        Attempts to develop co-operatives in India go back to 1904. Ex-
perimental credit co-operatives were organized in an effort to break

the poverty cycle of small agriculturalists. This poverty was brought about by frequent famines, low productivity and dependence on the money-lender merchants. The object of these early societies was to encourage thrift and the wise use of credit. In 1912, legislation was enacted to enable societies other than credit co-operatives to be incorporated; and in 1918, responsibility for co-operative legislation was transferred to the States. During the struggle for independence in the 1920s, 1930s and 1940s, many co-operatives were started in various forms, but the agricultural credit societies were the largest. Although thousands were organized by 1954, India's huge population meant that they barely met 3% of the credit needs of agriculturalists in the country.

The first five-year plan after independence gave an important place to the co-operatives in implementing programmes of national development. This occurred in small industry, marketing and processing of agricultural produce, supplying credit and other agricultural inputs. This role continued to be emphasized in subsequent five-year plans. In 1955, the All India Rural Credit Survey Committee made extensive recommendations that had a substantial impact on the shape of co-operative development. They proposed that a scheme of integrated rural credit be adopted, based on three fundamental principles: 1) State partnership at different levels; 2) Full coordination between credit and other economic activities, specifically marketing and processing; 3) Administration through adequately trained and efficient personnel responsive to the needs of the rural population.[8]

The Nehru government was well aware of the pitfall. Nehru himself is quoted as saying: "If it is to be a State-sponsored movement, with government officials running it, it may do some good — if the government officials are competent — but it does infinite harm in the sense that it provides few opportunities for the people to learn to do things for themselves, to develop a spirit of self-reliance and self-dependence, and even to make mistakes if they have to make mistakes."[9]

These plans led to a massive expansion of co-operatives, organized by government employees. The government provided considerable capital investment, with a rider that it could appoint up to three directors on the board of each co-operative in which it invested. A huge bureaucracy was quickly created, which, in the minds of many peasants, was inseparable from the government itself. The creators were well aware of the dangers inherent in these moves, but they saw no alternative. They were also committed to an independent co-operative sector and foresaw gradual government withdrawal as local leaders developed and the organizations became financially successful.

Thus, in the space of a decade, a full-blown co-operative super-structure was developed, involving literally hundreds of thousands of organizations and millions of members. The 135,000 multipurpose credit societies were the foundation of the movement at the village level. They were federated into 345 central co-operative banks at the district level with about 4,500 branches. These in turn were related to the twenty-five apex co-operative banks that operated at the State level. Their function was to pool liquidity for the central banks, drawing surpluses from some and providing credit to others as needs arose. They also served as a channel for the flow or production credit from the Reserve Bank of India. Credit at the primary level was available for productive purposes and not to meet the short-term consumption needs of farmers. By 1976, India's local credit societies covered 95% of the villages in the country. They reported a total membership of 40,100,000 families or 45% of the rural population.

Besides this huge system, there was a network of Land Development Banks (LBDs), which provided long-term credit on a sufficient scale to finance the cost of irrigation, land shaping and heavy agricultural machinery. There were nineteen State co-operative LBDs and 1870 primary LBDs with a membership of 15,700,000. By 1975-76, more than 70% of the loans granted were for sinking wells and installation of pumping equipment. The banks had financed over 2,000,000 wells to irrigate about 12,000,000 acres. More than 30% of the loans were in favour of small farmers who owned less than five acres of land each.

The statistics on marketing co-operatives were also impressive. There were twenty-five general-purpose apex marketing federations at the State level, and 3,278 general-purpose primary marketing societies covering almost all the important secondary markets in the country. There were also 590 specialized commodity marketing societies. These societies marketed agricultural produce collected through primary societies both as agents and through outright purchases. They handled agricultural supplies such as fertilizer, pesticides, seeds and implements, and building items such as steel sheeting and cement, which were supplied to local primary societies. About 90% of the multipurpose societies were members of the marketing societies. The average membership of individual farmers was estimated in 1976 at 840 per local society.[10]

Many agricultural products were perishable and had to be stored in temperature-controlled facilities. The co-operatives owned 133 cold storage plants with a combined capacity of 22 million tons. There were also 2,112 processing units, of which 1,360 units were operated by the network of marketing co-operatives described above and the remainder by separate co-operatives.

There were also seventy-four cotton spinning mills, of which forty were owned by handloom weaver co-operatives and thirty-four by cotton grower co-operatives. There were also 721 rice mills, forty-seven dal mills, seventy-one jute baling units and 148 oil mills for processing oil seeds. These represented the most important groups, but there were several hundred more involved in a vast variety of commodities.

Since the green revolution, chemical fertilizers have grown in importance. The Indian Farmers Fertilizers Co-operative Ltd. (IFFCO) was jointly owned by 27,000 co-operative organizations and was one of the top twenty industrial establishments in India. Although its plants were located in the state of Gujarat, its output affected an estimated 25,000,000 farming families spread over ten states. This complex was developed in the 1960s as a result of international collaboration between IFFCO and fertilizer co-operatives in the United States.[11] Of the network of 135,000 multipurpose co-operatives, 53,000 had established retail outlets for fertilizer by 1976. There were fourteen soil-testing laboratories, as well as countless test plants to help farmers make effective use of fertilizer. There were also 4,560 primary fishermen's co-operatives with a membership of half a million, which was about 20% of all fishermen in the country.

Co-operatives were not confined to rural areas. The structure of urban consumer co-operatives comprised about 15,000 primary societies stores with about 2,600 branches. There were a staggering 424 central/wholesales with 3,539 branches, including 178 department stores (Mehta, 1964). This four-tier structure was based on 41,000,000 members in urban areas of India. Only 20% of these stores had received any share capital contributions from the government, and nearly 83% of the total share capital was contributed by individual members.[12] As well as performing retailing and wholesaling functions, the wholesalers interfaced with the extensive industrial co-operative sector and also owned a number of their own processing plants.[13] There were also more than 17,000 non-agricultural credit societies, with a total urban membership of about 11,000,000.

This was a truly impressive achievement for a country that had been independent for only a little over thirty years. The policy in the central plans was based on principles to lay the foundations of a "genuine co-operative movement which should be self-supporting, self-contained and self-evolutionary."[14] But, there were problems. As Saxena says, "The co-operative movement is still floating in the air and it has not yet taken a permanent place in the Indian social system, even after strong backing and full support of the State." The organizations were introduced, not because they were desired, but because they were desirable. The need for development was urgent and a massive network of organizations was created, many of which functioned quite well. Yet "in most of the co-operative institutions, the members have not internalized the co-operative principles...[and] keep aloof from the organization except for getting the benefits for which they join."

There seems to be a fair degree of consensus that the Indian movement, despite its impressive size, had a number of major weaknesses. These include lack of local leadership, complicated rules and regulations, lack of resources, lack of imaginative management and a general frustration among the members because their hopes were not fulfilled. The movement failed to capture the imagination of the common man and this lack of impetus from the grassroots has severely handicapped efforts to realize the potential for co-operative development. As Gill points out, the impressive start to the agricultural co-operatives in the Punjab was stifled, not because of internal co-operative problems but because they were attractive to politicians and the State has taken them over.[15] There were two notable exceptions to this generalization that are very revealing.

(1) Sugar co-operatives

There were 106 sugar factories owned by over 1,000,000 cane producers. Most were located in the Bombay area in the state of Maharashtra. The co-operative plant capacity represented 53% of the entire sugar industry in India. Valuable by-products are derived from the processing of sugarcane, and the co-operatives developed twenty distilleries using molasses as the raw material and one factory to manufacture paper from the cane fibres. The cane growers voluntarily agreed to put part of their proceeds into a fund for economic development in the state of Maharashtra, the contributions from 1970 to 1975 amounted to RS. 250,000,000. The fund was used to "provide medical and educational services to the community and initiate a host of ancillary agro-based economic activities in the rural area." The co-operatives' leaders were elected and have become very powerful. One was recently elected as head of the state of Maharashtra. These organizations elected boards management was trained locally, not borrowed from the Indian government. The co-operatives developed a feeling of ownership amongst the farmers and were very successful.[16]

(2) Dairy co-operatives

When India became independent, this land with millions of cows was a major importer of milk powder from Europe. Dozens of people died each year from bacteria in the milk. Milk was collected by travelling middlemen who paid low prices to the farmers. When milk was in short supply they watered it down (often with contaminated water) and sold it in unhygienic ways in the cities. When milk was in surplus they bought only what they wanted and left the surplus with the farmers who had no other market. Under these conditions milk production stagnated.

The dairy co-operatives in the Anand area started in the 1940s. Their success drew national recognition in the 1960s and they were used as a model for development. The leadership from Anand formed the basis for the staff of the National Dairy Development Board, (NDDB) and its chairman (Dr. Kurien) provided dynamic and visionary leadership. Since the implementation of its programme "Operation Flood" in 1970, NDDB has transformed the dairy sector in India. The European Economic Community gave surplus milk powder and butter oil, which was used to supplement supplies when milk production was low. It was sold at regular prices and the profits were used to develop the co-operative milk marketing system.

The co-operative in Anand did four things: it bought all the milk the farmers would sell; it paid on the basis of quality, and gave honest measures; it supplied high quality feed for the cows; and provided-veterinary services and medicines at no cost to the individual member.

The 50,000 local societies are each managed by an elected board of seven farmers who appoint a secretary and hire three or four workers. The 800 to 900 local co-ops in a district own the regional union (165) which builds a modern dairy plant. Unlike many other agricultural co-operatives in India, the boards of directors of the unions are elected from the local co-operative chairpersons and are not government officials.

The unions operate modern clean plants which process the milk, a veterinary station that provides medicines, a herd of bulls for artificial insemination services to improve the local herd, a feed plant and other services. A farmer with a sick cow can get a veterinarian in under four hours!

But, it is the women who look after the cows and do the milking. The AMUL Dairy and many other unions developed a number of trainers who hold three-day workshops in the villages, open only to the women, to teach them animal husbandry among other topics. During the past three years 141,000 women have attended the AMUL Dairy-sponsored workshops in the Anand area.

The NDDB has been conscious of the problem of recruiting managers trained to run the Indian bureaucracies. The training centre IRMA (Institute for Rural Management) trains managers with the co-operative mental set. These professional managers are oriented to appreciate farmers, and are prepared to work for the farmers. The democratic values of co-operation are being taught in this two-year management programme which emphasizes practical application.

The development of the co-operative dairy industry and the sugar co-operatives in India clearly shows several points:

* Elected boards of directors are vital for building member confidence. Board members listen and talk to farmers.
* Managers are trained within the system and few are seconded from the government service.
* Members are treated fairly and receive a tangible improvement in their income and standard of living.
* Members have the power to remove corrupt and/or arrogant leaders.

Co-operatives persist as a vehicle for rural development in Third-World countries because they have as much promise of success as any other form. The peasants are usually blamed when they fail, but research shows that the causes of failure often rest with agencies that introduce them and the mental set of the managers who fail to understand the distinctive features that enable co-operation to emerge and allow organizations to become a vehicle for improving the quality of life for the members. Co-operatives are a difficult organizational form to develop. They often fail, but when they succeed can be a powerful force for rural development.[17]

Tanzania

Tanzania gained independence in 1961, but the development of the co-operative movement began in the 1920s and 1930s.

> There is no country in tropical Africa where marketing co-operatives have come to play a more central role in economic life than Tanzania. Moreover, while the movement there has achieved considerable successes, it has also met with its share of difficulties and setbacks.[18]

Economic exploitation was obvious to the peasants in the East Lake cotton growing area, and marketing co-operatives were developed from the grassroots. Roth notes that the movement began with independent African weighers at various cotton-buying stations, and expanded rapidly, though initially it had little significant external stimulus and support. It grew to become the Victoria Federation of Co-operative Unions, the largest in Africa. Economic exploitation in this case had an identifiable racial colouring and spurred peasant consciousness and action. The coffee growers in the Kilimanjaro area also organized during colonial times, and these growers' associations became the "natural centres of opposition to chiefly privilege."[19]

At the time of independence, marketing co-operatives were well developed in the densely populated areas near Lake Victoria, the Bukoka district and in the Moshi-Arusha area around Kilimanjaro. Following independence, the movement was viewed as the major mechanism for rural development and received the full backing of the State. The 172 societies of 1951 rose to 857 in 1961. There were 1,362 in 1964, 1,518 in 1965, and in 1969 a total of 1,737 registered societies were reported.[20] Vertical integration also had occurred. On the eve of independence, there were thirty-four co-operative unions. In 1962, legislation was passed to establish marketing boards, and the co-operative unions interfaced with the marketing boards to purchase most of the cash crops from the peasants.

In 1966, a Special Committee was set up to investigate the movement. It found that the general structure of the agricultural co-operative movement was sound and that the defects that existed in specific organizations were typically problems of growth. The committee listed five basic defects: uninformed membership; shortage of appropriate manpower; lack of democracy at the union level; lack of skilled people in the movement with special knowledge; susceptibility of the movement to political interference.[21]

The committee made two recommendations. It proposed the creation of a Unified Co-operative Service, which would be responsible for the engagement, discipline, terms of service and dismissal of all employees of registered societies. In addition, the upgrading of existing personnel and training of new personnel should be accelerated. The Co-operative College at Moshi was charged with this task, and it has since developed an extensive in-residence programme, field programme and correspondence courses for employees, elected officials and members.

In 1967, the Arusha Declaration marked a significant turning point in the development of Tanzania and the co-operatives. The Arusha Declaration, and the policies which flowed from it, emphasized five themes:

1)   Public control over the economy, involving public control of all financial institutions, large industrial and commercial concerns, and a major share of estate agriculture;

2)   Development through self-reliance, involving a high degree of
      domestic mobilization of local resources;
3)   Rural development, involving recognition that the society would
      be predominantly rural for many decades and that self-reliance
      implied rural development; this theme suggested the need for
      changes to adapt education, investment programmes and politi-
      cal thought more closely to the needs of the rural areas;
4)   Social equality, emphasizing the need to check growing economic
      inequality (based on wide income differentials and increasing
      private accumulation of capital, and aimed at narrowing the
      gap between rural and urban living standards) implemented
      through vigorous incomes and salaries policies and limitations
      on the forms in which leaders (i.e., all public office holders) can
      hold wealth;
5)   Rural Socialism, identifying the need to create a socialist society
      through he creation of collective, productive activities in the
      rural sector through application of the principles of Ujamaa;
      that is, through the spread of voluntary, co-operative forms of
      production.

These principles, enunciated in the Declaration of February 1967 and in
subsequent documents, were implemented through 1967 and 1968.[22]
      The establishment of *ujamaa* villages had started before 1967, and
many proved very successful.[23] By 1973, 2,000,000 peasants had
voluntarily joined *ujamaa* villages. Coercion was then used to complete the process, and the result was considerable turmoil in the
countryside.[24] By the end of that year, however, most of the peasants
were grouped in *ujamaa* villages. The co-operatives were consolidated with 220 consumer co-operatives, 360 credit co-operatives
and 1,387 primary agricultural co-operatives. By the early 1970s the
agricultural co-operatives were grouped into twenty-nine co-operative unions. Thus, there was a three-tier structure, with the twelve
marketing boards at the top responsible for marketing specific
products.
      The two main problems of democracy and efficiency continued
to plague the co-operatives. Major advances were made in educational programmes, and their success was considerable; but they failed to
resolve all the problems.[25] The central administration was operated
out of the Department of Agriculture. It had not eliminated corruption in co-operatives, and it had created a rigid bureaucracy, to the
great frustration of the peasants. The 1976 inquiry recommended extensive changes. Many unions were losing money and required constant subsidization. The movement was once again restructured. The

goal was to make the institutions reflect the new socialist conditions, to increase access for local people (farmers in particular) and to emphasize the participation of members, along with awareness of their rights. At the same time, responsibility for supervision was shifted out of the Department of Agriculture to the Prime Minister's Office.

But discontent continued. In 1976, the government made all *ujamaa* villages multipurpose societies by decree, and dissolved all the co-operative unions, confiscated their assets and debt, and turned their assets over to the crop authorities. Socialism and support for co-operatives had not been abandoned as an official policy. The government's stated intention was to make the system work better for the peasants and the nation in general. Renewed emphasis was placed on education. Manday outlined the role Commissioner's department as follows:

> As for specific legal functions, the Commissioner of Ujamaa and Co-operative Development in the Prime Minister's Office identified them as: (a) to train village leaders on Ujamaa and Co-operative activities in line with the new structure of the Co-operative movement in the country. (b) To check the villagers' books of accounts. (c) To provide consultancy services to the villagers on the operation of Ujamaa activities. (d) To represent villagers and Ujamaa villages together with town Co-operative activities at regional, national and international meetings. (e) To coordinate Ujamaa Co-operative activities of the villages in all matters relating to insurance and legal matters. (f) To give publicity to all activities in relation with the development of villages, Ujamaa villages, and other co-operative services in towns.[26]

The changes were meant to be a frontal attack on the problems of the *ujamaa* villages and the co-operative superstructure. Nyerere's resolve to develop a humane, decentralized, egalitarian society does not seem to have been altered, but the change did not work.

The problems that existed in the co-operative unions were magnified in the crop authorities, and by 1980 they were hated by the peasants who pressed for the return of the co-operatives. In response to the pressure, a commission was established to study the problem. It recommended that the political structures and the economic activities in the village be once again separated, and that a system of local multipurpose co-operatives and regional co-operative unions be re-introduced. The co-operatives act of 1982 made this possible and Tanzania reduced the activities of the government marketing boards to an export function, allowing new co-operative unions to emerge. The process was being done on a gradual basis. The co-operative leaders, were well aware of the difficulty of sudden massive changes, and deliberate attempts were made to develop sound organizations. This has become increasingly difficult as the economic infrastructure ages and breaks down.

By 1990, with the decline of planned economies in eastern Europe CCM, Tanzania's only party was faced with demands to open the market economy and do away with inefficient and corrupt State organizations. Co-operatives were gaining strength and confidence, and they also wished to be able to import and export product and to have an apex that they controlled rather than one dominated by government appointees. The revised act of 1992 gave them this power. The aid-weary Nordic countries are also withdrawing assistance and more of the agricultural decisions are now resting on the farm community and their organizations. The Co-operative College at Moshi is the largest in Africa, entirely staffed by Tanzanians, and it trains several thousand people each year. The movement has a strong educational focus to develop managers and elected people. It is well positioned to develop a movement which works for farmers, and one that farmers feel they own and can trust.

Peoples Republic of China

In 1949, Mao's forces swept to power in China. Unlike the Bolshevik revolution in 1917 which was based on industrial workers, the Chinese revolution was a victory for the peasants. The reconstruction period attempted to develop a place for both the landless rural population as well as the peasants who owned land, draft animals and agricultural tools.

Mao was concerned that the agricultural reconstruction get started and be successful quickly, as China has a huge population to feed. In 1943, Mao, "stressed that because individuals grouped in co-operatives can produce more than they can individually co-operation constitutes the springboard for mutual prosperity, and the ultimate bridge to collectivism."[27]

As a result co-operatives were organized rapidly. Co-operatives were not new to rural China as agricultural marketing and credit organizations had been organized earlier in the century. There was a long tradition of co-operation in the form of mutual aid teams to do the heavy work at critical periods, particularly during seeding and harvesting operations.

The co-operative development immediately after the revolution was largely voluntary, fostered by the sense of nation building.

Progress was slow and by 1955, Mao had lost patience and the process of collectivization was speeded up. Peasants were required to pool their land and form production co-operatives. By 1958, all the agricultural land was pooled into directed co-operatives and work was done collectively in teams. Production did not pick up so other measures were implemented.

During the great leap forward, launched in 1958, the co-operatives were merged into the giant rural communes. The political and economic organizations were merged. Each commune "was seen as a microcosm of China's transformed rural society each one a large autonomous cell that greatly reduced the tasks of government."[28] The communes provided food, owned heavy machinery, controlled transport and provided the political and the social-cultural infrastructure. The rural area was organized into about 50,000 communes. Each commune was organized into brigades which usually included twenty to thirty households. The smallest unit of organization in the commune is the team. About seven or eight teams make up a brigade.

The great leap forward had problems. The agricultural units were too large for effective decision-making. The work-point system was discontinued and everyone received the same, regardless of effort. The cultural revolution (1966-1976) was launched in the name of countering State monopoly, decreasing bureaucratic tendencies and removing counter-revolutionaries. Instead it led to even greater centralization of power and excessive bureaucratic control which inhibited the productive capacity of the country even further.

In 1978, two reforms were implemented that continue to transform the economy of China. The separation of political and economic functions and the responsibility system. This system provides economic rewards for performance and expands the decision-making power of peasants and workers.

> The most important element in the implementation of the system of producer responsibility is the use of contracts. Under that system collective responsibility now rests primarily with co-operative teams. In rural areas teams divide collective fields into strips which they allocate to smaller units by contracting most productive tasks to work groups or households or individuals. In urban areas too a growing number of industrial and commercial enterprises are being operated on the basis of various kinds of contracts with teams (or with the State) in which the material benefits of workers are linked directly with the quantity

and quality of their work.... These contracts enable the team to increase productivity by increasing incentives, allocating responsibility to smaller units more adapted to the work, and linking incomes to effort.... It is worth stressing that although the contract system and the responsibility concept in agriculture represent a significant shift of income, economic power and decision-making to individual households, nevertheless these household units operate under what is essentially a co-operative way of organizing production.[29]

The new co-operatives in China appear to be genuine co-operatives. They are moulded to fit the current socio-economic-political environment in China. They apply the values and principle of co-operation in a form that fits the economic reality of China. The communes were too large-scale and centralized, and too inefficient for farming.

Farming is labour-intensive and requires careful management of resources, timely execution of sequences of production, and individual initiatives by peasants. Hence the commune was not an appropriate level for decision making in farming, and the concept of the iron pot carried with it a strong work disincentive. On the other hand if the peasants are to optimize, they must increase the operational size beyond their family-based ownership size through some form of mutual aid co-operation.[30]

These changes have meant a return to private plots, as well as specialized farming activities like pigs, poultry, vegetables, fruit, etc. Households are now free to produce what they want as long as it does not damage the nation's resources or conflict with collective production or constitute speculation and hoarding.

The unified management of the collectives has been combined with the separate management of households. A limited market has been introduced. The State planning is still in place but bureaucratic centralized management has been reduced with more worker and peasant influence on decisions. This is not a retreat to capitalism as the western media like to portray the changes. It is still a socialized economy, and in many ways is closer to the ideal of Marxist socialism. It has had the effect of increasing the economic decision-making power of groups of peasants and workers as compared to bureaucrats. For "decentralist socialists" the new China represents a higher form of socialization than the China during the cultural revolution. The study team from the ICA found that co-operatives had considerable latitude in making economic decisions. They remain at a distance from the State political machinery which, as shown by the Tiananmen square massacre, is not open to democratic reforms. But, reforms continue in the economy.

In February 1985, the All China Federation of Co-operatives was accepted into membership in the International Co-operative Alliance. The All China Federation represents about 132 million individual members. These are the peasants who own the 35,000 basic supply and marketing co-operatives at the commune level. These have organized 2,010 federations at the county level, which in turn are organized into twenty-nine regional federations that form the All-China Federation.

Membership is voluntary, and joining means purchasing shares to finance the organization. All members are equal in terms of control, with one member one vote. Surpluses go to taxes, special reserve funds, increased production and payments on shares. Patronage refunds are being considered, but are prevented by administrative difficulties. Co-operative officials are no longer appointed by the State; rather they are elected by the membership.

A major emphasis of the supply and marketing co-operatives is to encourage and increase farm production. They devote about 15% of their surplus to support production. They do this by:

> helping agricultural co-operatives and/or households directly with technical advice, counselling services, training courses, financial support for example in the form of interest-free loans or lower prices for farm inputs and special discounts on equipment provision of fertilizers and insecticides, special strains and seedlings....
>
> However in China co-operatives have financial and economic autonomy. They are expected to implement general guidelines laid down by the State but beyond this the Government does not interfere with their activities.[31]

The co-operatives also get some direct support from the State. They have priority for State supplies of raw materials. They receive investment funds, loans and credits and only pay 40% tax rate as compared to 80% on State enterprises. These organizations are owned by the peasants and have a major objective of supplying the infrastructure and supporting and developing the agricultural production co-operatives.

Agricultural Production Co-operatives have replaced the communes as the unit of agricultural production. They usually comprise twenty to thirty households (former brigade size) and operate through contracts. These are three-part contracts signed by the State, the co-operative and the peasant household or households that are undertaking the work. The co-operatives are involved with the State in terms of planning, and they provide the organizational framework for organizing agricultural production. However, the actual production work and decisions are contracted to the co-operative members. Day-to-day production decisions are decentralized to the people who are doing the work, with a strong incentive to produce more each year.

The purpose of the agricultural production co-operatives and the marketing and supply system of co-operatives is to increase production in agriculture to feed the population. They do this by decentralizing decisions, and allowing innovation and specialization to occur without destroying the socialist society.

Credit Co-operatives were established by the peasants in the 1950s as mutual aid organizations. During the cultural revolution, they were incorporated into the agricultural banking system.

Today, however, rural credit co-operatives are the basic organizations through which the Agricultural Bank operates. They have been restructured to service peasants now benefiting from the responsibility system. The 55,000 credit co-operatives and their 31,300 sub agencies are being given independence in management and are assuming full responsibility for their profits and losses. They make loans to individual peasants and specialized households or groups according to State policies, and charge a floating rate of interest fixed by the Agricultural Bank of China.... Dividends are distributed to members of credit co-operatives according to their shares in a move to give them the initiative to expand their business.... Officials are elected by the members.[32]

Another type of co-operative in China is the Rural Industrial Co-operative. These are the organizations that have taken over the small and medium-sized industries operated by the communes. They are not worker-owned, but rather owned by agricultural co-operatives or groups of peasants that need their products in the communes. "These enterprises engage in the processing of agricultural produce; production and repair of farm implements; production of cement, bricks and other building materials; fertilizer manufacture; mining and quarrying; handicraft production, and repairing and tailoring."[33]

These are now well integrated into the rural community as a system of complementary firms that support agricultural production. In 1981, there were 1,300,000 rural enterprises, absorbing about 10% of the labour force and generating 33% of the collective income of the communes or 11% of the national industrial production. These enterprises are basically small scale and are owned by the peasants and the workers.

Handicraft Co-operatives (Worker owned co-operatives in light industry) are not limited to Arts and Crafts, but include light industry involving many consumer goods. These co-operatives developed during the early years of the revolution, and by 1955 there were 4,500,000 individual members. In 1958, they were denounced as having "capitalist tendencies." More than 100,000 were closed as their functions were integrated into huge State enterprises and the production of consumer goods dropped. With the reforms of 1978, the co-operatives were encouraged to reorganize. They were given independence to select leaders, make production decisions according to market demand and to determine the most efficient production methods.

> These policies have borne fruit in marked increases in value of output in some cases approaching 50% and in numbers of co-operative enterprises and employers. As of 1982 there were some 62,000 co-operative handicraft enterprises accounting for well over 40% of total national output of light industry, and employing about 6.5 million workers, i.e., half of the national total for light industry. Some 60% of the output of these co-operatives is intended for household use. Types of product or service include: clothing, plastics, furniture, arts and crafts, toys, hardware, electrical appliances, catering, furs and leathers, stationery, instruments, repair and farm implements.[34]

These organizations pay workers on the basis of performance. So far the income is about the same as workers in the State owned firms but with increased productivity incomes could exceed State enterprise workers.

Urban Co-operatives Formed by the Unemployed have sprung up in recent years due to the serious unemployment problem in the cities. In the late 1970s there were over 25,000,000 young people waiting for jobs.

In 1979, however, a number of young people became restless and began to organize themselves to form small businesses at their own risk and often with their own funds; in short they created jobs for themselves. These collectively-owned sales and service units came to be called "people-run enterprises."...In 1982 more than 12,000 labour services companies had been set up throughout the country. These companies had established 58,000 production and service networks and helped to create job opportunities for 1,260,000 people. In addition they had organized 1,610,000 people as casual labourers and labour service teams and provided professional training for 320,000 people.[35]

Most of these worker co-operatives are introducing democratic control. Practices vary; some of these require workers to buy shares while others do not. In general, 60% of the surplus is allocated to investment and 40% to workers welfare and bonuses.

China has made tremendous strides in many areas since 1949. These were achieved in areas where large, centralized decision-making made sense. However, in the area of agricultural production and consumer goods, smaller units with local decision-making is more appropriate. In these areas co-operatives seem to be taking root and developing. It will be interesting to study how these organizations develop in the future and how effectively they can serve the needs of a billion citizens!

These are three important developing countries. China and India have nearly one-half of the world population and economic development that benefits the majority of the population is important for world stability and peace.

PROBLEMS

By the end of the 1970s, studies were starting to show that co-operatives were developing in the developing countries beyond the influence of the government ministries. The use of action research and community development techniques meant co-operatives were developing in local communities without the top-down paternalistic approach, and a new wave of organizations was emerging. Laidlaw outlines the State of the movement at the end of the 1970s. He found that commitment by members was declining along with their participation, the neglect of member education was taking its toll and the potential of co-operatives was not understood by the general

public. The movements around the world had an image problem and were struggling in crisis.[36]
He concluded his global study with four recommendations.

1) In the years ahead, co-operatives everywhere should concentrate especially on the world problem of FOOD, all the way from farming to consumer. It is an area of great human need in which the co-operative movement is in a position to give world leadership.

2) Workers' productive and industrial co-operatives are the best means to create a new relationship between workers and the workplace, and to bring about another industrial revolution.

3) The traditional consumer co-operative should be orientated in such a way that it will be doing something more than merely trying to compete with a capitalist business. It will be known as a unique and different kind of business and will serve only members.

4) To serve the urban population, there should be a cluster of many different kinds of co-operatives that have the effect of creating villages within the city.[37] Interestingly these trends which Laidlaw saw as critical in 1980 have continued to develop and are gaining strength in the 1990s.

The agricultural co-operatives that developed independent of governments have made dramatic progress in addressing the food problem. Farmer-centred enterprises are once again emphasized by developers.[38] The Chinese reforms in 1978 allowed co-operatives to develop. By the mid 1980s, 132 million farm families were members of 35,000 agricultural marketing and supply co-operatives. India became self sufficient in milk in two decades as "operation flood" developed a network of co-operatives owned by milk producers.

The privatization drive by many governments in the 1980s meant that people were faced with either waiting for individuals to provide the services being abandoned by government or providing them for themselves in their communities. Day care, nursery, and other service co-operatives have been incorporated in record numbers. Community health clinics with an emphasis on preventative medicine have provided an alternative for increasingly expensive health costs.[39]

Worker co-operatives, stimulated by the outstanding success of Mondragon co-operatives in Spain and elsewhere in Europe, are emerging as a movement in Europe and North America. Their development is complemented by the transfer of manufacturing to lower-wage countries and the attempt by communities and workers to retain jobs. Communities are facing the reality that big government and big business cannot resolve their problems. Participatory development at the community level is gaining importance and co-operatives are being rediscovered.[40] Other forms are also developing, ESOPs (Employee Share Ownership Plans) are widespread in the United States and are growing in Canada. These are not worker co-operatives but they can be seen as a first phase in worker ownership. In Canada, the Co-operators Data Services Limited was converted to a multi-stakeholder organization that has given voice to the workers, users and capital suppliers.[41] The point is that the current era of co-operative development has seen a new emphasis on community involvement and organizing. The needs now are different from the last century or the first half of this century, so the organizations are different, but the goal of people co-operating is still strong. In 1989, the planned economies in eastern Europe collapsed. The State-sponsored co-operatives were unpopular and they also collapsed. Interestingly, the idea of co-operation is powerful and new co-operatives are emerging from their ashes. In Tokyo in October 1992, the ICA took steps to review once again the co-operative principles. The whole question of how the State relates to co-operatives is one of the major concerns.

There seems to be a fair degree of consensus that the Indian movement, despite its impressive size, has a number of major weaknesses. These include lack of local leadership, complicated rules and regulations, lack of resources, lack of imaginative management and general frustration among the members because their hopes have not been fulfilled. The movement has failed to capture the imagination of the common man and this lack of impetus from the grassroots has severely handicapped efforts to realize the potential for co-operative development. As Gill points out, the impressive start to the agricultural co-operatives in the Punjab has been stifled not because of internal co-operative problems but because they were attractive to politicians and the State has taken them over. There are two notable exceptions to this generalization. The sugar co-operatives in the State of Maharashtra and the dairy co-operatives following the Anand model.

CHALLENGES FOR CO-OPERATORS: BUREAUCRACY

Nehru's prophetic comment about the heavy hand of government officials has turned out to be true. Many studies have shown this heavy hand creates a situation resembling "bureaucratic feudalism" rather than the intended self-reliance. The action by government often came after problems were identified. Loan embezzlement and other practices meant members' assets were at risk and government action was needed.[42] But, Korten has documented the take-over of the co-operatives in Andhra Pradesh and the struggle of members to try to get them back.[43] Corrective action by government is justified; continual domination is not.

The most recent task force to look at national laws has recommended that the laws be changed so government officials cannot make equity investment in co-operatives and take control.[44] Studies on the successful co-operatives clearly show how autonomy from government officials is a critical factor.[45] The strong hand of the registrar was created by the colonial administration to keep control and prevent co-operatives from becoming a true expression of members desires. Unfortunately, India and many newly independent governments have not rescinded the registrar's power. This is proposed in the legislative changes for the Government of India and its implementation is critical for the development of true co-operatives in India. The survival of many co-operatives in India is at stake.[46] But...emancipation from government is only the first step. The second step, applying a self-help logic is just as important, and will be dealt with in the next chapter.

NOTES

1. There are few cases where this transition did occur, but it does not mean that it could not have happened. For example, see Seibel, H.D. and A. Massing. 1974. *Traditional Organizations and Economic Development Studies of Indigenous Cooperatives in Liberia.* New York: Praeger. For a detailed study of indigenous co-operatives in Liberia and their development into more modern forms.
2. See Gosselin, Gabriel. 1976. "Traditional collectivism and modern associations: the example of South Dahomey," June Nash et. al., eds., Popular Participation in Social Change. The Hague: Mouton: 55-70.
3. Singh, Mahindu. 1970. *Cooperatives in Asia.* London: Praeger: vi.
4. The argument is complicated because the technology usually available from North America and Europe is capital intensive, not labour intensive. Those who are involved in planning for development in Third-World countries must recognize that capital is scarce and labour is plentiful. The appropriate technologies maximizing available resources are critical for development.
5. Worsley, Peter, ed., 1971. *Two Blades of Grass.* Manchester: Manchester University Press: 39.
6. Worsley, 1971: 18.
7. Hyden, Goran. 1970. "Can co-ops make it in Africa." *Africa Report,* 15 (Dec): 71.
8. Tyagi, R.B. 1968. *Recent Trend in the Co-operative Movement in India.* New York: Asia Publishing House: 49-51. Also see Saxena, Suren K., 1992. *Cooperatives in India and Pakistan: Some Aspects.* New Delhi: ICA Domus Trust.
9. Gill, Manohar Singh. 1983. *Agricultural Cooperatives: A Case Study of Punjab.* New Delhi: Vikas Publishing: 533.
10. The source for these statistics is a booklet called *Indian Co-operatives,* published by the National Co-operative Union of India. Statistics are for 1976.

11. Craig, J.G. 1976 *Multinational Co-operatives: An Alternative for World Development.* Saskatoon: Western Producer Prairie Books.
12. Mehta, 1964.
13. Consumer co-operatives were established in Britain in the nineteenth century mainly for the purpose of supplying unadulterated goods. This need is still present in India. Sarkar, A. 1976. "Consumer problems and consumer protection in India," *Consumer Cooperation in South-East Asia.* I.C.A., eds., New Delhi: International Cooperation Alliance: 160-183: "According to a recent survey, 38.8% of the coconut oil sold in tins was found adulterated (Bombay area). The percentage of adulteration in loose coconut oil was naturally even higher, as much as 46.7%. Til oil was the worst of all showing 47.8% adulteration. Loose groundnut oil was also found adulterated. Consumption of mustard oil adulterated with toxic oil extracted from agrimony oilseeds (seeds of wild growth) often result in beri beri and dropsy disease...25,000 people in and around the district of Akola suffer from the effects of eating cooked food with adulterated oil. Many of them have swollen limbs and some have become permanently crippled."
14. Saxena, Krishna Kumar. 1974. *Evolution of Co-operative Thought.* New Delhi: Somaiya Publications: 335-336.
15. Gill, 1983: 556.
16. Baviskar, B.S. 1980. *The Politics of Development: Sugar Co-operatives in Rural Maharashtra.* Delhi: Oxford University Press.
17. These co-operatives have had been studied by many. See: Mascarenhas, R.C. 1988. *A Strategy for Rural Development.* New Delhi: Sage. Also Baviskar, B.S. 1986. "Dairy Cooperatives and Rural Development in Gujarat: A Case Study," *Cooperatives and Rural Development.* Delhi: D.W. Attwood and B.S. Baviskar eds., Oxford University Press. George, Shanti. 1985. *Operation Flood: An Appraisal of Current Indian Dairy Policy.* Delhi: Oxford University Press; Somjee A.H. and G. Somjee. 1978. "Cooperative Dairying and the Profiles of Social Change in India." *Economic Development and Social Change.* Vol. 26: 577-597 for a discussion on women-only dairies.
18. Saul, John S. 1971. "Marketing cooperatives in a developing country: the Tanzania case," *Two Blades of Grass.* Peter Worsley, ed., Manchester: Manchester University Press: 347-370.
19. Roth Warren J. 1976. "Traditional social structure and the development of a marketing cooperative in Tanzania," *Popular Participation in Social Change,* June Nash et. al., eds. The Hague: Mouton: 45-54.
20. Westergaard, Paul W. 1970. "Co-operatives in Tanzania as economic and democratic institutions," *Cooperatives and Rural Development in East Africa.* C.G. Widstrand, ed., New York: Africana Publishing Corporation: 124-152.
21. Westergaard, 1970:129-133.
22. Hyden, Gorun. 1980. *Beyond Ujamaa in Tanzania,* Berkeley: University of California Press: 9697.
23. Lewin, Roger. 1973 "Matetereka," *Socialism in Tanzania.* Lionel Cliffe & John S. Saul, eds., Vol. 2, Policies. Dar es salaam: East African Publishing: 189-94.
24. Raikes, 1975: 33-52 refers to turmoil in the countryside.
25. Hyden, Goran. 1974. "Co-operative education and co-operative development: The Tanzanian experience." *Agricultural Administration.* 1 (Jan): 35-50.
26. Manday, E.A. 1977. "A new structure for co-operatives in Tanzania." *Annals of Public and Co-operative Economy.* 48 (April-June): 239-244.
27. Stettner, Nora. 1984. *Chinese Co-operatives: Their Role in a Mixed Economy.* Oxford: Plunkett Foundation, Development Series No. 7: 3.
28. Dixon, John. 1982. "The Community Based Rural Welfare System in The peoples Republic of China: 1949-1979." *Community Development Journal,* Vol. 17, No. 1.
29. Stettner, 1984:22.
30. Stettner, 1984:23.
31. Stettner, 1984:43.

32. Stettner,1984:44-45.
33. Stettner,1984:45.
34. Stettner, 1984:49.
35. Stettner,1984:53.
36. Laidlaw, Alexander F. 1980. *Co-operatives in the year 2000*. Ottawa: Co-operative Union of Canada: 26-66.
37. Laidlaw, 1980:66.
38. Bottomley, Trevor. 1989. *Farmer-Centred Enterprise for Agricultural Development*. Oxford: Plunkett Foundation for Co-operative Studies.
39. Pestoff, Victor A. 1989. *Swedish Consumer Policy as a Welfare Service: Organizations in an Negotiated Economy*. Stockholm: University of Stockholm, Department of Business, Studies in Action and Enterprise. And 1991. *Between Markets and Politics: Co-operatives in Sweden*. Boulder: Westview Press.
40. See Quarter & Melnyk, 1989; Whyte & Whyte, 1988; and Fairbairn, Brett; Lou Hammond-Ketilson; Murray Fulton and June Bold. 1991 *Co-operatives & Community Development*. Saskatoon: Centre for the Study of Co-operatives, University of Saskatchewan.
41. Jordan, John. 1989. "The Multi-stakeholder Concept of Organization," *Partners in Enterprise: The Worker Ownership Phenomenon*. J. Quarter and G. Melnyk. Montréal: Black Rose Books: 113-31.
42. Saxena, Suren K. 1992. *Cooperatives in India and Pakistan: Some Aspects*. New Delhi: ICA Domus Trust: 7-9.
43. The calls for the end of bureaucratic meddling in co-operatives in India are extensive. The current law amendments before the national government are critical in allowing the movement to develop.
44. Planning Commission, 1991. *Report of The Committee on Model Cooperatives Act*. New Delhi: Government of India: 4-5.
45. Singh, S.N. 1992. "Anand Pattern Cooperatives The Indian Experience: A Cooperative Model for Asia." Paper to ICA Researchers Forum, October, Tokyo. And Korten, David C. 1990. *People Versus Government*. Hyderbad, India: Samakhya.
46. For a clear statement of this issue see Kurien "Cooperative Leadership and Cooperative Values." Kurien, V. *Cooperative Leadership and Values*. Anand: NDDB.

Chapter 6

THE PROBLEM: CO-OPERATIVES WITH LITTLE CO-OPERATION

It is well accepted that doing things for people extinguishes the self-help drive. Groups need to learn co-operation by doing things to help themselves. Some co-operatives are large, yet members are actively involved and new self-help programmes keep bubbling forward. The logic of stimulating self-help can be illustrated with an example.

In an uplands area of West Java, Indonesia, a young engineer had a project to assist rural villages electrify. He didn't go to villages and hold meetings to lecture the villagers on self-help. Rather, he would go to a village on his motorscooter. He would take a motorcycle generator, a short wire, a light bulb some rope and wood. When the children would come out to meet him he would get them to help him build a water wheel to turn the generator and produce light in the single bulb. He would then leave. A few weeks later he would return, and the adults would ask him to put the lights in their homes. He would explain that the small generator could run only a few lights. But, if they wanted he could show them how to develop the head-waters and install a turbine that would have the capacity to provide lights for all the houses. Electrification...self-help style with few resources.[1]

The idea of establishing contractual co-operation by using formal co-operatives has been attractive for the past 150 years. As a philosophy it is appealing but as we have shown the attempts to put it into practise often mean disappointment for those who truly want to create co-operating systems. What has caused the difference between promise and practise?

A group of experts at a 1984 conference in Washington DC indicated fifteen reasons why co-operatives fail. These are discussed in this chapter under three more generic topics: orientation of leadership and management necessary for development; membership characteristics; and legislative environment created by government. All three are critical to why co-operatives so often fail. These reasons are listed in Figure 6.1.

Figure 6.1

SUMMARY OF "IMPORTANT FACTORS CONTRIBUTING TO CO-OPERATIVE SUCCESS OR FAILURE"

a) Orientation factors (within the co-operative)

Leadership	The ability to articulate, motivate and stimulate others.
Sound management	The ability to deploy resources in such a way as to serve needs and create more resources.
Training	Learning skills required to operate an organization.
Education	The continual flow of information to develop members' capacities to participate effectively in decision-making.
Linkages	The need for relationships with other institutions and co-operatives.
Variety	The adaptation of the "co-operative model" to the particular community context.
Individualized Planning	The co-operative addressing situation specific needs in a phased manner.

b) Membership characteristics

Participation	Full and direct involvement in the planning of the co-operative's activities.
Open Membership	Membership open and voluntary.

c) Governmental environment

Favourable Climate	Conditions that allow co-operatives to flourish.
Sensitization	Education of the co-operative logic by government officials and others.
Legal Status	Legal recognition through legislation which grants co-operatives the right to exist and to function.
Integrated Development	Co-operative development seen as a part of overall socio-economic development plans.
Harmonization of Objectives	Co-operatives must work together for political/legislative ends.
Adequate Time Frame	New activities undertaken must not exceed the co-operative's ability to absorb them.

Source: The factors listed in this table come from the report "Why Co-operatives Succeed and Fail: A compendium of views by International Co-operative Experts." Washington D.C. USAID, 1984.

FROM DIRECTED TO CONTRACTUAL CO-OPERATION

The types of co-operation were explored in Chapter 1. The era from World War II to the 1970s was an era when the logic of directed co-operation and contractual co-operation were being tested. These dimensions are illustrated in Figure 6.2 along with the scope of co-operation (the topics of Chapters 3 and 4). The distinction between these types of co-operatives is important in understanding the dynamics of co-operation, and why so many co-operatives fail, while others succeed.

By building on these concepts, we move beyond the argument of traditional versus modern forms of co-operation. Contractual co-operation may be present or absent in both. Secondly, only service co-operatives built on segmental co-operation are a Western phenomenon. Forms of comprehensive co-operation are found in almost all human societies, in many cases in an explicit contractual form. Thirdly, whether the co-operatives were started as top-down or bottom-up is largely irrelevant. What is important is the nature of the internal dynamics and their relation to their environment after they are in operation. Often, when co-operatives are started by government officials, dependency is created and the officials, are not prepared to let go. However, noting this is conceptually different from arguing that all co-operatives must be started by the people in a community and never by outsiders.

Standards of Comparison

In order to analyze the reasons for failures — plus the continuing appeal of using co-operatives as a development vehicle — we need to establish our standards of comparison. Etzioni points out that there are two models to evaluate success or failure. The goal model and a comparative model.[2] In social science in general, and in the evaluation of co-operatives in particular, the goal model is often used quite inappropriately. For example, if the goal model were used by an electrical engineer to evaluate a light bulb, then he would conclude light bulbs fail! The goal of developing a light bulb is to convert electricity to light. A light bulb will only convert about 5% of the electricity into light the rest is dissipated as heat. But, a light bulb that will convert 7.5% into light is a 50% improvement and would be regarded as a major improvement by electrical engineers. Yet it is only a success using a comparative model, as it is still a failure in terms of the ideal goal. When comparing technology as reflected in machines, the comparative model is almost always used. Yet in assessing social technology, like co-operatives and

Figure 6.2

RELATIONSHIP BETWEEN TWO TYPES OF CO-OPERATION AND THE
INTERNAL POWER RELATIONS ILLUSTRATING THE DEVELOPMENT OF
CO-OPERATION WITHIN THE MEMBERSHIP

Contractual

A Grassroots co-operative activities	**B** Grassroots service co-operatives
C Government- sponsored community activities	**D** Government service co-operatives

Comprehensive
co-operation

Segmental
co-operation

Directed

Summary of key elements:

Type A and B are often referred to as grassroots co-operatives.

Type A co-operation occurs in all cultures and is not culture-specific.

Type B emerged in Britain and Europe with the industrial revolution and has
been widely diffused around the world as specialized co-operatives
in agricultural marketing, credit and supply co-operatives.

Type C and D are often referred to as top-down co-operatives. They are in-
stituted by planners rather than by local leaders. Research shows
that they rarely endure unless they take on contractual characteristics enabling bonding with the members. Type C and D may
have the same structures as A and B, but the processes are directed
by outsiders rather than internally. Type D is the common type of
planned agricultural marketing and supply co-operatives. Type C is
the common type of planned production societies.

Point: Who starts the co-operative is less important than what happens after
it gets started.

many other social changes, assessors may inappropriately use a goal model.

When co-operatives are compared to their ultimate goals, we must conclude that they are always dismal failures in developing rural areas in less industrialized countries as well as in the industrialized countries. Yet comparatively the picture changes. The *haciendas* (an example of capitalist development) in Latin America have produced food but have caused severe hardship and little development for the majority of the rural population. The same has been true of northern Agribusiness like the United Fruit Co. in plantations in central America. This is consistent with the body of analysis that asserted that colonialism and capitalist expansion went hand-in-hand, and that the several hundred years of capitalism within colonialism failed to produce much development in the colonies. Agricultural development in North America and Europe occurred in a capitalist framework, but with very unique conditions that are rarely found in the tropics. Similarly, socialist development has not been very successful either. As discussed in Chapter 5, the communes in China have largely been abandoned and replaced by individual and group initiatives organized around co-operatives. Socialist organizational forms in the less industrialized countries have not significantly improved the lot of the ordinary citizen. In short, neither capitalist or socialist organizational models have worked well in developing the rural sectors of less industrialized countries. And developers keep returning to co-operatives when they compare their results with other approaches. In order to assess co-operatives we feel that only a comparative approach is useful, and that attempts to analyze development using an ultimate goal approach are not very productive.

In Canada, which has a well developed infrastructure, we expect about 80% of new small businesses to fail within the first five years. Co-operatives also have a high failure rate and a review of the history of almost all successful co-operative movements in the industrialized countries shows that in the early organizational stages many are organized. Over the years, some succeed many others fail. The failures are usually amalgamated with stronger successful associations.

The point is that failure rates for all organizations have always been high. Co-operatives are no exception. They can succeed as a system when some local associations succeed, and organize a central organization that then provides training and other kinds of assistance to a growing movement. The chance of success for co-operatives started in isolation is and always has been very small. That is true of any small-scale business organization. However, acknowledging the problem of bureaucracy is important in understanding the nature of co-operation.

PARADIGMS AND OUR UNDERSTANDING OF CO-OPERATION

An important reason for this occurring has been the different perceptions of the nature of co-operation. The paradigm with which to understand co-operation differs from the one commonly used to practice it. The scientific community is now undergoing a paradigm shift. This new or emergent paradigm is more compatible to co-operative philosophy and an analysis from this perspective yields many insights as to what has been done wrong in the past.

A paradigm (illustrated in Figure 6.3) is the set of fundamental beliefs and assumptions that we hold that provide order and coherence to our perceptions of what is and how it works. It is our basic world view and how we understand the world. It can be viewed as our map, made up of the whole pattern of metaphors that consist of an individual's perspectives on and perceptions of reality. In a broad sense, a paradigm is the lens through which we see everything. For example, if we see and organization as a machine, we look for the faulty part to replace each time a mistake is made. This is different if we see it as an organism: then we look for a way to help the problem area to get well. Metaphors are a very important element in paradigms and in our understanding of the world around us.[3]

WHY CO-OPERATIVES FAIL

Leadership Orientation

There is a basic contradiction between the logic of co-operation and the logic of bureaucratic organizations. These logics often come into conflict, and over time the societal pressures squeeze out the co-operative logic, the bureaucratization of the co-operatives occurs and the organizations fail. This shift is a very prominent cause of co-operative failures in both the industrialized and less industrialized countries.

The bureaucratic mental set of leaders and management is a major obstacle to the development of co-operatives. The logic of co-operative activity is not only to market goods or satisfy consumer needs, but rather to provide as many benefits as possible for the people who are co-operating. Complexity and diversity is assumed in the logic. It is recognized that no one community is exactly the same as another and no group is the same as another. The logic is that

Figure 6.3

THE ROLE OF THE PARADIGM IN UNDERSTANDING THE WORLD

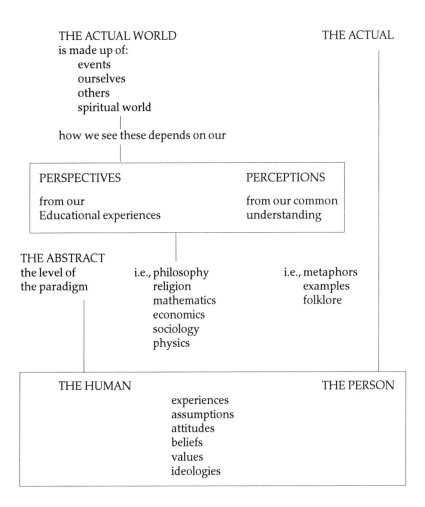

THE ACTUAL WORLD   THE ACTUAL
is made up of:
    events
    ourselves
    others
    spiritual world

how we see these depends on our

PERSPECTIVES   PERCEPTIONS

from our   from our common
Educational experiences   understanding

THE ABSTRACT
the level of   i.e., philosophy   i.e., metaphors
the paradigm   religion   examples
                          mathematics   folklore
                          economics
                          sociology
                          physics

THE HUMAN   THE PERSON
                          experiences
                          assumptions
                          attitudes
                          beliefs
                          values
                          ideologies

Modified from Peter Schwartz & James Ogilvy (1979), The Emergent Paradigm: Changing
Patterns of Thought and Belief.

groups can provide mutual self-help to each other and determine their own destinies. From diversity comes innovation and autonomous units provide freedom and flexibility for people to innovate and develop organizations that are responsive to their changing needs.

The logic of the co-operative activity of federating together is not the logic of hierarchy as assumed in the bureaucratic paradigm but rather the logic of heterarchy. Groups within a community co-operate, provide themselves with goods and services, and they work together through a federated structure with other groups in other communities. The bureaucratic paradigm assumed a hierarchy of external controls with a strong centre; but the logic of co-operation is of heterarchy, where there are internal controls and self-regulated groups co-operating with the centre but not dominated by it. Groups work together as equals in federations. The centre is controlled by the periphery and not the reverse, as is assumed in the logic of hierarchy.

The metaphor of mechanical order is compatible with the logic bureaucracies but not with co-operation. The co-operative movement cannot be seen as a machine made up of specialized parts. The logic of the co-operative movement is that communities will develop co-operatives to serve their needs. They will not exploit one another and they will function in a democratic fashion. Each of the co-operating units within a community embeds in itself the logic of co-operation and it relates to others not as a subordinate but rather as a part of the whole. Each co-operative and each co-operator is assumed to understand the values of co-operation and be capable of seeing the broader picture. This is far more compatible with a holographic metaphor than with the older mechanical metaphor inherent in the bureaucratic paradigm. For those who cannot think in holographic terms, the idea of co-operation beyond one's small group is difficult to understand.

The logic of autonomy and voluntary democratic action means that outcomes of decisions are indeterminant to outsiders. The groups must apply their own perspectives to situations as they arise and make decisions. The logic of co-operation is that there is an orderly process in which various groups can air their views and influence the outcome of decisions. Decisions are not determined by the controlling centre forcing its views onto others. The solution for one community may in fact be a major problem for another. The solution to problems are in-determinant and both the problem and the solution can best be defined by those who are involved in that community at that point in time.

Another feature of the logic of co-operation is multicausality as opposed to linear causality, assumed in the bureaucratic framework. Generalizing about causal effects across cultures and societies and then applying the findings without reinterpretation into the immediate context is extremely difficult and largely irrelevant in terms of the logic of co-operation. Yet development personnel from northern countries do it all the time in the south! The bureaucratic paradigm feature of blueprint change imposed from the centre does violence to the logic of democratic involvement to enable diverse elements to interact and make innovative connections. This is basic in the logic of co-operation. The bureaucratic logic of a central authority developing a blueprint for change does not fit the logic of co-operation, and attempting it has distorted the practice of co-operation in co-operatives.

The logic of an external objectivity in the bureaucratic paradigm has also distorted the logic of co-operation. The rationality used within a co-operating unit is either one of service to the members where an external criteria of objectivity (i.e., efficiency) can be applied, or one of meaning where the group develops its own rationale and then makes decisions. With a meaning rationality, the decisions can be viewed as rational if all affected by the decision have had the opportunity to discuss their ideas and their various views have been heard in developing a new perspective.

Co-operating groups are rational and objective only within their own framework of rationality. From the outside, one cannot impose an objectivity on the group because it is the perspective from within that group, which makes sense to that group, and the logic of co-operation is that this point of view should dominate. The logic that recognizes the rationality of outside experts to be superior to that of the co-operative members is not consistent with the logic of co-operation. This is not to deny the value of outsider's views. They may bring a fresh new perspective or important technical information. The point is that their analysis is not predetermined to be superior when applied in any local setting; it is a resource among others to be used in making the local decisions.

There are two categories of problems brought about by the application of the bureaucratic paradigm in relation to co-operatives. One is in the area of understanding co-operation and the other is in the application of co-operation in co-operative organizations. Co-operators have had great difficulty in communicating their paradigm to people who are well socialized within the bureaucratic tradition. It is difficult to create understanding when one is asked to think about things in a different way. When people try to incorporate the ideas of co-operation to be consistent with the bureaucratic logic they distort the meaning of co-operation. This is one reason why co-operative education has had difficulty making a major impact on the masses. To co-operators the ideas are clear and simple. But this clarity is only within the co-operative logic, not in bureaucratic logic.

The second set of problems relate to management and have meant that the promise of co-operation often goes unmet. Organizations have been premised on the bureaucratic logic for most of the past 200 years. Management in a bureaucracy assumes that organizations have narrow goals, that they are hierarchically organized with external controls through supervisors and specialist staff, they have complex communication channels which are premised on a hierarchical arrangement. Change within organizations can be made by experts on a blueprint basis. With increasing bureaucratization there is low risk-taking as risk-takers are punished and the emphasis shifts to following procedures. The logic of objectivity and linear causality are central in how organizations are thought to work best and how managers try to make them work. Bureaucratic organizations are important in society. They are crucial for the military and government administration. But that management style relies on directed co-operation from the centre and prevents contractual co-operation from emerging in co-operatives. Members do not see them as their own organizations and the promise of co-operation fades.

Unfortunately, co-operatives are usually organized in less industrialized countries by people trained in the bureaucratic traditions of the north and by bureaucrats in the less industrialized countries. Researchers point out:

> Once created...organizations reflect the prevailing meaning structures of their time in their internal pattern of social relations. Thus organizations originating in bureaucratized society will tend to be created with bureaucratic structure — even when, one might add, they are designed to overturn the political system.... This is because the founders of the organization whatever their aims, will usually take their ideas about efficient organization from the stock of knowledge characteristic of their society at the time.[4]

These pressures result in the shaping of organizations to fit the management approaches dominant in the country. The logic of co-operation has not been within the bureaucratic logic but the practice of co-operation in many co-operatives has been. This has done violence to the basic ideas of co-operation. In short, people well socialized into the logic of co-operation may create organizations which have been compatible with that logic. However, as the organization grows and new members and new managers take over who are well socialized into the bureaucratic logic, a displacement takes place. The organizations slowly but inevitably become transformed into organizations which lose much of the properties of co-operation. The lack of a well developed theory of co-operative management does not help. Existing managers feel very threatened when they are accused of not being co-operators. The harder they try to make the organizations work well the stronger the pressures to make them conform to the bureaucratic paradigm. This has been happening in the co-operatives in industrialized counties for decades and these are the blueprints for the bureaucracies in the less industrialized countries to use as models.

A careful analysis of the history of successful co-operative agricultural movements in Europe and North America shows quite clearly that none were copies of other movements. The Raiffison co-operatives in Europe inspired agricultural co-operatives in North America, etc., but the socio-economic environments differed, and organizational structures and processes emerged to fit the environments rather than a blueprint from elsewhere being used. Yet donor countries continually send people to the less industrialized countries who usually have little experience in co-operatives in their own countries, and who try to impose the back-home model in a completely different environment. As one researcher observed:

> It is vital that such services are organised to respond to particular requirements in each context — a "blueprint" approach is a recipe for failure. It is also essential to remember that the process of implementation is as important, if not more important, than the concept. Even the most carefully conceived projects can fail because the institutions responsible for implementation are unable to cope with the demands made of them. Co-operatives must be able to undertake the responsibilities of project implementation but even with technical support, they may not be able to overcome bureaucratic bottlenecks which public agencies are only too capable of creating. Anticipating implementation problems is an essential part of project design.[5]

In short, the aid agencie's approach is also very important in determining the ultimate success and failure of co-operatives. If the co-operatives succeed the agency will take the credit; if they fail, the problem is either the local people or the notion that "co-operatives just don't work."

Membership Characteristics

Successful co-operatives must take root in the membership they must be valued, and over time, institutionalized into the community. This is achieved when the basic functional requirements of organizations are met, plus the basic values inherent in co-operation are practised. These patterns within the group are necessary but not sufficient for the success of co-operatives. Groups are always surrounded by a broader economic, political and social environment which constrains and impacts on their day-to-day dynamics. This environment shapes the actions within co-operatives, but over time the environment is also shaped by the actions of groups of which co-operatives may be a significant force.

An important condition in a group is a clear, well understood need. This is a requirement of both the organizations and the logic of co-operation. Groups of people must share a clear goal on which they basically agree. It will be clear, straightforward and pragmatic. It will usually reflect the self-interest of what the community hopes to gain by co-operating.

These membership characteristics were discussed in Chapter 4 and will not be repeated here.

Legislative Environment Created by Government

Governments are clearly related to the success and failure of co-operatives. Frequently co-operatives have been seen as an important tool in rural development. The planners using a classical economic development framework wish to increase agricultural exports to provide a capital base for industrialization in the urban economy. Co-operatives are closely controlled and the surplus is in effect confiscated from the peasants to be used for industrialization. The peasants do not see these as desirable goals and do not support the organizations set in place to extract the surpluses. I do not argue the merits of this development assumption, but merely point out that co-operatives are designed to enable members to control the surpluses they produce. In the above situation they are the wrong organizational form and are bound to fail.

Insecure governments are also fearful of competing power actors in society. In the case of ex-colonies many of the existing leaders were involved in co-operatives prior to independence and understand that an effective co-operative helps people learn leadership skills and develop a local power base. This is feared, and legislation often provides for a close scrutiny of activities so leaders can be co-opted early. This often dooms co-operatives to failure.

Tropical countries often have so much that needs to be done, and rising expectations of the population that governments deliver. If co-operatives obtain initial success they are often given such huge development tasks that they are swamped. A realistic legislative environment is critical, and aid organizations need to be proactive in advising recipient countries of the roadblocks that are in the legislation. This needn't be an ethnocentric process of standard co-operative acts. It needs to be done in the context of each country's own conditions. In Canada, co-operatives have had an ongoing struggle to get fair legislation. The Canadian Senate, by a single vote, defeated the federal co-operatives act in 1907 and it took until 1970 before an act was passed. Current legislation in most provinces has been unfavourable to workers' co-operatives, and legislation to encourage Canadians to invest has discriminated against investment in co-operatives. Getting a level playing field has been an ongoing struggle.[6]

Understanding Co-operation

Co-operators have had great difficulty in communicating their paradigm to people who have been thoroughly socialized within the dominant paradigm. There are, however, many co-operators around the world who see co-operation within the new emergent paradigm, but it is difficult to create understanding in others when they are required to apply themselves and assess their actions in a different way. A review of the history of co-operatives demonstrates that although new patterns of organization have been applied at various times and places, when the co-operatives run into economic difficulties, experts trained in the bureaucratic paradigm are brought in and given a free hand to "clean up the mess." This has meant applying the dominant paradigm to the co-operative organization; this paradigm frequently distorts the meaning of co-operation and reinforces the popular wisdom that co-operation only works in small groups.

This process is also one of the reasons why co-operative education has had difficulty making a major impact on the masses in the Western societies. To co-operators who understand the logic of co-operation within the emerging paradigm the ideas are clear and simple; but this clarity is only present when one is thinking within the emerging paradigm not within the dominant paradigm.

I am arguing that the logic of co-operation and co-operative organizations have had a minimal effect because of the organizational logic of the environment within which they have been set. This goes beyond the Marxist argument that you cannot have an island of

socialism in a sea of capitalism. Co-operatives are also swamped by
the dominant bureaucratic paradigm used in socialist societies. For
co-operatives to be successful, organizational structures and processes need to be developed within the emerging paradigm.

PRACTISING CO-OPERATION IN CO-OPERATIVES

This challenge goes beyond India, China and Tanzania as discussed in the last chapter. Few co-operatives have training programmes that really address the teaching of the self-help logic to managers
and leaders. There are several ways to proceed:

1)   Management and Board training programmes focused specifically
      on the logic of co-operation and the contradictions of the
      bureaucratic logic when "one works for farmers." Co-operatives
      must be organizations that are constantly learning and respond-
      ing to the needs and aspirations of its members.

2)   Training programmes to enable students to spend time in the field
      observing the two logics in practice and documenting and view-
      ing the impact of each on the members.[7]

3)   Assignments for employees to critique existing ways of doing
      things and propose changes to improve efficiency, effectiveness
      and apply the co-operative logic for the benefit of members.

4)   The International forums where researchers who study co-opera-
      tives meet and talk need to continue. Papers addressing the
      theory of co-operatives need to be widely circulated.

5)   We need case studies where the co-operative logic is being applied
      and a learning organization is in operation.

Co-operatives are being challenged. In Europe, Japan and North
America the market forces are forcing co-operatives to change. Some
are rediscovering their roots and reinvigorating member involvement for a competitive edge, others are imitating their competitors
and losing their co-operative features. In Eastern Europe, the State-
directed co-operatives collapsed and genuine co-operatives are rising
from the ashes. In most of the newly independent countries internal
pressure is mounting to free the co-operatives from the bureaucrats.
State planners have failed. The challenge is to develop genuine co-
operatives as the State backs away. The ICA is evaluating the co-
operative principles once again. By 1995 these will be articulated, and
national movements will be pressing governments to amend legislation so that amended principles are included in the Acts. Embodying
the co-operative principles in legislation is an important defense to

keep bureaucrats from taking over. In short, the challenge is not only to help members to take back their co-operatives from government, but to apply the co-operative logic to have true member-owned and controlled co-operatives.

SELF-HELP LOGIC APPLIED IN CO-OPERATIVES IN INDONESIA

A development project in Indonesia during the 1980s provides some empirical insights into applying the logic of self-help outlined above. The project started with the problem of water management in the Citanduy river basin in central Java, Indonesia, and by 1987 the environment had been improved in terms of water management. As well, food self-sufficiency was achieved with surplus food production in many more of the villages and the surpluses were being used for local development. Two projects realized these objectives and will be compared in this paper. One was the traditional blueprint approach from the top and the other involved local participation and the development of grassroots pre-co-operatives (KUBES) in the villages.

The Citanduy river basin in Indonesia presented water engineers and agricultural experts with a problem. Due to improper management, wrongly placed infrastructures and facilities, and past natural processes, about 76,000 hectares in the upper watershed was critical in causing about 51,000 hectares of land in the lower watershed area to be flooded between four and twelve times annually. In the dry season about 72,000 hectares of rice fields lacked water for irrigation.[8]

The area involves a total of 446,000 hectares of farmland of which 27% is classified as uplands devoted to small cultivation. The peasants in the upland areas were living on old rubber plantations and most were barely producing enough food for subsistence. Many hamlets had no roads, only a walking trail to larger communities. The peasants were extremely poor and relied on subsistence agriculture. The poor soil management in this uplands area was the cause of the water management problems downstream. So development was needed to assist the surplus producers downstream.

The solution to the problem in the minds of the water management experts was clear. A project was developed, run by the government of Indonesia and funded by USAID. A comprehensive flood-control system was designed and constructed to protect the entire lower watershed from regular heavy flooding that occurs about every 25 years. At the same time selected irrigation systems both in the lower and upper watersheds were rehabilitated, and two new irrigation systems were constructed. The planning followed a blueprint approach. These improvements were purely technical and did not need the active participation of the local government and farmers to be achieved.

In 1981 the project entered a second phase where the small farmers in the upland villages needed to be drawn into the picture to improve their farming practices. Two projects were funded to undertake the task. One was undertaken by the government personnel and the other contracted to ITB (Bandung Institute of Technology) a nearby university. The approaches used in the two projects were very different and so were the outcomes.

The Government Development Project

Organizers selected the villages where terracing should be used to improve the uplands water management. They made contact with the local government and village leaders and gained permission to work with the farmers to develop a network of terraced fields. Peasants were hired to terrace the fields and the outside experts supervised the work to make sure the aid money was well used. By 1986 about 4,000 hectares of land had been terraced and better agricultural technologies were being used. Food production increased and the villagers were brought into the market economy as they now had surplus foodstuffs to sell. The existing marketing infrastructure was not disrupted. Rather it expanded to handle the increased production. Production continued on small plots and the credit needs of the farmers were supplied through the traditional channels. By development standards this was a successful project as the funding for the terracing was used for that purpose. The work was closely supervised and the objectives were achieved.

The Grassroots Involvement Project

The approach used by the engineers from the Institute for Technology Bandung (ITB) started the same as the above project. They told the villagers what to do, but were frustrated because the activities would only take place when the engineers were in the villages supervising. They involved personnel at the new Centre for Environmental Studies (PPLH, also located on the ITB campus) who advised a very different approach. They suggested focusing on two pilot villages in the area. They approached the local government and village leaders, gained approval and proceeded to work with the local farmers. In one village, the leaders were not prepared to let the local farmers be involved in making decisions, so this location was dropped and the efforts were focused on the village of Cigaru. It was selected because it was one of the poorest hamlets and was looked down on by the people in the other hamlets. The technique used was to hold meetings with the farmers, have them identify their problems and help the group come up with solutions. One solution was to increase rice production. The engineers showed the farmers how to terrace fields and develop the water channels. This became the model village. After the first crop was harvested with a dramatic increase in production, the field workers who were making contact with other villages suggested they visit Cigaru for ideas. They did and the other villages often improved on the techniques in the process. They started terracing and called on the outsider experts when they needed technical assistance. The work was done on a self-help basis and the only aid money was used for salaries for the organizers, travel and some specific technical inputs.

By 1986 the project was successful, with over 4,000 hectares of land terraced and over 80 subsistence hamlets becoming surplus food producers. As well, about 48,000 hectares "had been rehabilitated and made productive using physical inputs originally provided for 5,000 hectares."[9] The success of the project was achieved by the organizers through participatory action research programmes that addressed the critical needs felt by the peasants.[10] One observer has concluded. "The foundation of the success of the Ciamis Program was established by inducing one hamlet, Cigaru, to come to grips with the need to improve management of its land and water resource base, creating grassroots organizational structures compatible with the traditions and skills of its people, and incrementally building up their capacity to confront more and more complex problems."

An important dimension of the success of the project was that external aid was only used to provide organizers. The villagers achieved the development through their own efforts and in the process developed organizational skills so the process continues.

The organizers did the following:

- Spent the time with the farmers to let them define their needs and to decide what they wanted to do. When they had decided terracing was a good idea they,
- showed the villagers how to terrace some of the rich hillsides to catch the water and start growing rice and to combine/develop fish ponds in some of the terraces to increase the available protein.
- They showed the villagers how to plant more trees like coconuts and fruit trees, etc., to protect the soil, as well as when to harvest the coconut trees that were getting old, before they died, to produce lumber for construction and sale.
- They showed how to use the coconut husks to stop erosion on slopes in the village.

- They demonstrated how electric lights could be developed by building a small waterwheel using a motorcycle generator, and when hamlets wanted more lights they showed them how to develop the headwaters and install a turbine that would have the capacity to provide lights for all the houses.
- They involved the women in identifying needs and exploring solutions together to improve the quality of life. With better water supply, a larger range of foodstuffs could be grown.
- They also developed a pre-co-operative organization — so the villagers could have a regular forum to discuss needs and concerns — which provided an ongoing organizational framework for the villagers to address common problems, like credit and purchasing inputs togethers.

Like the government project, over 4,000 hectares of terracing has been completed. But unlike the government project the terracing is still in progress, plus other land upgrading is continuing that was developed by the farmers and that is beyond the original objectives of the project. The subsistence hamlets are now surplus food producers. Their standard of living has improved, with better homes and better diets. Many have built roads so that supplies can be brought in by truck rather than on motorcycles with an immediate decline in price for the inputs of about 20%. The (KUBES) pre-co-operatives now have a capital base to make small loans to members at about 15% per annum (bank rate) rather than 70-150% from the moneylenders.

This case study illustrates that rural development can take place with a minimum amount of outside resources. Locally organized co-operatives can be successfully developed amongst the poor if the process is right, and a self-help logic can emerge in communities where the people gain confidence that they can do things, and do not wait for the outside experts to come in and organize them. It isn't easy and requires a logical set and skills not usually found in bureaucratically oriented development officials.

These are different outcomes:

- Both projects achieved terracing of about 4,000 hectares by 1986. The terracing is continuing in the ITB project villages but has stopped in the government project area.
- The cost was twelve times larger in the government project compared to the ITB project.
- The money saved in the ITB project was used to rehabilitate an additional 48,000 hectares of farmland and increase its productivity.

- The cultivation patterns are by small peasant plots in both projects and production has increased. Inputs are easier to obtain and less expensive in the ITB project area because the emerging KUBES provide credit at reasonable interest rate compared to the traditional money lenders.
- Spin-off projects to improve the quality of life are continuing in the ITB project area because their is an ongoing organizational infrastructure controlled by the villagers to enable action to occur. (e.g., the development of small turbines to provide electricity).

Both projects had the same goal. Yet they proceeded in different ways and produced very different results. The Ciamis project cannot be replicated by others unless they have a mental set that enables them to think within a self-help paradigm. This can be contrasted to the bureaucratic paradigm that is usually used in development and fails to stimulate self-help and ongoing development.

The question can also be asked, can it be replicated by others from the same organization in a non-rural context? ITB is in the process of trying. The new project is in a local brick-and-tile manufacturing industry in Indonesia where the introduction of better and more efficient production methods, new technologies and marketing strategies through local co-operative organizations is carried out in a sustainable ecologically sound manner.

In 1989, two students, one Canadian and one Indonesian, spent three months living in the area, talking to people and doing preliminary data collection. Their report formed the basis for a funding proposal to the Canadian Co-operative Association. The methodology for intervention is based on the experience of the Centre for Environmental Research at the Institute of Technology in Bandung, Indonesia (PPLH/ITB). The objective is to develop a network of community organizations, mostly co-operatives and support organizations, that will create a symbiotic relationship and generate a sustainable development dynamic that creates non-farm jobs. This action research project is based on the model developed and used so successfully during the 1980s in Ciamis[11] and the Bandung scavenger project.[12]

The central assumption is that in order for development to be sustainable, it needs to proceed at the same speed as the learning process is progressing within the local population. External resources are used to help the population help themselves. External resources are introduced when the community wants them and the consultants work for the community, not for an external client. The point of intervention in this case is a savings and loans co-operative (credit union) that mobilizes community savings and is the focus of the self-help initiatives in the community.[13]

SUSTAINABLE DEVELOPMENT

Development is an active process in a community. The definition used here has been defined by Girvan;

> Development is a complex process involving the social, economic, political and cultural betterment of individuals and of society itself. Within the development process, women and men are viewed as active agents in, and not passive recipients of development.[14]

Sustainable development has been used in a number of ways. The Brundtland report, which gave high prominence to the term, defined it as "development that meets the needs of the present without compromising the ability of future generations to meet their own needs."[15] This sounds good at a conceptual level, but as Brooks points out, it is neither clear, nor complete. He goes on to point out that, "it is an alternative economics not an alternative to economics." It contradicts many conventional ideas about economic growth but does not define growth as bad. Growth means an increase in size by adding material, development is the realization of potential. Sustainable development means limits placed on potential — "quality can always be expanded and in many more ways than mere physical size."[16] It is a different mental set about development.[17]

The emerging paradigm of sustainable development integrates five requirements;

1) Integration of conservation of natural resources with development.
2) Satisfaction of basic human needs.
3) Achievement of equity and basic social justice.
4) Provision of social self-determination and cultural diversity.
5) Maintenance of ecological integrity.[18]

Co-operatives are one organizational form that can be compatible with sustainable development. Whether they are compatible or not depends on the way in which they are introduced and the manner in which they operate in the community. Established co-operative movements in Europe, North America and Japan along with their governments, have been providing aid to a number of countries in Asia for the past forty years to develop co-operatives.

The results have been painfully limited and all too often what has been called "bureaucratic feudalism" has emerged rather than the member-supported movement that was intended.[19] Asian countries are densely populated and the surplus population displaced as agriculture mechanizes cannot be absorbed into the cities. Non-farm rural employment must be developed. Pollution has an immediate impact in densely populated areas and sustainability is critical.

As people strive to bring forth sustainable development in the Asian context, it is valid to ask: Do co-operatives have a role in developing environmentally sound, sustainable, non-farm economic projects in rural areas of Indonesia? The experience at the Institute for Technology at Bandung suggests that this is the case. But it must be done with the population at its own pace.

Jasinga-Leuwiliang Project

This project involves the introduction of better and more efficient production methods, new technologies and marketing strategies. Most of the current brick and tile activities are small scale and done by hand. This provides employment for women and landless workers and a source of cash income for small landholders. Incomes of both the hired workers and the brick producers are at the subsistence level. The current methods present the following two problems.

a) The environmental problem — the source of clay is from the fields and unless the farmers are very careful, the process can be environmentally degrading. Fields can be lowered too far and/or the topsoil destroyed.

b) The bricks and tiles are of low quality and the family receives very little for the work involved.

When this small-scale activity takes place in the hilly waste land (currently used for firewood, as the timber has been long since removed), the quarrying of the clay flattens the land and it can be brought into agricultural production. Topsoil contains too much vegetable matter to be used for bricks. So by returning the top soil to the levelled land, the process need not be environmentally harmful. But even if the producers wish to produce higher quality materials, they face problems in improving and expanding operations.

a) *Capital:* is not available at reasonable rates. The villagers are dependent on the moneylenders and/or middlemen for capital.

b) *Marketing:* The only channel has been through middlemen. The producers have prevented themselves from filling large direct orders by producing bricks of varying size and quality.

c) *Technology:* Modest improvements could yield major results if they are appropriate and the changes well understood. These technological changes would also displace the women who currently are employed to shape the tiles by hand.

It is estimated that the population of Indonesia will reach 290 million people by 2018. The island of Java is already one of the most densely populated areas in the world with more than 100 million, or 60% of the country's population. The current densities of Java and Bali are 800 and 500 people per square kilometre, compared with only ninety-one for Indonesia as a whole. Java's population is expected to increase by 8% during the current five-year plan (1989-94) and the population of Jakarta is expected to reach 10.3 million, compared with a current population of 8.8 million.

While agriculture is the country's primary source of employment, tens of thousands of young Indonesians are leaving their villages to seek work in the industrial zones surrounding the nation's urban centres. Indonesia's 74-million-strong labour force is growing by 2.2 million a year. At present, only about 55% of the total labour force can find more than 35 hours of work each week. About three out of four Indonesian workers are employed in the "informal sector" as petty traders, retail vendors, cottage-industry employees or day labourers. Job creation is of vital importance, particularly in the rural areas.

Rapid economic growth combined with continued population growth is stressing both the ecology and the social systems. Awareness of the negative impact of growth-oriented development on the environment has put "sustainable development" on the political agenda. But it remains a concept that many have heard but few have understood or seen, including the foreign donors. This is particularly true of the Indonesian co-operative movement which is well placed to make a contribution to sustainable development.[20]

The proposed project location is in the area south west of Jakarta. It is a predominately agricultural area with a relatively low population density (438 people/km²). Agriculture is limited by poor soils (acidic and high in aluminum) and irrigation. Land use is dominated by mixed, treed areas, gardens, open fields and rain-fed rice fields. Surrounding the area are extensive plantations of rubber and coconut.

> It is difficult to provide a clear picture on sources and levels of income in the area as statistics are unreliable. According to the *lurah* (a local government official), 70% of the inhabitants are farmers. But given that agricultural productivity averages only 183 kg/person/year most people must supplement their incomes with employment outside the farm. The main off-farm, income-earning activities are provided by small family-run enterprises producing

firewood and planks for Jakarta's markets, the tile and brick industry and small trade. Statistics indicate that up to 50% of the people who migrate to Jakarta are young people. An increasing number of people who are selling immature fruit trees as firewood would indicate that sources and levels of income in the area generally poor.[21]

The brick and tile area closer to Jakarta is being overrun with industry. Production of bricks and tiles has been declining in the Jakarta area at the same time that demand is increasing. The Jasinga area has had small scale producers of bricks and tiles for many years as there is an abundance of high quality clay available. This provides employment for women and landless workers, and is a source of cash income for small farmers when they are not busy in the fields. Almost the entire tile and brick producing activity of Jasinga is concentrated in the project area. There are no official figures for the tile and brick industry but ITB research indicates there are about eighty-five small enterprises producing 30 million bricks annually.[22]

A typical enterprise consists of several open thatch-roofed sheds (*lio*) in which bricks are moulded and stacked to dry. In an adjacent oven or kiln the dried bricks are fired. The majority of the local tile and brick enterprises were established using personal savings and local resources (building materials, help from neighbours, etc.).

Most of the producers lack the capital with which to pay their workers and to purchase fuelwood. For an average-size enterprise (10,000 bricks per firing), this amounts to around Rp. 200,000 ($125.00) for each firing.[23] Obtaining credit has proven to be very difficult as the *lio* owners are seen as poor credit risks.

There are three sources of credit in the area:

1) Bank Rakyat Indonesia (BRI), a privately owned village mobile bank. The producers do not borrow from the mobile banks because loans are too small and repayment is daily. BRI is not a viable option either as often the producers do not have the collateral (land certificates) and cannot meet the daily instalments.

2) Brick retailers (*leveransir*). When they borrow from the retailer, payment is made in bricks at Rp. 30/brick (less than 2 cents) which is well below market levels.

3) Pre-selling to buyers. Brick producers sell to one of two types of buyers: buyers who buy on site and external buyers. Prices paid by the two buyers vary; Rp. 45 and Rp. 75 respectively, with the latter price including transportation costs.

4) Grameen Bank Indonesia. The Bank of Indonesia invited the Grameen Bank from Bangladesh to develop a pilot bank in this area.

Started in 1990, it now has five field workers and nearly 1,000 borrowers. It has closely followed the model so successful elsewhere. The target group is the poorest of the poor working in lending circles. This provides a valuable source of credit but is designed to meet the needs of a poorer segment of the population.

About 70% of the selling price of the brick goes to buy raw materials for firing and the remaining 30% covers the cost of hired labour, transportation cost and the cost of credit, etc. Net profit earned is negligible, about Rp. 1/brick. Imagine making 1,600 bricks to provide Cdn$1 in family income! Those with enough resources to finance production thus not needing loans can make more money.

If the producers could do two things — improve the quality of the product, and bypass the money lender and the middlemen and sell directly to contractors — they could substantially improve their incomes. This money would be spent locally, and a development dynamic would get started. Sounds simple, but it is actually quite complicated. For example over the years the buyers have convinced the producers that they are in competition with each other and have encouraged the production of different sized bricks. This prevents any one producer from producing the volumes needed to sell directly to a contractor.

The Jasinga-Leuwiliang sustainable development project is designed to break this dependency relationship, and has the potential to keep people in the area, rather than flooding into the Jakarta job market. The existence of good materials for tile and brick manufacturing in the Jasinga-Leuwiliang area represents a potential that can be developed.

Developing co-operative credit organizations could play a role in mobilizing local capital so that the community can retain control of its resources. Employment for both men and women can be increased and the intervention could head off future environmental degradation. In short, it is designed to meet the five criteria discussed above for sustainable development. The ingredients for this development need to come together at the right time or mal-development could easily result.

Method of Local Intervention

PPLH/ITB has developed the following approach to development.[24]

1) They view a project as an exercise in "social learning" for all the actors, including the government and commercial interests as well as the community.

2) They attempt to synthesize the top-down approaches used by others with bottom-up approaches, by using mechanisms for conflict

resolution both between and within the various groups, and by organizing locally controlled organizations. This is done through the local development consultant who lives in the community and speaks the local dialect.

3) The research done by PPLH over the past three years provides an information base to be discussed by the community and to assist in improving the quality of the decisions. This is done by providing information in an understandable form at key times.

4) Rather than dealing directly with a large, complex eco-region, PPLH/ITB starts with the smallest possible unit as an entry point for eco-development that is sustainable, and then replicates its development in the surrounding hamlets.

5) Participatory action research is used for limited purposes at critical times, such as at the beginning of the project, for the identification of problems and potentials at later stages in development of markets etc.

6) The engineering capacity of ITB and contacts in the modern sector enable technical expertise to be available to the hamlets.

The central assumption is that in order to be sustainable, the process needs to proceed at the same speed as the learning process within the local community. External resources will be used to help the population help themselves and will be introduced when the population want them. In short, a learning process is started and the community creates an organization that it democratically controls, an organization which becomes the gate-keeper to outsiders.

ITB provides a local "development consultant" (someone with social learning skills) to work with the people.[25] They get to know the people, and become trusted. As interest develops, a local forum is created for people to meet, talk and make decisions. The organization can take on the first task of developing capital (i.e., a credit union), and it will continue to provide a forum for those interested in exploring development options. There may be one forum, or it may subdivide, with one for brick and tile producers and one for ceramic producers, or one for women ceramic producers and one for men ceramic producers. These are community decisions. In the long term, co-operatives may be developed from these groups for marketing and transportation. They may be user-owned, privately owned or worker-owned co-operatives. The form depends on what makes sense to the community at that point in time.

From the preliminary research based on discussions with the people, three functions are needed at the village level to start sustainable development. It is important that control of these three functions rests in the community. They are:

1) A credit and savings capacity (credit union) to mobilize local savings and channel some seed capital to producers.
2) Technical Services Organization (TSO) to find and arrange for technical expertise when needed.
3) Management Services Organization (MSO) to find and arrange for management expertise when needed.

The backup experts are on-call by the community organizations. They will change over coming years but a number have been identified and will come into the communities when asked to do so by the credit union, Technical Services Organization (TSO) or Management Services Organization (MSO). This is important. Consultants always try to please their clients in order to get more work. These consultants will not be working for an external agency like York University, ITB, the Government of Indonesia or a foreign aid organization. They will be hired or fired by the community-controlled organization.

What is Possible
With the appropriate technology, sustainable development could be achieved. One of the mandates of ITB is to develop and introduce appropriate technology for development. The brick-tile-ceramic combination has a number of advantages over traditional technology.

1) An extruder can speed the process of shaping bricks and tiles, but will displace the women who currently do it by hand. The women released from the shaping of tiles can learn ceramics and make household utensils, water purifiers, etc., for use in the region's homes. Those who are artistically talented can make ceramic works of art. This is more pleasant work and should provide more income. Very few ceramics are currently produced in the area.

2) Poor-quality products take as much work as good-quality products. Clay selection, preparation and kiln design is very important for quality products and can be taught as the groups progress.

3) All the materials for the kilns, potters wheels, etc., can be made from local materials with the assistance of the local people. By making the machines themselves they will understand them and be able to repair them and not become dependent on the outside technologists.

4) Brick kilns and smaller ceramic kilns operate at high heats (1,000 to 2,000 degrees). As the heat rises it cools and this heat can be used to extract vegetable oils, or cook coconut sugar. The technologies are known; what is needed is creative organization.

5) Handmade bricks are dense and heavy. Chemicals can be added that produce light high-quality bricks that command a premium price. The chemicals needed for this technology are currently by-products of several industries operating in the Jakarta area. Indonesia has no hazardous waste disposal sites, so this waste is stored on the factory grounds. The Environment Ministry has awarded a contract to another university to explore uses of the waste and ways to dispose of it. PPLH/ITB is currently negotiating with the industries and government to fund a research project at ITB to answer three critical questions: How can the chemicals be mixed with the clay without presenting a health hazard to the workers? Will the temperatures used in the kilns be adequate to make the chemicals inert? Will the smoke from the kilns present a health hazard? This is in the future. Such technology is currently far too advanced for the area. But, if the project realizes its potential, it can continue to upgrade and expand non-farm employment.

With the introduction of simple improvements in quality, a tangible improvement in the quality of life should be realized. With an ongoing forum to address problems, the questions of how to utilize the newer advanced technologies plus how to organize to improve marketing and transportation can be addressed. For outsiders like the Canadian Co-operative Association (the funder) and York University, the organizational solution may be to develop unifunctional co-operatives and get to work. When using a learning approach the answer is less clear at the start. For example, the existing middlemen who are making large profits are not going to just go away. During the conflict management phase, the community may find other alternatives such as selling directly to housing co-operatives in Jakarta, using other truckers or being a bargaining organization and selling to competing middlemen, etc. — a good reason for the experts to work as consultants *for the community* not aid donors.

The credit union is being developed by the grassroots without external pressure and through that process, local leaders will emerge. The local worker will keep a local forum going (education programme) where the villagers will identify problems, analyze them and think about how to address them. The external resources will be invited to meetings and the work sites by the credit union's Technical Service unit or the Management Service unit. The community groups will be clients.

The Project and Sustainable Development?

1) Integration of conservation of natural resources with development.

Building in a learning dynamic means that awareness and knowledge about the natural resources of the community can be included. Large brick operations develop open pit mines and scar the landscape. Small-scale community-based operations can use hilly land, remove the top soil, level the land and then replace the top soil and put the land into agricultural use. The existing rice fields could be levelled for more irrigation by removing sub-soil for bricks. The excavation of brick-making sub-soil should enhance the natural resources in the area. This, combined with composting current waste can improve the field and reduce the waste material in the villages.

2) Satisfaction of basic human needs.

Subsistence living is hard. By improving incomes of both the producers and workers more basic family needs will be met. Displacing women workers, from the shaping of tiles and replacement with jobs in ceramics will not only mean employment, but also the availability of low-cost ceramic household products such as bowls, dishes and water purifiers. The artistically talented can develop their potential as the Jakarta tourist market is close. This should produce better incomes and better working conditions.

3) Achievement of equity and basic social justice.

Cutting the margins going to middlemen, ending the excessive interest rates charged by moneylenders (often in excess of 100% per annum) and putting more money into the community economy is a basic start on achieving equity and basic social justice. However the creation of people-owned organizations allows for a forum to address issues and an organizational capacity that can address questions of equity and basic social justice in the years ahead.

4) Provision of social self-determination and cultural diversity.

Community-based organizations provide for a major degree of self-determination. The day-to-day working of such organizations builds confidence, a sense of commitment, and pride in achievement. This mental state is important in strengthening self-determination and local culture. These are indirect things, yet they develop as people successfully experience co-operation.

5) Maintenance of ecological integrity.

The ecology of most areas is complex and two kinds of expertise are critical. The experts' general knowledge from scientific study, together with the particular local wisdom of centuries of observation of the ecology of a particular locality. The merging of these knowledge bases is built into the design of the project. Evaluation by participants and outsiders will enable a regular check to maintain the ecological integrity in the area.

If the research at ITB on combining chemical waste and brick making is successful in producing high-quality brick and tiles, a symbiotic relationship may emerge to reduce hazardous waste in the factory areas and making it inert in the bricks and tiles.

These examples show what can be done in developing countries, but what about in highly industrialized countries where capitalism provides massive competition? The remaining two chapters deal with contemporary problems and how farmers and consumers can be empowered by using co-operatives to improve their quality of life.

NOTES

1. Craig, J.G. & H. Poerbo. 1988. "Food security and rural development: the case of Ciamis Indonesia," *Journal of Rural Co-operation,* Vol. XVI, No. 1-2, pp. 111-124. Reprinted in UCE reprint series.
2. Etzioni, A. 1964. *Modern Organizations.* Engelwood Cliffs: Prentice-Hall: 10.
3. Morgan, Gareth. 1980. "Paradigms, Metaphors and Puzzle Solving in Organizations." *Administrative Science Quarterly,* 25: 605-622.
4. Silverman. 1970. *The Theory of Organizations.* London: Heinemann: 148, quoting Stinchcomb.
5. Alder, Graham. 1985. "The Role of The Cooperative Sector in Financing Urban Housing Development." Paper presented to "Why Cooperatives Succeed...and Fail. Washington DC: US Overseas Cooperative Development Committee: 15.
6. Holland, Douglas. 1981. *The Co-operative Movement and Taxation: A Study in Canadian Public Policy.* Toronto: York University, unpublished Masters thesis: 21. Also see Ish, Daniel. 1981. *The Law of Canadian Co-operatives.* Toronto: The Carswell Co: 11-13.
7. Senge, Peter. 1990. *The Fifth Discipline: The Art and Practice of the Learning Organization.* New York: Doubleday Currency: 17-26 outlines common learning disabilities in organizations. These include; I am my position; the enemy is out there; the illusion of taking charge; the fixation on events; the delusion of learning from experience; the myth of the management team.
8. Information for this case comes from two papers, Rachlan. 1987. "Grass-root Involvement in the Management Process of Agro Development and Land Management in the Citanduy Basin" paper presented to the International Conference on Local Resource Management for Livelihood Security and Livelihood Enhancement, Bandung, May 19-22, 1986; and Terrant, James and Hasan Poerbo. 1987. "Strengthening Community-Based Technology Management Systems," *Community Management: Asian Experience and Perspectives.* David C. Korten, ed., Kumerian Press: 181. Plus the authors involvement with the project. I have visited the Ciamis area twice and has talked extensively with field workers. Poerbo is the director of (PPLH) the Centre for Environmental Studies at ITB and has been involved in the project since it started.
9. Rachlan, 1986: 3.
10. For a detailed description of an action research project see Verhagen, Koenraad. 1984. *Co-operation for Survival.* Amsterdam: Royal Tropical Institute; or Whyte, William Foote. 1991. *Participatory Action Research.* Beverly Hills: Sage Publications.

11. Schwass, Richard. 1990. *A Study of the Implementation of the Ciamis Action Research Project in the Uplands of Citandy, West Java.* Indonesia. PPLH/ITB Bandung, Indonesia: University Consortium on the Environment; Student Publication Series No. 1.
12. Poerbo, Hasan. 1991. "Development Consultancy: Agent of Change For a Society in Rapid Transition?" Discussion Forum II, Graduate Programme on Development Studies. ITB, Bandung Indonesia.
13. Korten David C.1980. "Community Organization and Rural Development: A Learning Process Approach." *Public Administration Review*, Vol. 40: 480-510.
14. Girvan, Marnie. 1992. "Women in Development Process," Proceedings of the *ITB/York University Forum on Gender and Development*. North York: FES York UCE project: 12: 11-13.
15. Brundtland Commission. 1987. *Our Common Future*. Oxford: Oxford University Press.
16. Brooks, David. 1990. "Beyond Catch Phrases: What Does Sustainable Development Mean?" Ottawa: International Development Research Centre, *REPORTS*.
17. Several recent publications explore this paradigm in detail. See Cernea, Michael. 1985. *Putting People First.* New York: Oxford University Press. Ekin, Paul and Manfred Max-Neef. 1992. *Real Economics: Understanding Wealth Creation*. New York: Routledge. And Ekins,Paul. 1990. *A New World Order: Grassroots Movements for Global Change*. London: Routledge; Fals-Borda, Orlando. 1992. "Evolution and Convergence in Participatory Action Research," pp. 14-19 in Frideres, James S., ed., *A World of Communities: Participative Research Perspectives*. North York, Ontario: Captus University Publications; Holloway, Richard, ed., 1989. *Doing Development: Governments, NGOs and the Rural Poor.* London: Earthscan Publications.
18. Brooks, 1990.
19. Ledesma, A.L., A.Y. Ledesma, A.B. Quizon and A.M. Salinas. 1982. *The Cooperative Experience in Asian Cultures.* Manila: Centre for the Development of Human Resources in Rural Asia.
20. Walsh, Tom. 1992. "Funding proposal to Canadian Co-operative Association." Unpublished.
21. Walsh, 1992: 2.
22. Poerbo, Hasan and William Thomas. 1990. "Environmentally Sustainable Development: A Proposal for the Jasinga Area Based on Experience From the Ciamis Project and Studies of Rural Productivity and Non-Farm Employment in West Java." Paper presented to the Workshop on Sustainable Development, Bogor, December 12-13, 1990.
23. 1,600 Rupees = Cdn $1.00
24. See Poerbo and Thomas, 1990, for a more detailed description of this approach.
25. Poerbo, 1991, outlines this approach including the skills of such a person.

Chapter 7

SOCIAL INEQUALITY: GENDER, RACE AND CLASS

Conceptually, co-operation is a social process to overcome the problem of social inequality in society. Co-operatives were formed to reduce class exploitation. This is the ideal ... How has it measured up in practice?

An important aspect of sociology is the exploration of the impact of social processes on social inequality. Yet as feminist scholars have capably pointed out, sociology as a discipline has been blind to the contribution of female scholars in the early part of this century.[1] The empirical confirmation of many theories has been based on white males.[2] Patriarchy provides a powerful bias in most countries. Dobson defines patriarchy as "a culture that is slanted so that men are valued a lot and women are valued less."[3] Societies are created by humans, shaped by human activity and the impact on people varies. Modern society has been marked by inequality along the lines of gender, race and class. As outlined in the previous chapters, various groups suffering from unequal treatment have attempted to alter their dependent relationship with others by increasing their collective power through co-operating in economic and political endeavours. Many have organized co-operatives to help reduce this social inequality, others have used co-operatives to further their own power at the expense of others. But regardless of the motivation to co-operate, the fact of co-operating in a particular way within a particular framework has an impact on people who are co-operating and on others in their communities. Inequality is synonymous with patriarchy, and racism and class bias are deep-seated and passed on to generation after generation. The purpose of this chapter is to look at these developments specifically in terms of class, race and gender.

THE STATE AND CO-OPERATIVES

As described in earlier chapters many of the new leaders of the independent countries in Africa and Asia had studied in Europe or

North America and were well aware of agricultural co-operatives. Their countries faced severe rural poverty problems and a lack of rural infrastructure. The population wanted change and the only institution with enough immediate resources to address rising expectations was the State. Leaders like Nehru knew that the bureaucracy of the State and the dynamics of local democracy were in conflict, but it was perceived that there were no options. The State had to be the engine of development. As a result, co-operatives were organized and supervised by civil servants, so that they often seemed like an arm of the State, and not locally owned and controlled organizations.[4]

The research literature from India is rich in addressing this phenomenon and although it appears to be culturally specific, the more general problem of State-sponsored co-operatives is the case in almost all African and Asian countries.

Housing for the poor is an area where, in most countries, the State has pressure to act. In Canada, provincial governments have built 206,000 units since 1949. There has been strong opposition to this on both social grounds and economic grounds. Despite high expenditure, much of this housing stock could be classified as urban slum. Since the mid-1960s about 300,000 units of co-operative and non-profit housing has been built.[5] These are built for use, and not as a commodity to resell for capital gains. They still require government assistance in the form of long-term lower-cost mortgages, but have proven to provide quality housing. The primary reason is that residents are involved; they see it as mutual self-help, and a community subsequently emerges. The State must still be involved but as a partner rather than a manager.

SOCIAL CLASS AND CO-OPERATIVES

When co-operatives emerged in the last century in Europe, they were class-centred and were part of the struggle for more equality and freedom from the tyranny of the elite. The impact of the industrial revolution was to increase class awareness of the plight of the lower classes, and form the space for them to organize. Co-operatives were an organizational form for workers and farmers to increase their collective power in society and reduce the exploitive impact of the ruling class to some degree. The history of co-operatives in western countries outlined in the earlier chapters shows this class struggle.

The new co-operatives in the newly independent nations in Africa and Asia were often conceived of by their supporters as starting in a classless environment. To those struggling for independence, the perceived classes were the ruling colonizers (mostly Europeans) and the oppressed native population. With independence the educated elite of the native population moved into the positions of power vacated by the colonists and the new social dynamics generated a new class structure. In most cases, the laws and the legal institutions that supported the old colonial class system and gender bias were left in place. The dynamics of inequality were often addressed by well meaning policy and people, but the social dynamics worked the opposite way.

Agricultural co-operatives in the newly independent States were given monopoly powers and all farmers became members. It was forgotten that the colonial laws recognized only males as the farmers even in situations where the men were gone most of the year engaged in wage labour and the farming was done by the women. This meant that the older system of class, cast and privilege in the rural areas went unchallenged. The newly emerging elite (politicians and traders) who became wealthy were all members of the local co-operatives even though their personal interests were in conflict with the goals of the organizations. It is not surprising that the co-operatives quickly became dominated by a new elite and were seen as instruments of the ruling classes, not ways to empower the powerless. These trends have been well documented by the UNRISD studies in the late 1960s and early 1970s.[6]

Independence meant that change was desired and the levers for change rested in the newly independent countries. The new countries could make substantial changes to the colonial institutions and many did. But with all social changes, the impact of the changes are not known for years and the direct causes are never clearly known. Social change is by trial and error, and the tens of thousands of co-operatives and millions of members experienced these changes (as outlined in Chapter 5). The trickle-down model of development promoted by economists from the industrialized countries in the 1950s and 1960s has proved to be a dismal failure. Susan George shows how the model not only failed, but the immense debt has brought hardship to the masses in tropical countries.[7] With the failure of the State to achieve development, self-help approaches at the community level are now back as the development approach being promoted by aid agencies.

But the issue of top-down *versus* bottom-up still ignores the impact of class on co-operative development. Verhagen shows how an action research approach can be used to develop co-operatives amongst the poorest farmers, and demonstrates the importance of not letting the elite dominate.[8] The study also shows the suspicion and hostility of authorities when outsiders work with the lower classes. Such outsiders are suspected of being *saboteurs* and the wealthy class feel threatened.

The literature shows quite clearly that class-based co-operatives can play an important role in strengthening the resources of the members, and can be a vehicle to reduce the power of the upper classes.[9] However, the research is also clear that the impact of credit co-operatives in India strengthened the cast biases rather than reducing them as Nehru had dreamed, as upper-cast farmers moved into leadership roles and credit went to the higher cast members, at the expense of the poor casts that the co-operatives were intended to help.

Co-operative values of equity and equality stand in opposition to class politics in class-based societies. However, in practice, co-operatives may reduce the impact of class or they may increase class exploitation. The context is very important. Marx dismissed co-operatives by definition in the nineteenth century as being utopian because they minimized the resistance of the elite to give up power to the poor. Co-operative leaders and law-makers today that fail to address class as a basis of social inequality are still dismissed by many members as utopians.

CO-OPERATIVES AND RACE

Co-operative values and ideology are strongly egalitarian and opposed to racism. Yet agricultural co-operatives were well developed by white farmers in South Africa during the apartheid era and most Afrikaner farmers are members and supporters. The whites-only leadership was silent on the issue of apartheid and exclusion of blacks occurred in the co-operatives as well as elsewhere in white society. The agricultural community of what is now Zimbabwe is a case in point. Before independence the white farmers developed strong co-operatives to market agricultural products and obtain supplies. With independence, the black army has been settled and an active co-operative movement has emerged.[10] Older, racially segregated organizations have adapted as society changed and have moved to becoming racially integrated. These co-operatives reflected society, and were neither a force for either social change nor a means to maintain the status quo.

Israeli agriculture is practically all organized in *kibbutzim* or *moshaves* (both co-operative forms). Across the Jordan river and in the Sinai, co-operatives flourish among Jordanian, Palestinian and Egyptian farmers. The values held by the farmers in these situations are both those of the broader society and co-operative values. They are reconciled by compartmentalization. Members are supportive of their ethnic roots, their governments and the problems that they face as a nation-State. They see co-operative values of equality and mutual self-help as applying within their membership base in the organizations. They would argue that races or ethnic groups are not mixed in membership because of law or social norms — so the co-operatives are not racist in the application of their rules and by-laws, all members are treated fairly. Further, they would argue that if others want the benefits of co-operatives they are free to start their own! Criticism from outsiders strengthens the internal bonds and the criticism is dismissed as meddling in internal affairs.

The research findings are clear. Co-operatives are mechanisms for local empowerment and local change. They are not necessarily forces for the social change of national institutions at the nation-State level. In practice they may under certain conditions be a force to further entrench racism and sexism in a society.

EMPOWERMENT AND CO-OPERATIVES

A general understanding of empowerment implies the notion or the experience of psychologically "feeling powerful," the opposite of feeling dependent.[11] Power is not only understood as something groups of individuals have; rather, it is a social relationship between groups that determine access to, use of, and control over the basic material and ideological resources in society. Fundamentally, then, empowerment is a process aimed at consolidating, maintaining or changing the nature and distribution of power in a particular cultural context.[12] It takes twists and turns, includes both resistance and consent, and ebbs and flows as groups with different relations to the structures and sources of power come into conflict.[13] In terms of the management literature, the reasons for the interest in empowerment given by Conger and Kanungo, are namely that total productive forms of organizational power and effectiveness grow with superiors sharing control and power, and empowerment techniques play a crucial role in group development and maintenance.[14]

Empowerment is a concept which is coming back into the management literature.[15] Conger and Kanungo point out that there is a growing interest in empowerment and cite three reasons. First, studies on leadership and management skills suggest that the practice of empowerment is a principle component of managerial and organizational effectiveness. Second, analysis of power and control

within organizations reveals that the total productive forms of organizational power and effectiveness grow with superiors sharing
control and power. Third, "empowerment techniques play a crucial
role in group development and maintenance."[16]

Empowerment has been used in two different ways. Power may
be defined as the ability to make others do something even if they do
not wish to. Power has a perceived quality, as the perception of
power is adequate for power or control to be used. As Tannenbaum
has shown, power is not necessarily zero-sum.[17] Often when power is
delegated, co-operation occurs and the total power is increased. So
managers that share power not only make others more powerful but
also make themselves more powerful. Power also has a relational
quality. We cannot assess the power of an individual or group in
isolation. It is always in terms of others, and empowerment of a
group is specific to a given situation.

To empower implies the granting of power or the delegation of
authority (legitimate power) to others.[18] This would suggest that all
delegation is empowerment. But, because of the perceptual quality of
power, individuals or groups that do not perceive that real power has
been delegated are not empowered.[19] They may hear the words but
when they see that the behaviour is not consistent with the words
they rarely believe that empowerment has occurred. On the other
hand they may believe it, but it takes time for groups to learn the
skills and structures that must be in place for groups to exercise
power. If either is lacking, empowerment does not occur.[20]

Empowerment becomes the process by which a leader shares
power with others.[21] That feeling of power must have a basis in
reality, and usually there are mechanisms which enable members to
participate, to discuss ideas and have managers or leaders listen,
learn and respond.[22]

Empowerment is basic to the idea of co-operation, where people
work together to achieve goals that they could not achieve as individuals. The logic of organizing a co-operative is to empower
people to provide themselves with goods and services. This often
means to influence the market place.[23] Yet, after co-operatives have
been in operation for a long time, members increasingly feel relatively powerless to influence the organization.[24] A common observation
by researchers is that power has gravitated to the management (men)
and members, particularly women or lower-class members, are largely irrelevant and powerless.[25] Management practices in co-operatives
converge more and more over time with the practices of competitors,
and the logic of managing a process where staff and members are
empowered gets lost in the day-to-day activities.[26] The strength of the

co-operative idea is that power is based in the membership when it is incorporated, and it is assumed that leaders will provide mechanisms to enable the power to be realized through participation and that leaders will listen and learn from members. The idea of power-sharing through democratic processes is central to co-operatives. Lambert, states: "In my view, democracy is the cardinal principle. It distinguishes co-operative business most sharply from capitalist business, and it can be applied uniformly to any type of co-operative...."[27]

Democracy is a global term with many interpretations.[28] A level of participation is a necessary condition of any form of democracy, and participation is vital for empowerment to be realized.[29]

The key word here is power, but power can mean different things to different people depending upon the cultural and social norms of the society in which the co-operative operates. It is generally agreed that co-operatives are organizational forms in which people can be empowered. They are strong in agriculture, and 60-70% of the world's population is engaged in agriculture. Farmers around the world use marketing co-operatives to deliver goods to market. Canadian farmers began organizing co-operatives during the nineteenth century.

EMPOWERMENT: FARMERS AND CONSUMERS IN CANADA

Saskatchewan Wheat Pool (SWP)

The Saskatchewan Wheat Pool (SWP) is the largest Co-operative in Canada with annual sales volume of $1.8 billion in 1988 and earnings of $27.5 million. It is one of Canada's largest corporations. It was founded in 1924, has about 3,200 employees and about 65,000 members. It has marketed most of the wheat and oilseeds grown in the Province of Saskatchewan for the past 50 years. By any standard it is a very successful business; but, it is more. The three prairie wheat pools represent the empowerment of western Canadian farmers in the market place.

In 1919 the Canadian government enacted a compulsory wheat marketing board to market Canadian wheat. It was implemented as an emergency measure and was discontinued in 1920. This agency operated on the pooling principle to market wheat. A fixed initial price was made to all farmers at the time of delivery. The wheat was then sold on the basis of market price from day to day, and at the end of the pool period a final payment was made to the farmers. This was the first experience western Canadian farmers had with orderly marketing. The discontinuance of the Wheat Board meant the return to speculation, wide fluctuations in wheat prices, and lower returns for the farmers. All the farm organizations advocated a return to orderly marketing. When the federal government refused to act, the farm organizations launched a drive to organize a voluntary pool. From August 1923 to the spring of 1924, over two-thirds of the wheat acreage was committed to the pool by five-year contracts. Thus in less than a year, following a very emotional organizational drive, SWP grew from an idea to the largest grain-marketing co-operative in the world. The organizers asked fellow farmers to sign a five-year contract to deliver all their wheat to an organization that had no assets, no past record but a promise to treat farmers fairly and to be controlled by farmers. The idea was seen as empowering farmers. Its control structure provided the guarantee.

From the time SWP was organized, the province was divided into sixteen districts and 160 sub-districts with a delegate from each sub-district; the delegates elected sixteen directors. Over the years as the farm population decreased, the number of subdistricts has varied from a high of 168 to a low of 138; there are now 144 subdistricts. From 1924 until 1966 every delegate was elected annually. Six farmers can nominate a delegate and a mail ballot is held. Each shipping point (grain elevator), plus a number of locations where elevators are no longer situated, has a committee of farmers.

But these formal mechanisms are not what makes democracy work. The processes that are built into the operations are the key to democracy and empowerment. In SWP, each delegate meets with the delivery-point committees several times a year and the directors meet with the delegates in their district several times a year. There are lots of meetings and lots of ongoing discussions. This activity is culminated with a delegates annual meeting each November that lasts about two weeks.

The delegates do not spend all this time and effort just on SWP business. They also concentrate on agricultural policy in general, and since the 1920s SWP has been a major voice for Saskatchewan agriculture.

In order to assist the flow of information from farmers to the Board and senior management, the organization has an Member Relations Division which works with the local directors and delegates. This division reports to the Executive Director, Policy and Member Services (who reports directly to the Board of Directors) rather than to the Chief Executive Officer who is responsible for operations.

Most shipping points (about 475 and approximately eighty inland committees where no elevators are located) have a committee elected at an annual meeting of members in the area. There are five to ten members on each committee. They meet about four times a year and discuss the business of SWP plus agricultural policy in general. If they want something changed they draft a resolution discuss it and vote. If it is approved, they send it to head office for action. About 400 to 500 resolutions are sent in each year. A senior staff member reads all them and if s/he deals with operations, sends them to the right manager for action. If they are about policy matters they go to a resolutions committee made up of delegates. They combine similar ones and prepare them for debate at the delegates meeting.

SWP has 6,000 to 7,000 farmers that hold elected positions on an annual bases. About one-half of the farmers in Saskatchewan have been Committee Members at on time or another. A study in the early 1970s found that the democratic process provides a forum for a wide cross-section of farmers' views, and delegates are very sensitive to the changing views of farmers. If they are not in touch, they can be defeated in the spring election. Over the years when SWP policies were out of step with farm opinion, there was an increase in the number of delegates seeking election and SWP policies subsequently changed.[30] Since the 1920s, SWP leadership has been the voice of farmers.

But times have changed. Agriculture is being severely squeezed in Canada as the Americans and EEC are aggressively subsidizing farm exports. The pressure for value added to farm products has meant the involvement of the prairie pools in strategic alliances to ensure the usage of prairie raw materials and enable farmers to share in the value added of the produce sold to consumers or to reduce the cost of farm inputs. To gain a higher return they have organized. These organizations are briefly described in Figure 7.1.

Calgary Consumer Co-operative

The Calgary Consumers Co-operative is the largest consumer co-operative in North America with membership of over 250,000 and annual sales in excess of $440 million in 1988.[31]

It was founded in 1956 and has had a steady growth in terms of members and sales every year. It markets out of thirteen shopping centres, plus a Home-Agri unit that sells hardware and lumber in conjunction with a pre-fabrication plant. In the early 1980s, a severe depression hit the Alberta economy with the decline in the price of petroleum products. The economic crisis hit most organizations in Canada and has been blamed for the collapse of many businesses including a number of consumer co-operatives. Interestingly, the Calgary co-operative continued to grow during the hard times as well as during the boom years of the 1970s. In 1985 despite a stagnant market, sales increased 4.9% and

Figure 7.1

STRATEGIC ALLIANCES INVOLVING THE WHEAT POOLS

A) TO INCREASE RETURNS FOR FARMERS BY BETTER EFFICIENCY

1   X Can Grain — Owned by MPE, SWP and AWP
    Purpose: Market Canadian grains internationally.
2   IPCO (Inter-provincial Co-operatives Limited)
    Owned by UCO, FCL, CA, La Fédérée, MPE, SWP and AWP
3   CanAmera Foods — Owned by MPE, SWP, AWP, and CENTRAL SOYA
    Purpose: Processing and marketing vegetable oils
4   Philom Bios — Owned by, SWP, Dow Elanco, and Philom Bios
    Purpose: R&D in Biotech area
5   Prince Rupert Grain — Owned by MPE, SWP and AWP
    Purpose: Transferring grain to ships
6   Vancouver Terminals — Owned by MPE, SWP and AWP
    Purpose: Transferring grain to ships

B) VALUE ADDED TO RAW MATERIALS FOR GREATER RETURNS TO FARMERS

7   Poundmaker Feedlot — Owned by SWP, Mohawk Oil and local owners
    Purpose: Produce Ethanol (10m liters); use the mash by-product to
    feed (18,000) head of cattle per year.
8   Robins Donuts — Owned by, SWP and Robin
    Purpose: Supplies to franchise Donut-shop owners.

savings to $14.1 million. This was an increase of $1.3 million over 1984. The patronage refund for 1985 was 3.8% on retail purchases and 1.7% on travel purchases. The strong financial performance has continued. Calgary Co-op has been economically successful through good times and bad. Even when retail sales and the population in Calgary has declined the co-op has continues to grow.

Calgary Co-op, like the other urban retail co-operatives in the west, purchases supplies from Federated Co-operatives Ltd., and is an active supporter. But what does Calgary Co-op have that most of the other urban co-ops in western Canada lack. The following short overview is an attempt to identify some of the elements that may be contributing to the success of this co-operative.

In the 1950s and early 1960s, corner stores were replaced by small super markets and Safeways dominated the food market. With a near monopoly situation and many small and aging supermarkets the food margins were higher in Calgary than in other western Canadian cities. This helped in the first few years, but as the Co-op grew, the market place became more competitive and margins dropped as they did in most Canadian cities. The Calgary management has always been cost-conscious and has kept costs under control as the economic environment has shifted.

As plans for expansion developed, the Calgary Co-op went to it's membership for advice and also with financial instruments to finance the expansion. They sold debentures, etc., to raise the long-term capital. This was seen as win/win, as it meant the Co-op got long-term capital at a good rate and members got a good interest rate. It meant more work for management, but in the long term it seemed to help build commitment and a feeling of ownership amongst the members.

The leadership has had a vision of Calgary Co-operative being the "best" food supplier in the area. They are constantly conscious that they are responsible for creating a "favourable shopping experience." They firmly believe that the image of being responsive to members is very important, and they work at creating a favourable image in all the stores. They have a regular monthly newsletter. One of the most widely read section is "You asked for it." Management and directors respond to questions sent in by letter or via the member-suggestion box located in each store.

> Every request for information or complaint about products is responded to first by letter or phone call and a sample of these comments, requests etc. is published in the newsletter. This immediate response to a member concern has been well received...we have demanded that we have a quality product available with competitive prices, and that we offer service second to none in this city.

This strong commitment by the leadership permeates the organization and is evident to shoppers. It isn't just a series of words — rather it is a guideline for action that is believed and practised.

Involvement processes

Calgary has a conventional control structure with one membership meeting per year. It attracts several hundred members but with a total membership of about 296,000, this is a small percentage. It does however have some interesting ways of involving those who want to be active.

- It has a regular monthly newsletter distributed to all the members. Input of news, etc., comes from volunteers.
- It advertises for volunteers to make up its many committees of volunteers. One important committee in the planning committee,

in which an interesting dynamic has occurred. As the co-op grew, the status and profile of the Board of Directors increased. There was lots of competition to be a director, but the trouble was to get known. One way to get known was to volunteer, particularly for the planning committee and do some important work. As a result, experts in the membership scanned the retail environment for changes, researched the issues and given presentations at management and members meetings. Topics like computerization, laser scanners at the checkout, etc., were studied, and reports given to management long before the changes were imminent. As a result the co-operative has been an innovator rather than a follower.

- The innovations have been done with the members support. For example when the competitors dropped check out "boys" to let shoppers pack and carry their own groceries the Calgary Co-op Food stores improved this service. This gave more part-time work to students and was a service the members appreciated. Part of the cost was offset by having the shopping carts managed and not spread all over the neighbourhoods and damaged as had happened at the competitors. Gas sales are important and there is a gas bar at all the shopping centres. The Co-op found that by giving full service they could pump more gas per pump, thus keeping the capital investment lower and providing more jobs. In a climate like Calgary's this is a competitive advantage over self-service stations. The price is the same and you don't have to get out of the car.
- Other committees are also busy. Some test products and advise the purchasing department. Others organize member activities.

In 1985, the co-operative offered thirty-two free consumer courses to members on a wide range of subjects. The co-op has been criticized over the years for not being more socially aware, engaging in boycotts or taking stands on social issues. The leadership has resisted this and has seen its mission as providing goods and services to meet the members' needs.

> The mission of Calgary Co-operative Association is to provide each member with the opportunity to participate in the ownership and direction of an organization of their own and to improve the economic position of members through co-ordinated procurement, manufacture and distribution of goods and services.

It seems to be doing it very well.

Credit Unions

The bond of association is the way a credit union defines it environment and fits into each organization's mission statement. It specifies who to focus on to meet financial needs. In the process, it defines who are included and who are excluded. Their community may be a workplace definition, an ethnic group or a geographic area. Traditionally, the common way to respond to members' needs has been on an individual basis. However, people as social animals also have community needs as well as personal needs. A responsive credit union will develop financial instruments and provide leadership for these needs. That is the social implication of the organization.

In times of uncertainty and community stress, credit unions have challenges and opportunities to help members improve their quality of life. This need is as great in the 1990s as it was in the 1930s and 1940s. But they must do some things differently to fit the realities of the changed environment.

Confédération des Caisses Populaires et d'Économie Desjardins du Québec

In 1900, Desjardins started the first *Caisse Populaire* in his home town of Levis, Québec. The *Caisses Populaires* were started to provide savings and loan services to the working class. They were parish-based, and often supported by the local clergy. Emphasis was placed on organizing local *Caisses Populaires* which were managed by volunteers. As they grew, seven regional federations were organized and they worked closely with the locals. The regional federations are members of the Québec Confederation. As the locals grew in number and size, many differences emerged and over the years, six centrals were organized by splitting away, or started by newly organized locals. These were often critical of each other and provided many lines of communications and options to members and potential members. If a system was not responsive there were other *caisses populaires* only too happy to provide services. Although outsiders have criticized the democratic process as being paternalistic there has been an active debate and dialogue for over eighty years. The base for the *Caisse Populaire* was the church parish. People traditionally knew one or more directors and every *Caisse* sent delegates to the regional meetings, plus every region sent delegates to the provincial organization.

In the mid-1980s they started a process to define what they stood for by developing a statement of their values. This was not done in the traditional manner of forming a committee, hiring a consultant then sending the result to a meeting for approval. They used a process to involve people. The local *caisses,* were involved in brainstorming sessions and organized grassroot discussion sessions. The ideas were sent to the Confederations offices and circulated several times. It culminated in a meeting which drew over 2,300 representatives to discuss and finalize the statement.

The 1,400 *Caisses Populaires* are relatively small in size but can provide economy of scale because they are closely integrated to the central. Because of the small size of the organizations they can provide more services by being operationally integrated yet autonomous in policy-making. There are 18,700 elected positions. The structure is not unusual and many credit union systems in North America are similar. What is unique is that the involvement processes work on a regular basis.

Debate has been lively in this system in a variety of forums. *Caisses Populaires* are the most important financial institutions for Québecers, and there has been lots of competition for the over 18,000 elected positions elected by the 149,000 (1991) members who attend annual meetings.

Credit Union Central of Saskatchewan (CUCS)

Saskatchewan, like Québec, was a "have-not" province until very recently. The local credit unions were first organized in 1937 and numbers increased until the mid-1950s. During this time the chartered banks were consolidating and closing branches. Agriculture was depressed and farm loans were hard to obtain. Western alienation against the financial centres in eastern Canada was a major incentive for people to support credit unions.[32]

Once again, by any standard the Saskatchewan Credit Union system is financially successful. The over 200 local credit unions have over $5 billion in assets which, as in Québec, represents about 40% of the personal savings in the province. It has a strong financial base and has helped several other provinces over the past twenty years when they were faced with financial problems.

Like most other credit union systems, it was started with the structure that worked and is working well in Québec. The problem was the structure didn't fit the conditions in Saskatchewan. Distances were greater and size of the member credit unions varied considerably. Things happened too fast for one annual meeting a year to keep members informed. Delegates needed to be more active and have more responsibility. This was achieved by reducing the number of delegates from one per member credit union to having the number of delegates reflect the membership size in the credit unions. Delegates now represent districts and in some cases a delegate will represent several small credit unions.

Since 1970, the system has had a very active delegate structure that combines planning with the activities of the delegates. The delegates hold an annual meeting which controls the business of the organization (i.e., reviewing operations, financial statements, and setting policy). Every two years a Convention is held where all delegates and any other interested people can attend. The agenda focuses on critical issues facing Saskatchewan in general and credit unions in particular. It is forward-looking, with presentations by experts, and workshop sessions so participants can discuss the ideas. This generates ideas that are then discussed in the series of regional and local meetings. In this process policy gets discussed and debated, and when decisions are needed the delegates and directors of local credit unions are well informed.

The delegates are elected by the local credit unions and they in turn elect a director from each of the twelve districts. Delegates meet six times a year in different forums, enabling them to become well informed and capable of providing direction to the system.

Both the Québec and Saskatchewan systems have a long tradition of involving local delegates in the long-term planning process. Debate is often heated and lively but out of the series of meetings plans evolve which reflect the changing needs and aspirations of the members.

These successful co-operatives have developed some common features.

- They have opportunities for delegates to participate in real meaningful ways, with real things to do.
- They help new delegates learn and develop the skills to carry out their functions.
- Management has an orientation to listen and learn from the delegates.
- They have periodic assessment that regenerates the processes.

It is interesting to observe that the credit unions have the greatest market share in areas that are more removed from our larger cities — the prairies, British Columbia and rural Québec, the Maritimes and Ontario. They are seen as local organizations responding to the ever-changing needs of people in the community rather than to "Bay Street." In 1991, the combined assets of the 2,600 credit unions and *caisses populaires* in Canada were very close to the assets of the Toronto Dominion Bank, Canada's fifth largest chartered bank ($70 billion). The TD Bank has one Board of Directors and one senior management group making policy: perhaps 200 to 500 people. In contrast, credit-union policy is made by an estimated 30,000 volunteers with another 10,000 managers close to the process. This is a fundamental difference in enabling credit-union policy for savings and loans to be shaped to the unique needs of diverse groups of Canadians.

The Diversity of Credit Unions

Both the strength and the weakness of credit unions in Canada springs from their diversity. Credit unions' inherent advantage in the market place rests with their fundamental organizational features: first, the duality of being a social organization as well as an economic organization; second, the bond of association that identifies the group of people to be focused on and served. If credit unions develop these features to fit with the needs of the 1990s and the twenty-first century, they can grow and prosper and make a major contribution to the quality of life for ordinary people across Canada. Many may not and will disappear! Let's explore the features that respond to members needs.

1) Managing the Duality

As self-help democratic organizations, credit unions are social organizations. This implies the meetings, reporting, elections and checking with members to see what should be done. Unfortunately, this side of credit unions has often stagnated. Many managers see working with volunteers as a hassle. Boards are seen as a group to manipulate, rather than a group with whom to work. Other managers look at credit unions and see that the manager has a competitive advantage. He/she has a regular focus group to find out what members may be thinking. They have a mechanism to involve the community and build loyalty. Usually this opportunity is missed by holding the most boring meetings that can be devised and chasing people away.

When credit unions manage the people side of the organization as well as the economic, they have a competitive advantage that few can challenge. The difficulty is developing the processes to manage the social side. It is different from managing the economic side. We do a better job of training accountants and supervisors than we do facilitators, community development people and people with group problem-solving skills.

Credit unions often do the economic side well, but the skills in listening and involving members and doing social audits are not as well developed. But the credit unions and co-operatives that manage this social side and work on the democratic process also have more successful business results.

2) Managing the "Bond"

Credit Unions need to define their own bonds of association and develop business plans based on the needs of the people in the bond. As self-help organizations, credit unions are designed to provide an organizational framework for a particular community of people to help-themselves. Over the years many have tended to fall into the pattern that self-help is only possible through savings and loans to individuals. This is important, but increasingly, communities need to work together to improve their quality of life. For the past two decades many communities have looked to big business and big government for help. Increasingly we are learning that little has changed. If we want life to improve we must act. Communities need some leadership and this leadership responsibility rest with credit union managers, employees and elected volunteers. You are the stewards of your bond of association. What leadership are you providing to identify and respond to the needs of your community?

Some credit unions are providing this leadership. Here are some examples:

a) Prince Albert, Saskatchewan

The Bank of Montreal announced that it was going to close its branch in Duck Lake, Saskatchewan, in 1983. Without full services the writing was on the wall that this community of 700 would slowly decline as people would start shopping where they had to go for banking services. The community investigated how these services could be provided. The Prince Albert Community Credit Union did a feasibility study and agreed to open a branch if the members of the community were prepared to help themselves and invest a minimum of $2,000,000. The branch opened in August 1984 with $2.4 M in assets. The credit union emphasized service, and by 1989 the credit union employed five people, and had assets of $6.5 M and 1,300 members. The impact on the community has been significant. Several new businesses have opened, a nursing home has been built and this historical community, a focal point of the Riel rebellion, is taking pride in its history and has a mural programme underway.[33]

The people living in the community have decided they do not want their town to decline and decay, and with the help of the P.A. Credit Union its leaders have changed the dynamics of decline. This is an example of opening a branch where it was wanted and involving the people in a meaningful way. Much more can be done.

Credit unions can play a significant role in community regeneration. The CUCS has launched a research project to assist local credit unions. They are developing an information programme to provide credit union and community leaders in the province with the following information:

1) Information about the community and rural municipality where a credit union or branch is located.

2) A provincial outline showing growing, declining and stable communities over the 1961-1989 period.

3) An analysis of trends in how communities have changed. This will include rates of change, number and location, distance between centres, population and proximity to large centres.

These facts are a start. What is done with this information is up to the communities. Credit unions are a natural focal point for the leadership to allow communities to discuss and shape their own destinies in innovative ways that fit the community. Here are a few more examples.

b) Niverville, Manitoba

Housing for elderly members in many small communities is a problem. But, is it a problem for credit unions? Should credit unions provide leadership?

The Niverville credit union acquired a plot of land in the downtown area of the village. The Board and management looked for ideas for what to do with the land and recognized the clear need for seniors' housing. They surveyed their members and got a strong positive response. "The credit union acted as the general contractor for the $500,000 project, tendering virtually all the work to members of the credit union."[34]

The fourteen-unit, one-storey apartment block is designed for seniors, with common areas to meet, and space for organized crafts and games. It is home for sixteen elders who can no longer maintain their homes.

The project is owned by the credit union. Is not subsidized, it provided work for some members who built it, and clean comfortable accommodations for others members to live in. The homes vacated by the seniors adds to the affordable housing stock for younger people and are an incentive to stay in the community. It provides a good example of leadership helping to serve member needs.

c) Cornwall, Ontario

Providing jobs and helping single parents to get off welfare is a problem for many communities and for many people within the bonds of association. But, is it a problem for credit unions? Should credit unions provide leadership?

The Cornwall Credit Union Chapter, four Cornwall credit unions and the Ontario Credit Union Charitable Foundation have developed a joint venture to provide loans to women (single parents) to start their own businesses. The purpose is to enable single parents to get off welfare, improve their self-image and feel they are more productive members of society. The loans finance the equipment costs of setting up a home-based small business to allow the recipients to become self-supporting.

In 1988, a division of the Ontario Social Development Council called Self Employment Development Initiatives started a support programme for women in Cornwall. The council, among other things, provides an eighteen-week seminar where women on welfare can learn business skills and develop plans to start small home-based businesses. After the seminar, the government-subsidized programme ends and the women are on their own.

In February of 1989, the Self Employment Development Initiatives group surveyed graduates of the programme and found several projects couldn't get started because of lack of credit to purchase basic materials. They raised the problem with the Ontario Credit Union Charitable Foundation and the credit unions. A partnership was formed to provide the loans, but minimize the financial risk for the credit unions.

The four Cornwall credit unions made a $6,000 contribution to the Ontario Credit Union Charitable Foundation. The Foundation matched the funds and provided a loan guarantee to Landmark Savings and Loans. In April 1989, $11,600 was lent to five women to start their own businesses.[35] By December 1989 all the payments were on schedule. By June 30, 1990, only $3,000 remains to be paid and several are ahead of schedule. The first stage was a success, so new loans are being made to new graduates and the programme is being expanded. The $12,000 represents a revolving fund to help single parents on social welfare break the poverty cycle and regain their dignity. Each had a poor credit rating and could not borrow money from any other sources.

How does the programme work? Social workers in the area refer people on social assistance to the Social Development Councils' project. The council staff organize the training and introduce potential graduates to the credit unions. The people go through the standard loan application process to the credit unions. The loans are assessed by a loan-review committee of the four participating credit unions and the successful loans are forwarded for a commercial loan review by Landmark Savings and Loans which issues the loan guarantee.

The applicants do all their transactions with the local credit union as they pull themselves up by the bootstraps. They get to know the local credit union people and get needed financial advice like any other member. They also meet regularly with the other graduates. This provides a social connection and a forum to discuss their triumphs and problems. In short, they develop a self-help co-operative support group with other graduates. The credit unions provide the credit and financial advice and the new members learn business skills.

The four credit unions through their local chapter are making a significant economic and social contribution in Cornwall and the Ontario Credit Union Charitable Foundation plays its role as a partner in the background. The loan repayments go into the revolving fund to be lent to other social assistance recipients, the borrowers gain self-confidence, self-respect and a better standard of living, and the taxpayer gets a smaller social-assistance bill. The credit unions are helping develop people and put their community commitment into practice by helping individuals and the community as a whole. The people involved in the Ontario Credit Union Charitable Foundation feel good that they can provide a mechanism for credit unions to address a local social problem in a constructive manner.

d) Bread and Roses Credit Union (Toronto)

Some credit unions were established specifically to serve the collective needs of groups in their community. Bread and Roses was founded in the 1960s in Toronto by a group of activist interested in helping groups help themselves. They have "bread" accounts that pay a competitive interest rate and "roses" accounts that are not interest bearing. Loans are made on a business-like basis, but with reduced interest rates to self-help groups creating jobs. Many of the "roses" accounts are placed by local church congregations. Each year the congregations get a report on how the interest that they are forgoing is assisting groups in their community. They are providing assistance not through charity but by helping people be more productive and help themselves.

The above examples are not cases of credit unions giving their members' money away. The credit unions in Prince Albert, Niverville or Cornwall did *not* give their members money away. Rather they are sound business decisions. Not conventional business decisions — but sound. Bread and Roses credit unions with their roses accounts make the difference between businesses going under in times of high interest rates or staying afloat. Parents often do this for their children — why can't it be broadened for the welfare of the community. In this case the credit union is not giving money away, but those with a social concerns are providing assistance without creating dependent relationship.

The above examples are breaking with conventional lending practices — but, that is what made credit unions unique. Lending money on "character rather than collateral" is sound — but when it was started in the early part of this century it was a break with the tradition. The notion that "the debt should die with the debtor" is also sound, but a major innovation of the time. Many feel it's time credit unions got back to their communities or "membership bond" and did things that respond to collective as well as individual needs. Credit unions should be the focus for community self-help. They are not charities, or do-gooders, but community-oriented businesses.

Creatively Empowering Members in the Financial Market Place
Credit Unions have made numerous innovations to empower communities. Credit unions started with a major innovation in consumer lending that was a hallmark of early credit unions that made sense to farmers, self-employed and wage earners. It was captured in the slogan "The debt should die with debtor." Credit unions were the first to automatically insure loans so the loan was repaid by the insurance carrier in the event the borrower died. This was also an era when many people had no life insurance and families suffered severe financial stress if the main income-earner died. Share accounts were automatically insured for the amount of the deposit, to a maximum of $2,000. In the first half of this century many people who had no savings and could not afford life insurance would borrow money from the credit union, deposit it in shares and pay the loan with payroll deductions. This taught thrift, regular savings as well as providing low-cost insurance.

The focus on members' needs gives credit unions a competitive edge. Here are some examples:
1) A strong desire by members of *Caisses Populaires* in Québec was to be able to carry out financial transactions when they were in other communities. In the 1960s, the Caisse Populaire Desjardins Federation in Québec developed the specifications for an integrated computer banking system and asked computer companies to bid. In the early 1970s the Québec *Caisses* were the first financial institutions in Canada to computerize and to offer inter-branch banking. Banks followed.

2) In the 1970s the first Automatic Teller Machine was introduced by Sherwood credit union in Regina with the assistance of CUCS and the Co-operators Data (now CDSL). Banks followed.

3) Weekly mortgage payments emerged from a *Caisse Populaire* in Oka, Québec. Many of its members were paid on a weekly or bi-weekly basis. With high interest rates in the early 1980s it made sense to innovate to reduce interest payments to help members cope and get through the period of high rates without losing their homes. The change was popular, many credit unions and other financial institutions followed.

4) Cross-border shopping has received a lot of media attention, but small towns have long suffered from people going to the big town to shop as well as to the U.S.A. Altona Credit Union, six kilometres from the Manitoba-North Dakota border came up with the idea of no-interest Christmas loans ($1,000 maximum, repaid in six months) when the money was spent with local merchants. In 1990, loans to 259 members meant $203,611 stayed in the community. The programme has been adopted by credit unions across Canada and banks have come up with similar programmes in order to compete.

5) The aging population has created the need for reverse mortgages. Products developed by banks and trust companies don't work in the interest of the mortgager. When a member of Cataract Savings & Credit Union was going to lose her house to a trust company for her grandson's default on a business loan, the credit union developed a people-oriented reverse mortgage. The idea was picked up by the Central and "Homefund" is now offered under licence by other credit unions. Credit unions now have the best reverse mortgage product on the market.

6) The "Ethical Growth Fund" was developed by VanCity to direct equity capital to firms that lived by a set of ethical standards. This was the first ethical growth fund in Canada. The sceptics who said "you can't mix ethics with business" have been proven wrong as this fund was the fourth-best performing fund during the 1980s. It left most "unethical funds" far behind.

7) Interest-free or reduced interest loans have been used by many credit unions to help particular groups. For example:

• Bread and Roses Credit Union in Toronto have bread accounts (those that pay interest to depositors) and roses accounts (those that pay no interest). The roses accounts enable groups to get low-interest loans to create jobs for themselves, or socially desirable projects that are viable if debt capital is not to expensive.

- Mennonite Credit Union in Kitchener-Waterloo has created a fellowship fund that puts mutual aid into practice. Members are encouraged to deposit in low yield or no yield accounts, and this is loaned by the credit committee to members in need.
- Sudbury Regional Credit Union made an interest-free loan of $400,000 to the local hospital to enable the cancer unit to continue cancer treatment for 11 people and expand to take on 12 more. It's a long way to Toronto for treatments. This loan touched the medical community with a $1 million medical foundation fund being transferred to the credit union along with a number of new members.

The ideal of co-operation is what defines the ideals of co-operatives. People aspire to apply co-operation in their communities and their personal lives. Co-operatives are merely organizational structures or forms for co-operation to emerge and persist. If the underlying logic of co-operatives is to enable people to co-operate, then how are they different from other organizations? This is not an empirical question where we go and observe. Rather it is a question about how co-operatives are conceived of. The examples above are an attempt to show how the mental set of co-operation is applied in the real world.

GENDER: WOMEN AND CO-OPERATIVES

Most societies are patriarchal: male-dominated with women having subordinate roles. Interestingly, this was not the case in many ethnic groups in pre-colonial Africa, but with colonialism came patriarchal social institutions and subservience. As Susan Dean points out, "The struggle of women to achieve equality with men in social, political and economic spheres is now nearly worldwide. While the emphasis might differ…the demand is the same: Women want their fair share."[36]

Women are confronted with four major obstacles that prevent more participation in co-operatives.[37] These include:

1) Traditional constraints. This is perhaps the most formidable obstacle as traditional roles, customs and religious practices are deeply rooted in social attitudes, with the underlying assumption that many men and women hold that women are unsuited for and incapable of most things outside the home and family. While this has been demonstrated as false it is still a widely held view that is a major roadblock to the increased participation of women.

2) Legal constraints. The laws that discriminate against women with regard to wages, property and personal rights take generations to amend and still exist in most countries.

3) Lack of education and training. In most developing counties the literacy rate of women is lower than men. Even in the industrialized countries where boys and girls receive similar years of training the number of females in business and related courses is usually lower.

4) Lack of time. Women, whether highly educated or less educated, are caught in the "Double Ghetto."[38] This means that the average work day for many women is twelve to sixteen hours. That leaves very little time or energy to go to meetings and be involved in organizations, even if women think their involvement would be valuable. Acknowledging these problems and the fact that co-operatives reflect the broader society in which they are located, we would expect to find gender inequalities. There are two thrusts that seem to reverse this gender inequality: an awareness of women's issues and a gradual change in the role of women within particular co-operatives; and women using the co-operative form to empower themselves within society.

Research in Africa has provided the following conclusions:

- Women are able to participate more freely where there is no strict traditionalism banning them from full membership in co-operative societies. From our findings, agricultural co-operatives are the largest, and perhaps most important. Participation of women in these co-operatives is limited because agriculture is tied to the land which is traditionally owned by the men.[39] So the women in Africa do most of the productive activities on the land, but have no control over the productive activities, except the food for home consumption. Insofar as the cash crop is concerned, control is in the hands of men, including the money accrued from it. Membership is tied to ownership of the land.[40] It therefore happens that the participation of women is in the names of their husbands. They may attend meetings as long as they are not vocal, and since they are not members, they may not vote.

- In Swaziland, we had discussions with committee members of Mahlangatsha Multipurpose Co-operative Society. In this rural society, tradition more than anything else limits against full participation of women. Out of 370 members only fifteen are women. These women members are all widows. The members of the society see no reason why women should be members when their husbands are. This is tantamount to separation. Women can participate in meetings. They can vote but they cannot be elected.

- It is mostly the women who participate in the co-operative activities. Purchasing of farm inputs is 80% by women. Consumer good purchasing is 100% done by women. The majority of attendants at general meetings are women. But these women remain passive. When voting, they vote for men. In Swaziland a woman does not stand before men. Even in the absence of a husband the women will delay decision-making in all important matters, including accepting new ideas from an Agriculture Extension Officer until she has consulted her husband.

- In rare cases, women can receive the money on behalf of their husbands, but they must have written consent. This society represents features typical of rural co-operatives in Africa. Men still dominate the rural life, even when they are out in towns for wage employment for periods of over 10 years. The co-operative framework has, however, facilitated economic activity in the village in which women are active. This is an aspect of development. Full participation of members is hindered by a tie between the co-operative demand of membership and the traditional pattern of ownership. Legally, there is nothing to prevent women from becoming members. But they do not own land or property on the land.

- One of the greatest motivators is achievement. People become encouraged to perform more when they appreciate their past performance by seeing the things they have achieved. Since women do not have full control of produce in their own co-operative, the sense of achievement is greatly impaired.

- If, on the other hand, women were allowed fuller participation, production in rural areas would increase. The women would make decisions relating to production at farm level instead of having to wait to consult their husbands at month-ends when they come home from their work places. The women would control the primary marketing society which handles their produce, and this would probably result in less of the corruption presently rampant in agricultural marketing societies.

- How to have women participate fully in agricultural societies has been a subject of discussion in many seminars and conferences organized by the International Co-Operative Alliance and other organizations. In some countries it is thought that it may be necessary to amend the Co-operative Society Act to expressly state that both husband and wife can be members of an agricultural marketing society. In other countries, opinion has it that the solution to this problem will be a change of attitude of men so that they may consider it proper for part of the farm produce to be marketed in the name of their wives, thus making them full members of the society.

Whatever has been done, the problem remains. Only a few women either as widows or whose husbands are more enlightened, have joined marketing societies. Presently, working women in Botswana are becoming members of cattle-marketing societies, since they can purchase cattle.

- We believe that the problem cannot be solved by looking only at co-operative legislation. The whole legislation regarding the pattern of ownership and inheritance of property in Africa must be reviewed if women are to participate fully in economic activities. In addition to amending legislation or enacting new laws, education directed towards changing of attitudes of men and women insofar as ownership of property and participation in decision-making must be propagated throughout the community.

- We would recommend that while we wait for the wall of traditional attitudes to be broken, more of co-operatives whose membership is not tied to tradition be started, both in the rural and urban areas. For promotional purposes, then, anyone aiming at greater participation of women in co-operatives would be advised to begin with savings and co-operative societies for working women, industrial and handicraft societies for all types of women and consumer co-operative societies for all types of women. What has been said about training and real benefits would very much need to be taken into consideration.

- In any organization one finds some people who work for the organization much more than others. These are the ones who sacrifice to keep the society going. Some women work until very late in the evening, visiting their society every day and acting in the forefront whenever there is any problem. Such individuals are very important in a society. There are others who cannot do so, either because they are selfish or because their family structures do not allow them to participate fully in activities outside their homes. A married woman who is a member of a co-operative society may have first to satisfy home needs before going out to a co-operative society. Many married women have to first consult their husbands before accepting any idea given to them. It is not surprising thus that many women who are in the leadership position of co-operatives are either widows or single.[41]

That's Africa. How well are we doing in Canada? A study by Holland of directors in Canadian co-operatives showed that nationally 77% of the directors were males and 23% females. However in the largest sectors of credit unions, retail and agricultural co-operatives males were 80%. In housing co-operatives there was a 50-50 split but in daycare co-operatives 90% of the directors are women. When size was controlled co-operatives with less than 100 members had a 50-50 split while those with over 100 members directors males dominated with 80%.[42]

Barclay studied nineteen of the largest co-operatives that are members of the Canadian Co-operative Association. A total of 220 men and twenty-nine women (12%) were in powerful leadership roles. Interestingly these women directors are in credit unions, retail co-operatives, financial and health co-operatives. The powerful grain-marketing co-operatives in western Canada had no female directors in 1991. When we look at the degrees of power held by these elected leaders we find none of the board chairs/presidents were women and only 8% of the vice-presidents/chairs and 7% of the executive committee were women. The senior management showed a similar pattern. Of the 593 management positions, 93 were held by women. Of those senior managers that report to the Board only 4% are women, 20% of the senior managers that report to the chief executive officer are women, but the next level down in middle management only 15% are women.[43]

In Canada, the housing co-operatives movement has seen dramatic growth during the 1970s and 1980s. It is a young, vigorous movement with high degrees of participation and 60% of the members are women. Brenda Doyle Farge's study showed that women were well represented on committees (60%) and Boards of Directors (52%). A different pattern emerged in more powerful positions. Only 32% of the presidents were women, but in the traditions role of Board secretary 70% were women.[44]

Managers/branch managers in credit unions in Ontario are 45% women and 55% men. Compared to other financial institutions in Canada this is impressive. However, these women are more apt to be managers in smaller credit unions. Of the 10 largest credit unions 27.5% are women.[45] The president of the Credit Union Managers Association is a women and the meetings of both managers and volunteers as usually well represented by women. The Board of the professional association (Executive Society, Managers Association and Lenders Association) is 85% men.[46]

Annual meetings and male-based methods of participation also pose a problem. They were designed by men to facilitate discussion between people. The problem is that the people were men and most of the processes have not been looked at critically to see if they are gender neutral or biased towards men. Recent research by Korabik, Ayman and Helgesen present a strong argument that there is a gender difference. The process of change needs to occur with a critical look at how the assumptions of patriarchy disadvantage women. An equal-opportunity policy is not enough.[47]

The member credit unions of the Credit Union Central of Ontario (CUCO) send one delegate, one alternate, plus visitors to the three-day meeting. This meeting of about 1,000 people presents an imposing situation. At the annual meetings from 1986 to 1992, only one or two women of the 30-40% women delegates went to a microphone to speak on a substantive issue. The debate on the floor is between men. The Board of Directors of CUCO consists of eighteen with six being elected each year from the floor of the annual meeting. Candidates must become known to the delegates from across the province and they must address the gathering with a campaign speech. In 1990, three of the eighteen elected directors were women and this is the largest number ever.

Doyle Farge also observed a similar phenomena at the 600-person national annual meeting of the housing co-operatives. She observed that of the twenty-four reports, seventeen were given by men, only seven by women and when it came to speaking at the floor microphones, twice as many men than women were involved. At large meetings, floor debates on resolutions and aggressive campaigning seems to favour men rather than women.

In both situations the sentiment is to increase participation of women. The main obstacles appear to be structural. The democratic structures and processes that were designed decades ago by men need to be examined to enable more equitable participation.

The issues of inequality are important in any society. For a researcher, establishing that social inequality exists is a first step, but documenting the social dynamics at work in society that create forces for equality is more important. Retail co-operatives in western Canada were important to women, but males dominated the leadership positions. The Co-operative Women's Guild was organized to address a number of the problems. The guild in the province of Saskatchewan successfully lobbied to have the legal roadblocks removed and carried out an extensive educational programme to assist women to take hold leadership positions. They also provided lunch and coffee at meetings and organized social activities. By the 1960s it became painfully clear to the provincial leadership that this strategy to empower women had failed. They had become stereotyped by the men as food providers and their role was still seen as being in the kitchen.[48]

One of the ways to increase equality is for women to organize their own co-operatives. Even in highly patriarchal societies there can be forces that empower the powerless and the dynamics of inequality can be questioned and changed. The consumer co-operatives in Japan provide such an example and are discussed in Chapter 8. In India there are a number of very successful co-operatives where only women can be members.[49] These co-operative banks lend only to women, but in a way that understands the needs of women who are creating their own businesses.

If women had equality would co-operatives evolve differently? Unfortunately this is a question that needs much more study but the anecdotal evidence suggests that this might be the case. The Grameen bank lends to poor women with an amazingly high repayment rate. Lending is done through groups that provide both emotional and practical support to each other. The bank comes to the women where their work and child-care is taking place. Loans and repayment schedules fit with the cash flow of the individual woman.

Many educational functions within the Indian dairy co-operatives are for women only. This lets their voices be heard without being dominated by men. But female wisdom is often overlooked. All to often all things local and rural are put down. An example:

> Women in Gujarat, India, used to cook their cottonseed and feed it to the buffaloes. They claimed that when fed cooked cottonseed their animals produced milk with more fat and that the clarified butter — ghee — they made from the milk was superior. The dairy experts convinced the women "to stop this wasteful process." But...thirty years later we have learned that cooking of cottonseed protein leads to denaturation of cottonseed protein which then bypasses the rumen. Bypass proteins are now accepted throughout the world as more efficient sources of feed proteins: they avoid conversion into microbial proteins in the rumen and are directly converted into milk and protein. Here is an example of centuries old wisdom, wisdom that we scientists and professionals did not accept...the women were right.[50]

Milk payment in the Indian dairies is made to the person delivering the milk. This does not guarantee that the women gets the proceeds, but it is a vast improvement over issuing a cheque in the husbands' name. Being able to market milk and buy cows has enabled many landless and very poor families to improve their incomes and buy other necessities for the family. This means less milk is given away in communities, a hardship for the very poor who once were given the skim milk. Plus the gain for rural women is not always accepted by middle-class urban women. Their traditions are changed and they pay more for milk.[51] This large project provides an interesting setting to study social change for both cast and gender. It shows that simple explanations are not appropriate.

Women around the world face family violence. When men get violent it is women and children that must leave, especially if the family home is in the men's name. Women's housing co-operatives, like St. Peter Clavel Women's Housing Co-operative in the slums of Kingston, Jamaica, provide more stability for women and children. Here the woman has title to the house and it is the man that leaves in the event of family breakup.

In Canada, where both men and women share the title, housing co-operatives like Jackson Point Housing Co-operative in Georgina, Ontario, found that the victims of violence, women and children, often became homeless when violence occurred. When the Board learned that at least six women members had been beaten by their husband, they responded by declaring the co-operative a violence-free zone. They amended their bylaws to allow the victims of violence to petition the board to expel the abuser. A subsidy provision is in place where necessary to allow the victims to remain in their homes while they find financial assistance and support payments and to develop a close working relationship with the local police force. Many housing co-operatives across Canada are now adopting similar by-laws.

Women-only credit unions are few in Canada, but one in Ottawa does things very differently. It was organized by middle-class women to provide themselves with savings and loan services but also to provide work experiences for destitute women. The credit union works with a social welfare agency and trains women who need job skills and helps them move into jobs in other credit unions and banks. They receive a training grant because they turn over the bulk of their employees each year. The training is intensive as most of the women were formerly on social assistance because they lacked job skills. Once they gain job skills, they move on to other jobs but most now use the Women's Credit Union as their financial institution. This is a case where the gender dimension is stronger than the class dimension. Women-only organizations provide a valuable contribution.

But women-owned co-operatives are not enough. They can still be vulnerable in a male-dominated world. The plight of the Transnzoia Consumer Co-operative and the Cherongo women's investment club in Kenya is a sad example.[52] In 1974, twenty women started an investment club, saved their money, bought a building and rented part and started a consumer co-operative. The male manager they hired was corrupt, so they appealed to the government officer. "The ladies watched the situation desperately. The shop was declining. The manager, the supervisor were rude to them. Being thus blocked, the ladies secretly went to the District Commissioner. The Commissioner promised to investigate." This did not help as the two colluded and the co-operative folded with the women losing their money to the males in the power structure.

Co-operatives can build in structural features to provide more equality for women. So far most co-operative movements have not achieved this vision of implementing the value of equality into everyday life. As co-operatives do, it is assumed that the organizational model will be profoundly changed. The anecdotal evidence from case studies around the world suggest that gender is much more than just another variable that needs to be analyzed. The essence of co-operation is not gender bound, but the practice has been in a male-dominated world. Most of the past research has been to test economic, sociological and psychological theories based on studying men. Research on Third-World women shows that they have a different appreciation of the environment than men.[53] Would the empowerment of women in the tropics through co-operatives also change the environmental impact?

The next chapter is an initial study of the consumer co-operatives in Japan where over 90% of the members are women. The difference in these organizations is often attributed to cultural differences and the uniqueness of Japanese society by white male academics. But how much of it is due to the gender difference? It would seem that gender is a very important fact and needs much more study and theory development.[54]

NOTES

1. Deegan, Mary J. 1988. "Transcending a Patriarchal Past: Teaching the History of Women in Sociology." *Teaching Sociology*. Vol. 16: 141.
2. Andersen, Margaret L.1988. "Moving our Minds: Studying Women of Color and Reconstructing Sociology." *Teaching Sociology*, Vol. 16: 123.
3. Dobson Gray, Elizabeth. 1982. *Patriarchy as a Conceptual Trap*. Mass: Roundtable Press.
4. Gill, Manohar Singh. 1983. *Agricultural Cooperatives: A Case Study of Punjab*. New Delhi: Vikas Publishing.
5. Quarter, Jack. 1993. *Canada's Social Economy*. Toronto: James Lorimer & Co. 117.
6. Fals-Borda, Orlando. 1971. *Cooperatives and Rural Development in Latin America*. Geneva: United Nations Research Institute for Social Development. Vol. III. And Worsley, Peter, ed., 1971. *Two Blades of Grass*. Manchester: Manchester University Press.
7. George, Susan. 1988. *A Fate Worse Than Debt*. London: Penguin.
8. Verhagen, Koenraad. 1984. *Co-operation for Survival*. Amsterdam: Royal Tropical Institute; and 1987. *Selp-Help Promotion: A challenge to the NGO community*. The Netherlands: Cebemo/Royal Tropical Institute.

9. Agricultural co-operatives in Europe and North America were used by farmers to gain bargaining power and reduce the power of urban-based commodity speculators. See contributions to the economy, Chapter 3.
10. Mitchell, Don and Adrianne Pavo. 1988. "To Zimbabwe with Love from Saskatchewan." *Worker Co-ops*, Vol. 8, No. 1, Summer: 23-24.
11. Emerson, Richard D. 1962. "Power-Dependence Relations." *American Sociological Review*, 27: 31-41.
12. Kanter, Rosebeth Moss. 1983. "Power Failures in Management Circuits," *Harvard Business Review*, Vol. 57, No. 4: 65-75.
13. Bookman, Ann and Sandra Morgan, ed., 1988. *Women and the Politics of Empowerment*. Philadelphia: Temple University Press.
14. Conger, Jay A. and Rabindra N. Kanungo. 1988. "The Empowerment Process: Integrating Theory and Practice," *Academy of Management Review*, Vol. 13, No. 3, 471.
15. For example, see Neilson, E. 1986. "Empowerment strategies: Balancing authority and responsibility," *Executive Power*, San Francisco: Jossey Bass; Pfeiffer, J. 1981. *78-110. Power in Organizations*. Marshfield, Ma.: Pitman; 1982 *Organizations and organizational theory*. Marshfield, Ma.: Pitman; Morgan, Gareth. 1988. *Riding the Waves of Change*. San Francisco: Jossey-Bass Publishers; Peters, Tom. 1987. *Thriving on Chaos*. New York: Perennial Library, Harper and Row; and Mintzberg, H. 1983. *Power In and Around Organizations*. Englewood Cliffs, N.J.: Prentice Hall Inc.
16. Conger and Kanungo. 1989: 471.
17. Tannenbaum, A.S. 1968. *Control in Organizations*. New York: McGraw Hill.
18. Burke, W. 1986. "Leadership as empowering others," *Power in Organizations*, S. Srivastra, ed., Nashville: Vanderbilt University Press: 3-48.
19. Lehman, Edward W. 1969. "Toward a Macrosociology of Power." *American Sociological Review*, Aug, 34: 453-465.
20. Leif, Irving P. and Terry Nichols Clark. 1972. *Community Power and Decision Making*. The Hague: A Trend Report and Bibliography International Sociologial Association.
21. Conger and Kanungo. 1988: 473.
22. Bennis, W. and B. Nanus. 1985. *Leaders*. New York: Harper and Row.
23. Brown, Leslie. 1985. "Democracy in Organizations: Membership Participation and Organizational Characteristics in U.S. Retail Food Co-operatives." *Organizational Studies*, Vol. 6 No. 4: 313-334.
24. Ostergaard, G.N. and A.H. Halsey. 1965. *Power in Co-operatives: A Study of Democratic Control in British Retail Societies*. Oxford: Basil Blackwell: 100.
25. Ostergaard and Halsey. 1965: 86-87.
26. Block, 1987. *The Empowerment Manager*. San Francisco: Jossey Bass.
27. Lambert, Paul. 1963. *Studies in the Social Philosophy of Co-operation*. Manchester: The Co-operative Union: 64.
28. Craig, 1975. Democracy in Insurance Coops
29. Craig, J.G. and E. Gross. 1970. "The forum theory of organizational democracy: structural guarantees as time-related variables," *American Sociological Review*, Vol. 35, Feb.: 19-33.
30. Craig and Gross. 1970: 20.
31. The information for this was obtained from B. Friesen's presentation to the Symposium on the Future, Yokohama Japan, April, 1989.
32. Bromberger. 1976.
33. CCCS. 1990. *Briefs*. Vol. 16, August 24.: 1.
34. Eggertson, Eric. 1990. "Keeping The Home in Home Town" *Credit Union Way*, Vol. 43, No. 3: 14.
35. The projects include a glass-etching operation; sewing women's clothing for hard-to-fit sizes; a carpentry operation manufacturing cabinets for stereos and VCRs and a wooden toy-manufacturing operation.

36. Dean, Susan. 1985. *Women and Cooperatives*. Rome: COPAC publication: 2.
37. Cobbald, Elizabeth. 1987. *Women in Agricultural Co-operatives*. Oxford: The Plunkett Foundation for Co-operative Studies. And Lamming, G.N. 1983. *Women in Agricultural Cooperatives: Constraints and Limitation to full Participation*. Rome: Food and Agricultural Organization.
38. This term is used by Pat Armstrong and Hugh Armstrong to depict the double bind of women, working in low paid jobs in the economy, plus the responsibility and long hours of looking after the family.
39. This was introduced by the colonial powers and has remained after independence.
40. This is in the law, but is not inherent in co-operatives. Once again it is a holdover from the colonial period.
41. Meghji, Zakia; Clement Kwayu and Ramadhan Meghji. 1985. *The Woman Cooperator and Development: Experiences from Eastern, Central and Southern Africa*. Nairobi: Maarifa Publishers Limited: 114-118.
42. Holland, Doug. 1986. *Directors in Canadian Co-operatives*. Ottawa: Canadian Co-operative Association.
43. Barclay, Myrna. 1991. "Toward Gender Balance: Women and Co-operatives." Ottawa: Canadian Co-operative Association, unpublished paper.
44. Doyle Farge, Brenda. 1985. *Women and Leadership in Co-operative Housing Sector*. Toronto: University of Toronto, unpublished Masters Thesis, OISE.
45. By asset size and members of the Credit Union Central of Ontario.
46. Ellman, Eugene. 1988. Ontario Credit Unions Lead Banks on Equality but Still Need Policies to Eliminate Barriers. *Spectrum*. Sept: 3.
47. Korabik, K. & R. Ayman. 1989. "Should Women Managers Have to Act Like Men? *Journal of Management Development*, Vol. 8, No. 6: 20. Helgesen, Sally. 1990. *The Female Advantage: Women's Ways of Leadership*. Toronto: Doubleday.
48. Hammond-Ketilson, Lou. 1992. "The Saskatchewan Co-operative Women's Guild." Saskatoon: Centre for Co-operative Studies, University of Saskatchewan, proceedings of the Canadian Association for Studies in Co-operation meetings.
49. Saxena, Suren K. 1990. "Cooperatives and Women Enterprise Development in India: Note on a Women's Cooperative Bank." *Transnational Associations*. 1/1990: 12-17.
50. Kurien, V. 1991. "Towards a New World Order," speech in Toronto to the Eighth World Congress of Food Science and Technology. Anand: NDDB: 11-12.
51. George, Shanti. 1985. *Operation Flood: An Appraisal of Current Indian Dairy Policy*. Delhi: Oxford University Press.
52. Meghji, et al., 1985: 42-44.
53. Dankelman, Irene and Joan Davidson. 1988. *Women and the Environment in the Third World: Alliance for the Future*. London: Earthscan Publications Ltd.
54. Vacek, Gunther. 1989. "The Consumer Co-operatives in Japan," in J. Brazda & R. Schediwy, eds., *Consumer Co-operatives in a Changing World*. Geneva: International Co-operative Alliance: 1063.

Chapter 8

EMPOWERMENT OF WOMEN IN CONSUMER CO-OPS IN JAPAN*

Japanese women are on average highly educated, but are denied access to power in society by strong traditional cultural values. During the past two decades, women have developed ways to exercise power in the control of the consumer co-operatives and they are having a major impact on shaping retail policy in the country. This chapter uses the case of Co-op Kanagawa, which is a good example of management within the emerging paradigm (Chapter 6), and of the active involvement of women in the policy direction and control of the organization. This co-operative has been growing rapidly. It has sales in excess of US$1 billion, nearly 800,000 women members with 350,000 active in electing and advising the eighteen women on the 28-person Board of Directors about policy. Women active in the housewives role have been empowered to play a meaningful role in the market place.

Working within the socially accepted norms of Japanese society, the consumer co-operatives have developed into organizations that attract and utilize the power of the Japanese housewife. Any discussion of empowerment and consumer co-operatives in Japan, therefore, is best understood against the background of the meaning and the role of the Japanese housewife since the membership of consumer co-operatives is 99% women.

Japan is a country where behavioural expectations for both sexes are strictly defined. Surprisingly, the Western observer finds that role-playing within the household is still strictly practised.[1] Culturally, the proper place for women is in the home, while men control the business environment. This does not imply that women do not work outside the home, for in fact one-half of all married women work part- or full-time in order to supplement their household income.[2]

The *Japan Times,* reports the results of a nationwide survey. They concluded the principle reasons for unfavourable working conditions for women were: traditional attitudes that women belong in the

---

*Written in collaboration with Deborah Steinhoff

home (28%), and unequal opportunity for job training and promotion (17%). Twenty-one percent of the men agree that ideally, women should continue working and 18% advocate they stay home. Only 9% of women felt they should stay home.[3]

The typical accepted pattern for women can be described as follows. After completing college or university they go to work in offices or the service sector until reaching their mid-twenties, at which time they are expected to get married and voluntarily leave the company.[4] Starting salaries for women are generally 10% less than for men hired the same year, and this gap generally widens by about 30% the longer they stay in the work place.

Once children are in school many women return to the work force in their thirties or early forties. At this time they come back as part-time workers, which means working as many as eight hours per day with little or no benefits and for minimum wage.

It is taken for granted that men should dominate the business world while women should take control of the home front. This does not imply that women are discontent with their role nor powerless in society. It is well documented that women are the powerful members of the family who single-handedly make the decisions in the home about such important matters as the allocation of income, investments and children's education.

Many younger women who may doubt the value of such role-playing and endeavour to enter the business world soon realize that it is close to impossible for a woman in Japan to be both accepted in business and be the model housewife and mother that society expects. It is neither smiled upon nor easy for a women to work the long hours that are expected of men in an equivalent position and still leave time for household and child care.

In industries which are more open to women than others, such as foreign companies, banking, insurance, government offices or department stores, women are increasingly pursuing careers and foregoing the idea of marriage. Still, the pressure to leave voluntarily at marriageable age is great, and the women who do not are a very small minority.

Men in Japan work longer hours than their counterparts in other industrialized countries and are expected to devote as much as eighteen hours a day to their respective companies. This includes commuting time, which on average is over an hour each way, and after-hour socializing with clients and fellow colleagues. Obviously husbands spend very little time at home, which makes it very difficult for women to both hold down a full-time job and run a household.

Married women who continue to hold full-time jobs generally live in two-generation homes where they can relegate household duties to their mothers or mothers-in-law. These women, however, continue to be a minority. One explanation is that working women are still viewed as an oddity which society tolerates, but does not gladly accept. Women, therefore, ask themselves, is the challenge worth it, especially in a society where being a housewife is not only a very accepted role in society, but one that is glorified through the media.

Being a housewife today is not necessarily the full-time job that it once was considering that the average home in Tokyo is 750 square feet and is continuously refurnished with the latest high-tech household appliances. Japanese couples usually have no more than two children and once these children enter school, women today, perhaps more than ever, have time and energy to spare. More than half of all women hold jobs, almost all attend or attended some type of continuing education classes, and more and more are becoming social activists in their communities.

One of the keys to understanding the continued growth of consumer co-operatives is understanding how the co-operatives have capitalized on the role that women play in society and how women themselves have transformed certain aspects of the co-operative into an organization where they can expend their energy for useful educational and social causes and community development.

The nature of Japanese society and the role of women has largely influenced the continued development of consumer co-operatives. In terms of a retail business, co-operatives have very effectively taken advantage of the female work-force which is available to them. More than two-thirds of any co-operative work force is now made up of part-time female employees. The majority of these employees are of course members of the co-operative, and if employees were not members before coming to work for the co-op, they soon become members.

Women's labour gives the co-operative a certain flexibility in terms of adjusting the work force to suit the flow of business. As stated above, co-operatives like their competitors pay minimum wage with no benefits, but on one account they have been more accommodating: adjusting work schedules to suit individual women's household schedules.

Secondly, the co-operative has continued to expand and develop its social nature through the energy and efforts of women. Since women naturally are in control on all aspects of society related to the home environment, child care and care for the elderly, the co-operative has developed into an organization where women can address various social problems related to these issues.

Because women's interests within the organization generally concentrate on and remained confined to issues such as food, safety and problems which concern homemaking, areas in which women show dominance, the male-dominated management of the co-operative does not feel threatened by the role that women play, and women and men sit comfortable on the same Board of Directors. The reverse can also be said to be true. This is that women generally accept that men are "better" at running the business and gladly relegate this task to them. On most consumer co-operatives Boards throughout the country, generally about half of the members of the Board of Directors are women.

The co-operative has developed a rather unique system which successfully utilizes the socially accepted roles of Japanese society. By organizing *Han* groups and various committees, women can have input into the male-dominated management side of the organization. Management also values such input from the membership. Through *Han* groups, and such committees as joint buying committees, women members can make their opinions known to management. And management, on the other hand, relies on hearing the voices of its membership as a means of knowing how best to serve its customers and stay competitive with other retail stores in Japan. Co-operative management never forgets that if members are not satisfied they can easily go elsewhere. The Japanese retail environment is highly competitive: on every corner where you find a co-operative store, you are likely to find a competitor.

One must also remember that the system of business management in most corporations, as in co-operatives, with its many meetings and constant flow of information can easily be made to accommodate input from members.[5] Japanese business management practices obviously have a big influence in the degree to which women are empowered in consumer co-operatives. Although this may be too large an area to discuss at this time, it does bear noting.

By joining a consumer co-operative, women are able to be empowered in two ways. If they choose to get involved in the many social and environmental projects and causes for the co-operative, they gain a personal sense of self-assertion outside of the home front. By banding together with fellow housewives through their local co-operative they are able to make a difference in the quality and price of merchandise that they will consume. Through the many committees that members have formed or insisted be formed by management, members are confident in the quality of merchandise, particularly those that bare the co-operative's brand label.

In other words, women members shape the policy of their local co-operative and in turn are able to shop with confidence. Grouping together the 657 co-operatives throughout the country under the national organization of the Japanese Consumer Co-operative Union, (JCCU) these co-operatives have a meaningful input in the market place. Together the co-operatives are the main force in the small but growing consumers' movement (Consumers Advocate Group). Through their co-operatives women are addressing larger issues that their "workaholic husbands" are too tired to think about.

Through co-operatives women have slowly made some impact. In the high economic growth years of the sixties, industry was allowed to produce mass merchandise and make products without regulations on standards and quality. As prices sky-rocketed and manufacturers did not act responsibly, consumers felt powerless and turned to their consumer co-operatives to address problems that affected their lives. Some successes included spearheading a consumer campaign to the government to make manufacturers of canned fruit juices indicate the percentage of real fruit juice on the label. They also disclosed that the first manufacturers of colour TV sets were unlawfully controlling the price of TV sets.

In achieving the economic success that Japan now has, its citizens (consumers) have not been terribly demanding. As the citizens today take a look at the world, they are deciding that they now deserve to partake in the fruits of their success and enjoy a higher standard of living. Through these co-operatives, women are thinking about ways to improves their lifestyles. They form committees to address problems of how to achieve a cleaner environment, question education and investigate ways to care for the elderly.

What do they do with the information they collect and the thoughts they debate? They produce monthly magazines for their members to spread the ideas and hopefully gather more support or at least debate, among the membership. They petition the government to consider new ideas in policy formation. This gives them a feeling of power,, the ability to have a say in the community a place where men have long dominated the scene. With this feeling of power, women develop a strong sense of empowerment through the co-operative and thus become loyal supporters of the co-operative and regular shoppers.

Consumer co-operatives in Japan have not tried to change the business style of retailing. It is a business which is dominated by men, just like all other business in Japan. What Co-operatives have successfully done is to allow the business style to incorporate and address the concerns of its membership. It has been able to do this because of the cultural peculiarities that we have described above.

The system of meetings in Japanese management allows for the opinions of members to be heard by most levels of management.

Women have let the men attend to what they know best, that is the running of the mechanics of the retail operation, while men have likewise not interfered with the movement side of the organization nurtured by the women membership. Effective participation means a regular process in which members, thoughts, ideas and aspirations can be communicated to other members and decision-makers of the organization, and can influence the long-term plans of the organization. Participation must be forward-looking, related to the planning process and have an impact on the direction of the organization.

The conventional wisdom in Europe and North America is that member democracy and participation can only be minimal in large urban co-operatives in industrialized nations. Leaders must raise capital and make decisions without involving members as the process will take too long. But failures have been a frequent result of such strategies.[6] Member participation is thought to be the luxury of rural or very small co-operatives, and is always a victim to growth and economic development in large co-operatives.[7] The popular wisdom of many leaders and managers in co-operatives in western Europe and North America holds that if one wants economic efficiency in the organization, then participation must go. You cannot have both![8] But does this popular wisdom fit with reality? Schumacher, argued that large isn't necessary and small is beautiful.[9] Certainly management with a bureaucratic framework tends to dismiss empowerment and member participation.[10] Interestingly, a cursory look at the state of co-operatives in the industrialized countries suggests that the co-operatives that are financially strong have also worked hard at member participation.[11]

The consumer co-operative movement in Japan provides evidence that the conventional wisdom about participation is indeed wrong. Member empowerment through participation appears to be a central ingredient for the massive growth of the past two decades. During this period consumer co-operatives have become a competitive force in food retailing. The Japanese case will be analyzed in terms of the five-stage process of empowerment developed by Conger and Kanungo and illustrated in Figure 8.1.[12]

CONSUMER CO-OPERATIVE MOVEMENT IN JAPAN[13]

Japan has a population of 120 million people with 39 million households of which 12 million are members of the 650 consumer co-operatives. Although the roots of the movement date back to the last century this is a new movement that developed since the pacific war

Table 8.1

STATISTICAL SUMMARY OF THE URBAN CO-OPERATIVE MOVEMENT

A — RETAIL CONSUMER CO-OPERATIVES

	1988 (March)	% change from 1987
a) Member information		
No. of Societies	654	-0.8
No. of retail outlets	2,190	+2.2
No. of members	11,801,752	+6.6
No. of *Han* groups	746,474	+13.2
No. of *Han* members	4,685,397	+9.5
Ratio of *Han* members to total number of members	39.7%	
No. of full-time employees	47,890	+2.5
b) Financial information		
Total turnover (Y million)	Y2,209,894 US$16.4 billion	+9.6
Retail sales	US$14.5 billion	+7.4
Services sales	US$ 1.9 billion	+30.0
Share Capital (Y million)	162,149 US$ 1.2 billion	+17.7
Share capital per member	US$ 102.00	+10.4

Calculated at US$ = 135 Y.

ended in 1945. Like many other consumer co-operative movements it faced a severe economic crisis in the 1960s when food retailing changed from small shops to supermarkets. Its response to the crisis was to renew its membership base and develop participative structures to respond to the changing urban environment. Consumer co-operatives have been among the fastest growing retailing organizations in Japan with annual membership and sales growth of about 10% per year from 1980 to 1985. It slowed during the late 1980s but still remained higher than other retailers.

The other parts of the consumer co-operative movement include the medical co-operatives which serve 1.08 million families through 118 co-operatives that operate eighty hospitals, 187 clinics, for a total of 12,336 beds employing 1,500 doctors, 7,700 nurses and 6,900 other staff for an annual turnover of US$1.06 billion. The co-operatives emphasize preventative health care. Insurance co-operatives are also consumer-owned and provide many kinds of insurance products through forty-seven societies with 25.8 million policies and 2,278 full-time employees. Housing co-ops, through forty-nine societies have 866,000 members. These co-operatives supply houses and housing plots to workers.

The growth in the retail co-operatives has been achieved to a large degree through the development of *Han* groups that enable Japanese women to exercise control of key aspects of the organization.[14] In effect, these are organizations where women have a meaningful influence to shape the market place. New members contribute US$ 20.00 to $30.00 investment to join and are then invited to join a *Han* group, which is the basic foundation of modern day urban co-operatives in Japan.

The numbers are impressive yet they do not show the vitality of the participation in the system that has evolved to provide the consumers (housewives) with real power in the organizations. To do this, we will look more closely at how it is done in one local consumer co-operative.

THE CASE OF CO-OP KANAGAWA

Co-op Kanagawa was established in 1975 with the merger of five consumer co-operatives in the Kanagawa prefecture which includes the port city of Yokohama. By 1980, three more consumer co-operatives in the prefecture merged to form a large centralized and efficient organizational unit. In 1985, Co-op Kanagawa had 573,000 members, 5,212 (including 1,134 full-time) employees operating 134 retail outlets, and had sales of US$ 968 million, of which 85% was food. Growth has continued with membership in 1988 at 750,000, with 5,900 (1,160 full-time) employees and sales of US$ 1.06 billion. By 1988, Co-op Kanagawa had two warehouses, three production units and one laboratory where food is extensively tested, 54 supermarkets and 93 small shops for a total of 147. Interestingly, 24% of the sales volume goes directly from the warehouse to the consumers through joint buying activities of the *Han* groups. This increases the efficiency of the organization considerably in high density urban markets where the cost of display space in retails is very expensive.

Before-tax earnings in 1988 amounted to US$ 25 million or 2.3% on sales. Co-op Kanagawa paid 3.3% interest on member shares (compares well to Japanese bank interest on savings accounts) and 2.4% dividend on purchases.

The organization has total assets of US$ 381 million. With US$ 124 million of share capital plus US$ 72 million in reserves. This is a strong financial base in a large, efficient retail organization. It continues to grow, make money and increase its market share.[15] This economic growth and strength happened during the 1970s and 80s.

The consumer co-operatives are largely urban-based. Agricultural co-operatives are also well developed in the rural area where they provide services to farmers as well as operating retail food stores. They are not included in this study.

The organizations in Figure 8.1 are all consumer food co-operatives. However the Japanese distinguish between five types. These include Citizen Co-ops, serving local residents through stores, joint buying and catalogue sales; Institutional Co-ops, serving workers in their work places through stores, canteens etc.; Expanded Institutional Co-ops, serving both workers and local residents; University Co-ops, serving students, staff and faculty members in universities and colleges through book stores, food stores, canteens and other services and; School Teachers' Co-ops, serving teachers at both the public and private schools mainly through catalogue sales and joint buying.

EMPOWERMENT THROUGH CO-OPERATION

In the 1950s and 1960s, the consumer co-operatives in Japan had a traditional control structure where members were advised of the location of the annual general meeting. The meeting consisted of reports from the Board, management and auditors; the members listened, approved the reports and elected the Board. Activities were focused on the past year with little opportunity for member input. The market place had become highly competitive with the advent of supermarkets and the co-operatives small shops were financially weak with a poor capital structure. In sum, members (housewives) had little opportunity to express their concerns and had the option of electing men to the Board of Directors.[16]

As several co-operatives got into financial difficulty, the Board and management appealed to the membership for capital and support. Housewives had a forum and told management what they disliked. The first *Han* group was set up in 1963 by Tsuruoka Consumer Co-operative now known as Kyoritsusha Tsuruoka Co-op. In those days the *Han* consisted of fifteen members and was mainly organized by store managers and female members on a voluntary basis. Store managers worked overtime without pay to develop the *Han* groups. By 1970 the average size of the *Han* was reduced to seven members. Since 1975, the average number of members has been five. These days

Figure 8.2

ORGANIZATIONAL CHART

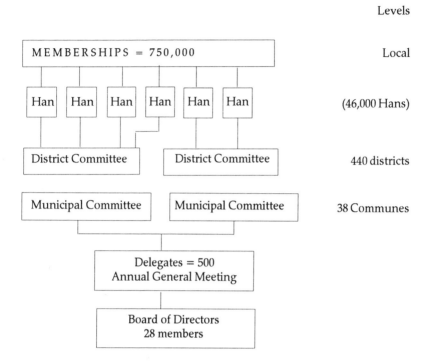

members basically organize themselves in *Han* groups, but employees sometimes assist and support members within their working time. The *Han* was the participative organizational structure to involve and empower housewives in the critical decisions of the organization, and economic success followed.

Co-op Kanagawa management put the necessary structures in place and actively involved the members (see Figure 8.2). Today the co-operative has 750,000 members, mostly women, involves nearly 40% or 304,000 members in its democratic administration through *Han* groups. The *Han* groups meet about three times a year. They are involved with product testing and development, issues related to shop operations and community involvement like festivals, crafts and dialogue with agricultural co-operatives. The *Han* groups are linked to the Board of Directors through 440 district committees that involve 7,200 members. These district committees are represented at the community level with 38 municipal committees involving 820 members. These are the most vital organizations for community involvement. Five hundred delegates (all housewives) are elected to attend the annual general meeting that formalizes policy and elects the Board of

Directors that meets monthly. The housewives elect eighteen women to the twenty-eight-member Board of Directors.

Co-op Kanagawa predecessor (Kawasaki Co-op) had eight women members on a fifteen-person board in 1974. With the merger of five co-ops to create Co-op Kanagawa, the Board expanded to twenty-five with fifteen women. In 1988 it was expanded to 28 with eighteen women board members. Each of the women directors heads up a policy team to review co-operative policy in various fields and recommend policy changes to the Board. Each will spend fifteen to twenty days per month attending meetings and working on co-operative activities. They are very active volunteers! Through this elaborate structure the women consumers shape the policies and long-term plans of Co-op Kanagawa in real and tangible ways.

As more and more women who were involved in the *Han* groups went into the labour force they proposed changes in their consumer co-operatives. Those who lived a distance from the store proposed that their group become a buying club. This innovation was viewed favourably and together with management, an efficient home shopping programme has been developed through experimentation and a learning process. The result is a win/win situation. The stores can become more efficient and solve some of management's problems and food shopping is much easier and convenient for women. However, it is not clear what the long-term impact will be. Some members can save time by having the merchandise delivered to their door, but for others this may not be convenient and they may drift away if new solutions are not developed.

Joint buying groups operate very well within the group-oriented society of Japan. Sometimes, however, women may resist joining a neighbourhood *Han* group because of the added pressure and responsibility that this entails in a community that already requires her to act according to her role. When women become *Han* members they feel a certain responsibility to the group, and this means being home to receive and sort the weekly merchandise of the group. As deliveries are done during the daytime the *Han* leader, or at least one on-duty member, must be home to receive and sort the pre-ordered merchandise and hand in the computerized order sheet for the next week's order.

Since Japanese houses and refrigerators are generally small, it is very difficult for one member to keep goods, especially those that require refrigeration for other members of the group if they are working until the evening. Members are of course trying to adjust the system to accommodate working women by requesting evening deliveries, but they are being met with opposition from employee labour unions.

Han groups which have become buying clubs meet at a pre-scheduled time each week. The joint-buying delivery centres arrange delivery according to neighbourhood. *Han* groups are informed when to expect the delivery truck. For example, a *Han* group can expect delivery every Monday morning. It is the responsibility of the group to be waiting to meet the truck and they are alerted of its coming by the sound of familiar bell or song that can be heard from down the street at a distance. When the sound of the truck is heard the members gather at the home of the on-duty member or *Han* leader to meet the driver and receive and divide-up the order they had placed the previous week.

The average size of *Han* at Co-op Kanagawa since 1975 has been only five members. The national average is between five to eight members. The number of members per *Han* in Sapporo Co-op is only four. The smaller the *Han* group, the more difficult it is for the cooperative to organize the system efficiently. In recent years although the number of *Han* members has increased the number of members per *Han* has significantly decreased. This trend may be a reflection of the increased number of women in the work force.

The joint-buying system is a separate operation apart from the retail outlets. Orders for dry goods are filled at one of the Kyodokonyu (joint-buying centres), and orders for perishables are filled at a delivery centre for perishable foods. A delivery truck may have to make two stops in order to complete an individual *Han* group's order.

The centres operate six days per week from Monday to Saturday, although delivery is done only five days per week. In Sapporo Co-op which has 16,000 *Han* groups servicing 68,000 *Han* members there are 190 full-time delivery men working out of eleven different centres to serve the members.

These delivery men have a very important job as the direct link between members, buyers and management who are responsible for the quality of the produce. Management has developed various systems/routes to receive and answer members' questions and complaints.

If a driver receives a complaint from a member *en route* or s/he cannot respond to the members' problem, s/he reports the complaint to the delivery centre manager, who will either contact the member or report the complaint to the appropriate buyer at the head office. In addition, each driver is requested to file a daily report of complaints and comments received from the *Han* groups and give this to their respective delivery-centre managers. All delivery-centre managers come together once a week in a meeting to discuss the members' complaints in order to see problems, understand common trends and come up with short- and long-term solutions.

A member is also free to fill in a blank complaint form which is attached to the back of the weekly order catalog. These complaints are all collected through the delivery centres and are directed to the appropriate buyer at the head office, who will then either phone the member directly to address the problem or write a letter of explanation. Generally, thirty to fifty complaints per week are reported to the head office.

At any time, members are free to phone the head office or the joint-buying delivery centre to voice complaints. Delivery centres receive scores of calls every day.

In addition to this constant source of members' input the most valuable source of information about merchandise is brought to the attention of buyers and management alike through the committees of the joint buying groups. These committees are organized at the retail outlet level, the regional level and the central level.

According to the Kanagawa prefecture co-operative union's survey, 25% of the membership hold part-time jobs.[17] This is far below the national average, which shows that more than half of all women hold part-time jobs. One explanation is that the *Han* tends to attract young housewives who are more confined with young pre-school children since *Han* provides them with the opportunity to socialize with their neighbours on a regular basis and offers the convenience of home delivery when it is often very difficult to go shopping with infants or toddlers.

Co-op Kanagawa, like all co-operatives in Japan, faces the difficulty of members leaving the joint-buying system once their children are in school and they feel more mobile. Co-operatives accept the situation for what it is and continually campaign for new young members while activist members work hard to inform *Han* members about the many activities that are available to them with the hope of maintaining their continued support and interest in the co-op.

At the moment, Co-op Kanagawa, like all other co-operatives is facing criticism from members that co-op stores are not as pleasant a place to shop as their competitors. In designing new stores, co-operatives are now looking toward North America to gain ideas about how to incorporate the idea of putting pleasure into shopping, a concept they believe to be a part of shopping in North America.

Co-operative stores are always striving to be as good as the competition and today this means developing shopping centres where shopping can be fun for the whole family. They are very interested in adopting ideas, for example.

The display of talent and interest shown by the members of Co-op Kanagawa in 1989 at the Yokohama Exotic Showcase is testimony to the fact that a significant percentage of members sees the co-operative as more than just a retail outlet. The co-op developed a pavilion to showcase the local amateur cultural achievements. In preparation for this pavilion, 533 local committees at the store level, thirty-nine committees at the district level, and a central prefectural committee, planned the programmes and content of a thousand performances with the advice of professionals provided by the co-op. This event showed that they valued members' initiatives.

Member involvement is more than joint buying, cultural activities and food tasting. When Co-op Kanagawa have stores in a deficit position they take the problem to the municipal committees and local *Han* groups. Housewives understand that stores must make money or be closed. If they want the service they have a responsibility to help provide answers to make it more efficient. Centralization of buying, marketing and financial management enable economies of scale to be realized but political decentralization allows the local members to provide input directly to their stores. This works because of the willingness of leaders and management to learn and listen, make decisions and follow up by monitoring members' responses to make sure they made the right decision. In Co-op Kanagawa business decisions are a co-operative effort involving shoppers (mostly women), management and staff (mostly women) at the store level.

They have found that the volunteer activities are not only important for the co-operative but are important for the individuals involved. Involvement enables housewives to learn to make decisions together. Public speaking and listening skills are learned by doing and co-operatives can provide this opportunity. The eighteen women directors on the Board of Co-op Kanagawa head policy committees made up of members interested in the specific themes. They spend many hours in meetings brainstorming, developing policies and thinking through the impact of such policies. If they sound good to them they must then convince other members that the policies should be implemented. It takes time but it provides a lot is learned about democracy and leadership.

Handicraft groups are provided space at the stores and meet on a regular basis. All the larger stores have a room designed for member's activities where various groups can meet on a regular basis. This increases store traffic and lets members perceive the store as community centres rather than just another store. These activities also enable the aging generation to pass on the cultural heritage to the next generation.

One of the plans concerns the environment. The plan that is described here is the result of many years of discussion and learning. The environment committee has travelled to the U.S.A. and Europe to try to find the best environmental practices. The president visited Toronto in May 1990, and consulted with a number of environmental groups including Pollution Probe. As they developed their conceptual framework they returned in May 1991, for further discussions. Their conceptual model indicates that they see the journey to change their organizations as a start, and further plans will emerge through a democratic process in the years to come. A practical example of "environmental demo-cracy."[18] The Ecology Programme is outlined in a booklet and is being studied by the *Han* groups. It contains specific measurable goals for the next few years. It is ambitious but, because it will be implemented through the active involvement of about half a million women, it is indeed realistic. It focuses on both the individual member level and the organizational, with the aim of "developing a community in which the individual, society and nature are in harmony." Further, whilst striving to improve the quality of life and of lifestyle in accordance with the demands of its members, the co-op must be constantly aware of the global environmental problems that can threaten the achievement of these aims. The co-op will accordingly:

1) Enhance its ability to contribute to society by attaining the long-term objective of progressively increasing the scope of its activities and operations to develop an ecology-conscious society and economy.

2) Encourage study by it members and reshaping its operations and activities to fit the aspirations that emerge from the membership.

3) Encourage co-operation at the community level, with other co-operatives in Japan and among co-operatives around the world.

The programme is setting the direction for the future. However the organization has already been acting to create an ecologically sounder world. Specifically:

1) Co-op Kanagawa has established a laboratory to test food products. The tests measure food for: microorganisms; radiation; antibacterial agents; food additives; heavy metals; pesticide residues; and nutrients. The information is used by the buyers in purchasing food as well as for programmes for the members. Ten other large co-ops have similar laboratories and tests are shared within the network of consumer co-operatives.

2) They started a milk-carton recovery programme in April 1990. Members are asked to rinse and flatten milk cartons when they are emptied and return them to the stores. So far, about 70% of all cartons sold are returned. They are then shipped to a paper producer and where they make up 10% of the raw materials for the production of toilet paper.

3) The Yokohama area is densely populated and air quality is a problem. To put pressure on the appropriate private and public authorities the co-operatives have started a programme to monitor the levels of nitrogen dioxide. The equipment is strategically located and operated by volunteers. The results are tabulated to develop a data base. The results will go to the groups for discussion and the development of action programmes.

4) Since the co-operative is a major purchaser of food, the co-op is working with agricultural groups to produce "ecology-friendly, safer agricultural products" by conducting experiments in cultivating rice and vegetables without using chemical fertilizers or other agricultural chemicals, or by eliminating such chemicals as much as possible. Economists portray the interests of consumers and producers as being in conflict. However it is in the interest of both to produce safe food, but a closer linkage between the two needs to be established.[19] The Co-op has provided this linkage between Japanese consumers and groups of producers in the Mindanao island in the Philippines. These producers are now cultivating bananas that are free of all agricultural chemicals, for export to the Yokohama-based co-operatives. These command a premium price for the producers and result in less toxic residues being ingested by Japanese consumers.

5) In co-operation with ISUZU truck manufacturer, twenty co-operatives have jointly established the co-op, Electric Vehicle Development Company. The first prototype is being tested. So far it is still too expensive to mass produce, however from what has been learned a second will be on the road in 1993 to test improvements, and it is hoped the truck will be in mass production by 1994. The consumer co-operatives currently use 10,000 diesel delivery vehicles of this size. So a conversion to electricity will make a substantial reduction in air pollution in residential neighbourhoods.

6) Stores are being equipped with energy-saving devices. Rain water is being caught in tanks to supply water for washing floors, etc., to reduce the demand on the city water supply. Garbage separation is underway for recycling, and more and more co-op brand products have less packaging and are utilizing refillable containers.

7) They have recently opened a processing plant to manufacture tofu and other food products. The roof has been covered with solar

cells which generate enough electricity to recharge the battery in one of the warehouse trucks. The soybean pulp left over from making tofu and soya sauce is sold as an organic fertilizer. The cooking oil left over from processing the foodstuff is used to make soap. This soap is used to wash the machines and keep the processing plant clean.

8) The Co-operative Research Centre conducted a survey in 1990. A random sample of members was drawn and 10,000 questionnaires were sent out with 4,300 returned. The results showed that 45% of the women were employed either full- or part-time and another 30% would like to have a job, certainly an indicator that the activity of the volunteers and the *Han* groups is undergoing change. The survey also showed that 11% of the members would like to work at the co-operative in either a full-time or part-time capacity, another 9% wished to volunteer for roles other than just the *Han* group. 3.8% would like to be more active as monitors or testers of new products and nearly 1% would like to start their own business to supply products to the co-operative stores. This group was invited to take part in an "idea factory" with two projects started in 1991.

a) A group of women responded to the idea of making chopstick holders out of a kind of cider that gives off an odour that kills bacteria. With the move away from disposable chopsticks a holder that kills any bacteria left on the washed chopstick is appealing. This group found a nursery that is planting this type of tree and obtained seedlings that are being culled to make the holders. No wood is wasted!

b) The second group of fifty women could be called weeder feeders. This is a group that lacks space for gardens at their own home and has volunteered to do the weeding from a farmer planting organic veggies. The women pull the weeds rather than having the field sprayed with chemicals, then purchase the harvested product and sell to the co-operative. An interesting win-win-win combination. The farmer gets the labour he needs to grow organic vegetables, the co-operative increases the supply available to buy and the women, the weeder feeders, increase their family income by acting as wholesalers and selling the vegetables to the co-operative.

The co-operative regularly surveys the members for ideas on how to do things better. Panels are organized to evaluate how well the changes are working. This involves 1,600 women and the idea factory has been organized to put members' ideas into new products to be marketed by the co-op that are produced by members: an example of how the participative system can be used by groups to improve their quality of life.

The consumer co-operative movement members and the environmental movement are working closely together in Yokohama. They see the programme as a start, but when viewed from afar it is a long way ahead of many other retailers whose management teams have been forced to act and are content to do the minimum amount in order not to lose to many customers. Consumer co-operatives are declining in many countries.[20] Craig and Saxena (1990) show that the ones that are growing seem to be ones that are responding directly to consumer needs. The environment is such a need, and the behaviour of most retailers, both corporate and co-operative, is far behind the expectations of consumers. Best practices need to be documented to show the reluctant managers and policy makers what can be done.

In conclusion, it seems obvious that since consumer co-operatives are patronized by women they should be run for the benefit of women. This means involving women in meaningful ways. The 340,000 women active in the *Han* groups in Co-op Kanagawa debate issues and provide input to leaders *before* decisions are made. In many cases they test products and advise buyers what items to stock *before* the new products are purchased and given shelf space. They have eighteen members on the twenty-eight-person board and are actively involved in policy development. But, perhaps the greatest aspect is they are respected and listened to by management. In short, women in Japan can meaningfully affect their lives and Japanese society by being active in consumer co-operatives.

Is participation only possible where most homemakers are not in the work force? The unique structure and activities in Co-op Kanagawa have developed and evolved in Japan to fit the socio-economic cultural context of Japanese life. But that does not mean that participation and empowerment of women consumers in other countries is not possible. The women's guilds were once powerful in the British consumer co-operatives, but they have declined with the movement.[21] The women's guilds in the western Canadian consumer co-operatives were organized to improve women's roles in the organizations, instead they were only more marginalized.[22] Increasingly, retail systems in all industrialized countries are looking for ways to learn about changing consumer needs. This should be a natural for consumer co-operatives, yet they are in decline in many countries as the older members leave and co-ops are seen as a thing of the past by young consumers.

Shouldn't all co-operatives be managed within a conceptual framework complementary to the processes that build contractual co-operation?

NOTES

1. The term "housewife" is used in this article, as this is how Japanese women view themselves. In a North-American context the term has negative connotations and the term of "homemaker" might be more appropriate.
2. Steinhoff, Deborah Ann. 1988. *SEIKYO: Japanese Consumer Co-operatives, Organization and Management.* Sapporo Japan: Hokkaido University, Unpublished Ph.D. dissertation.
3. *The Japan Times,* March 19, 1990, 4.
4. Hindry, J. 1987. *Understanding Japanese Society.* London: Croom Helm.
5. Steinhoff, 1988.
6. Bariteau, Claude. 1983. *Lessons from a Failure.* Saskatoon: Co-operative College of Canada, Working Papers Vol. 1, No. 6; Schediwy, R. 1989. "The Consumer Co-operatives in France," *Consumer Co-operatives in a Changing World.* J. Brazda & R. Schediwy, eds., Geneva: International Co-operative Alliance: 671-814.
7. Dufler, Eberhard and Walter Hamm, eds., 1985. *Co-operatives: In a Clash between Member Participation, Organizational Development and Bureaucratic Tendencies.* London: Quiller Press.
8. Furstenberg, F. 1985. "Problems of Member Participation at Different Stages of Co-operative Development." in Dufler, Eberhard and Walter Hamm, ed., *Cooperatives: In a Clash between Member Participation, Organizational Development and Bureaucratic Tendencies.* London: Quiller Press: 103-117.
9. Schumacher, Ernst.1973. *Small is Beautiful.* New York: Harper and Row.
10. Dulfer, E. 1985. "The Co-operatives Between Member Participation, The Formation of Vertical Organizations and Bureaucratic Tendencies." Dufler, Eberhard and Walter Hamm, eds., 15-39;
    Craig, J.G. 1989. "Paradigms and the theory of cooperation." *Learning Works: Searching for Organizational Futures.* S. Wright and D. Morley, eds., Toronto: ABL Publications, Faculty of Environmental Studies, York University: 63-82.
11. Craig, J.G. 1986. "Business Success and Democratic Process" in Juhani Laurinkari, ed. *Co-operatives Today. A Tribute to Dr. Laakkonen.* Published in German and English. Geneva: International Co-operative Alliance: 93-11.
12. Conger, Jay A. and Rabindra N. Kanungo. 1988. "The Empowerment Process: Integrating Theory and Practice," *Academy of Management Review,* Vol. 13. No. 3, 471-482.
13. Information from "CO-OP Information." (JCCU) Japanese Consumers' Co-operative Union, March 1989.
14. Kurimoto, A. 1983. *Research Activities-Studies, Project on the Future of Consumer Co-operatives.* Tokyo: Japanese Consumer Co-operative Union.
15. Yamagishi, M. 1989. "Democratic Administration in the Co-operatives," *Proceedings of the International Forum on the Vision of the Consumer Co-operative Movement towards the 21st Century.* Kurimoto, ed., Yokohama Japan: Co-op Kanagawa.
16. Vacek, Gunther. 1989. "The Consumer Co-operatives in Japan." *Consumer Co-operatives in a Changing World.* J. Brazda & R. Schediwy, eds., Geneva: International Co-operative Alliance: 1026-1105.
17. According to the Kanagawa prefecture co-operative unions's survey, 25% of the membership holds part-time jobs and 18% of the membership holds full-time jobs. Co-op employees consist of 1,220 full-time employees and 5,912 part-time employees as of January 21, 1990. Among the full-time employees 117 are female and among the part-time employees, 4,728 are female. The remaining 1% are part-time student help. Ninety-nine percent of female employees are members of the Co-op.
18. Commoner, 1989: 52.

19. Lovell, Alyssa. 1989. "Community-Supported Agriculture," pp 105-109 in C.& J. Plant, eds., *Green Business: Hope or Hoax*. Philadelphia: New Society Publishers: 105-109.
20. Brazda & Schediwy, 1989.
21. Muller, Franz. 1989. "Consumer Co-operatives in Great Britain." *Consumer Co-operatives in a Changing World*. J. Brazda & R. Schediwy, eds., Geneva: International Co-operative Alliance: 45-137.
22. Hammond Ketilson, Lou. 1992. "Co-operative Models of Community development: What makes Them Work and Why They Make Sense." Saskatoon, Centre for the Study of Co-operatives, paper presented at ICA Researchers Forum, Tokyo.

BIBLIOGRAPHY

Abarbanel, Jay S. 1974. *The Cooperative Farmer and the Welfare State: Economic Change in an Israeli Moshav.* Manchester: Manchester University Press.

Abel, I.W., 1976 *Collective Bargaining: Labour Relations in Steel, Then and Now.* Pittsburgh: Carnegie Mellon University Press.

Alder, Graham. 1985. "The Role of The Cooperative Sector in Financing Urban Housing Development." Paper presented to "Why Cooperatives Succeed ... and Fail." Washington DC: US Overseas Cooperative Development Committee.

Andersen, Margaret L.1988. "Moving our Minds: Studying Women of Color and Reconstructing Sociology," *Teaching Sociology,* Vol. 16: p. 123.

Antoni, Antoine. 1968. "Workers' control in the French co-operative societies," *Review of International Cooperation,* 61: 228-234.

Arbess, Saul E. 1966. *Social Change and the Eskimo Co-operative at George River, Quebec.* Ottawa: Northern Co-odination and Research Centre, Dept. of Northern Affairs and Natural Resources.

Axworthy, Christopher. 1985. *Worker Co-operatives in Mondragon, the U.K. and France; Some Reflections.* Saskatoon: Centre for the Study of Co-operatives.

Banks, J.A. 1972. *The Sociology of Social Movements.* London: Macmillan.

Barclay, Myrna. 1991. "Toward Gender Balance: Women and Co-operatives." Ottawa: Canadian Co-operative Association, unpublished paper.

Bariteau, Claude. 1983. *Lessons from a Failure.* Saskatoon: Co-operative College of Canada, Working Papers, Vol.1, No. 6.

Baviskar, B.S. 1986. "Dairy Cooperatives and Rural Development in Gujarat: A Case Study," in D.W. Attwood and B.S. Baviskar, eds., Cooperatives and Rural Development. Delhi: Oxford University Press. George, Shanti.

———. 1985. *Operation Flood: An Appraisal of Current Indian Dairy Policy.* Delhi: Oxford University Press.

Baviskar, B.S. 1980. *The Politics of Development: Sugar Co-operatives in Rural Maharashtra.* Delhi: Oxford University Press.

Bellas, Carl J. 1972. *Industrial Democracy and the Worker-Owned Firm.* New York: Praeger: 92-94.

Bennis, W. and B. Nanus. 1985. *Leaders.* New York: Harper and Row.

Berman, K. 1967. *Worker-Owned Plywood Companies.* Pullman: Washington State University Press: 213.

Bertram, B. 1938. *The Lord Helps Those...How the People of Nova Scotia are Solving their Problems through Cooperation.* New York: Vanguard Press.

Blau, Peter M. 1964. *Exchange and Power in Social Life.* New York: John Wiley & Sons.

Block, P. 1987. *The Empowered Manager.* San Francisco: Jossey-Bass.

Bonner, Arnold. 1970. *British Co-operation: The History, Principles and Organization of The British Co-operative Movement.* Manchester: Co-operative Union.

Bookman, Ann and Sandra Morgan, ed., 1988. *Women and the Politics of Empowerment.* Philadelphia: Temple University Press.

Bottomley, Trevor. 1989. *Farmer-Centred Enterprise for Agricultural Development.* Oxford: Plunkett Foundation for Co-operative Studies.

Boyd, Leslie S. 1991. *Co-operatives, Communities and Culture: An Assessment of the Arctic Co-operative Development Program.* Toronto: York University, Unpublished Masters thesis in Faculty of Environmental Studies.

Bromberger, Norman. 1973. *Conflict and Co-operation.* Regina: Saskatchewan Co-operative Credit Society.

Brooke, Marcus. 1977. "The Real Bali," *Thai International Magazine,* Nov.:31-34.

Brooks, David. 1990. "Beyond Catch Phrases: What Does Sustainable Development Mean? Ottawa: International Development Research Centre, *REPORTS*.

Brown, Leslie. 1985. "Democracy in Organizations: Membership Participation and Organizational Characteristics in U.S. Retail Food Co-operatives," *Organizational Studies*, Vol. 6, No. 4: 313-334.

Brundtland Commission. 1987. *Our Common Future*. Oxford: Oxford University Press.

Burke, W. 1986. "Leadership as empowering others," pp. 3-48, in S. Srivastra, ed., *Power in Organizations*. Nashville: Vanderbilt University Press.

Carpenter, Susan M. 1977. "Some problems arising from the structure of the West German agricultural co-operative organization," *in Research Report, Second Co-operative Research Seminar*. Oxford: The Plunkett Foundation for Co-operative Studies.

Carr-Saunders, A.M., P. Sargant, Florence and Robert Peers. 1938. *Consumers' Cooperation in Great Britain*. London: George Allan & Unwin.

Casselman, P.M. 1952. *Cooperative Movement and Some of its Problems*. New York: Philosophical Library.

Catalano, Bruno. 1984. "Work Cooperatives: What will be their evolution?" Paper presented to the General Assembly of CICOPA - Hamburg Germany.

Cernea, Michael. 1985. *Putting People First*. New York: Oxford University Press.

Childs, Marquis William. 1947. *Sweden the Middle Way*. New Haven: Yale University Press (revised and enlarged edition).

Cholaj, Henryk. 1969. "The changing functions of co-operatives in socialist countries." *Proceedings of the sixth International Conference on Co-operative Science*: 30-57.

Coady, M.M. 1939. *Masters of Their Own Destiny*. New York: Harpers and Fowler.

Coates, Ken. 1976. *The New Worker Co-operatives*. Nottingham: Published for the Institute for Worker's Control by Spokesman Books.

Cobbald, Elizabeth. 1987. *Women in Agricultural Co-operatives*. Oxford: The Plunkett Foundation for Co-operative Studies.

Cohen, Erik and Menachem Rosner. 1973. "Problems of generations in the Israeli kibbutz," pp. 534-544 in R.M. Kanter, ed., *Communes*. New York: Harper & Row.

Cole, G.D.H. 1944. *A Century of Co-operation*. Manchester: Cooperative Union.

Colombain, Maurice. 1976. "From Rochdale rules to the principles of co-operation," *Co-operative Information*, Vol. 52, No. 3, pp. 5-18.

Colquette, R.D. 1957. *The First Fifty Years: A History of United Grain Growers Limited*. Winnipeg: Public Press.

Commoner, Barry. 1989. "Environmental Democracy is The Planet's Best Hope," pp. 52-56 in C.& J. Plant eds. *Green Business: Hope or Hoax*. Philadelphia: New Society Publishers.

Conger, Jay A. and Rabindra N. Kanungo. 1988. "The Empowerment Process: Integrating Theory and Practice" *Academy of Management Review*, Vol 13, No. 3, pp. 471-482.

Cooper, Donald and Paul O. Mohn. 1992. *The Greenbelt Cooperative*. Berkley: University of California Press.

Coser, Lewis A. 1968. "Conflict: social aspects," *International Encyclopedia of the Social Sciences*. No. 3, pp. 232-236.

Cotterill, Ronald. 1982. *Consumer Food Cooperatives*. Danville, Ill.: The Interstate Printers & Publishers.

Craig, J.G. 1986. "Business Success and Democratic Process," in Juhani Laurinkari, ed., pp. 93-111. *Co-operatives Today*. A Tribute to Dr. Laakkonen (Finland). Published in German and English. Geneva: International Co-operative Alliance.

———. 1975. "Democratic control in insurance cooperatives," *Annals of Public and Co-operative Economy*, Vol. 46 (April-June), pp. 187-200.

———. 1989. "Paradigms and the theory of cooperation," in S. Wright and D. Morley, eds., *Learning Works: Searching for Organizational Futures*. Toronto: ABL Publications, Faculty of Environmental Studies, York University, pp. 63-82.

———. 1976. *Multinational Co-operatives: An Alternative for World Development*. Saskatoon: Western Producer Prairie Books.

Craig, J.G. and E. Gross. 1970. "The forum theory of organizational democracy: structural guarantees as time-related variables," *American Sociological Review*, Vol. 35, Feb., pp. 19-33.

Craig, J.G. & H. Poerbo. 1988. "Food security and rural development: the case of Ciamis Indonesia," *Journal of Rural Co-operation*, Vol. XVI, No. 1-2, pp. 111-124. Reprinted in UCE reprint series.

Craig, J.G. and S. Saxena. 1986. "The Co-operative Principles and the Community," in Yair Levi and H. Litwin eds. *Community and Co-operatives in Participatory Development*. London: Gower.

Curtis, Russell L. Jr. and Louis A. Zuncher, Jr. 1974. "Social movements: an analytical exploration of organizational forms," *Social Problems*, Vol. 21 (3), pp. 356-370.

Daniel, Abraham. 1975 "The Kibbutz movement and hired labor," *Journal of Rural Co-operation*, Vol. 3 (1), pp. 31-40.

Dankelman, Ireene and Joan Davidson. 1988. *Women and the Environment in the Third World: Alliance for the Future*. London: Earthscan Publications Ltd.

Davidovic, George. 1966. *Reformulation of the Co-operative Principles*. Ottawa: Co-operative Union of Canada.

Davis, K. and R.L. Blomstrom. 1975. *Business and Society: Environment and Responsibility (3rd ed.)*. New York: McGraw-Hill.

Dean, Susan. 1985. *Women and Cooperatives. Rome: COPAC publication*. Deegan, Mary J. 1988. "Transcending a Patriarchal Past: Teaching the History of Women in Sociology," *Teaching Sociology*, Vol. 16: p. 141.

Demarest, Henry. 1963. *Wealth Against Commonwealth*. Englewood Cliffs, N.J.: Prentice Hall.

Dixon, John. 1982. "The Community Based Rural Welfare System in The peoples Republic of China: 1949-1979," *Community Development Journal*, Vol. 17, No. 1.

Dobson Gray, Elizabeth. 1982. *Patriarchy as a Conceptual Trap*. Mass: Roundtable Press.

Downs, Anthony. 1957. *An Economic Theory of Democracy*. New York: Harper & Row.

Doyle Farge, Brenda. 1985. *Women and Leadership in Co-operative Housing Sector*. Toronto: University of Toronto, unpublished Masters Thesis, OISE.

Dufler, Eberhard and Walter Hamm, ed., 1985. *Co-operatives: In a Clash between Member Participation, Organizational Development and Bureaucratic Tendencies*. London: Quiller Press.

Earle, Jhon. 1986. *The Italian Cooperative Movement: A Portrait of the Lega Nazionale della Cooperative e Mutue*. London: Allen & Unwin.

Eccles, Tony. 1976. "Kirby manufacturing and engineering," pp. 141-169 in Ken Coates, ed. *The New Worker Co-operatives*. Nottingham: Published for the Institute for Workers Control by Spokesman Books.

Eggertson, Eric. 1990. "Keeping the Home in Home Town," *Credit Union Way*, Vol. 43, No. 3: pp. 14-17.

Ekin, Paul and Manfred Max-Neef. 1992. *Real Economics: Understanding Wealth Creation*. New York: Routledge.

Ekin, Paul. 1992. *A New World Order: Grassroots Movements for Global Change*. New York: Routledge.

Ellman, Eugene. 1988. Ontario Credit Unions Lead Banks on Equality but Still Need Policies to Eliminate Barriers. *Spectrum*. Sept: 3.

Emerson, Richard D. 1962. "Power-Dependence Relations," *American Sociological Review*, Vol. 27, pp. 31-41.

Etzioni, A. 1964. *Modern Organizations*. Engelwood Cliffs: Prentice-Hall.

Fairbairn, Brett; Lou Hammond-Ketilson; Murray Fulton and June Bold. 1991 *Co-operatives & Community Development*. Saskatoon: Centre for the Study of Co-operatives, Univ. of Saskatchewan.

Fairbairn, Garry L. 1984. *From Prairie Roots: The Remarkable Story of Saskatchewan Wheat Pool*. Saskatoon: Western Producer Prairie Books.

Fals-Borda, Orlando. 1976. "The crisis of rural cooperatives: problems in Africa, Asia, and Latin American," pp. 439-456 in June Nash et. al., eds., *Popular Participation in Social Change*. The Hague: Mouton.

Fals-Borda, Orlando. 1992. "Evolution and Convergence in Participatory Action Research," pp. 14-19 in Frideres, James S., ed., *A World of Communities: Participative Research Perspectives*. North York, Ontario: Captus University Publications.

Fals-Borda, Orlando. 1971. *Cooperatives and Rural Development in Latin America*. Geneva: United Nations Research Institute for Social Development, Vol. III.

Fauquet, G. 1951. *The Co-operative Sector*. Manchester: Co-operative Union. (4th edition).

French, David and Elena French. 1975. *Working Communally: Patterns & Possibilities*. New York: Russell Sage.

Friedrich, D. 1984. *Direct Charge: The Common Sense Approach*. Saskatoon: Co-operative College of Canada, Working Papers, Vol. 2, No. 1.

Fullerton, Michael, ed., 1992. *What happened to the Berkley Co-op?* Berkley: University of California Press.

Fulton, Murray E., ed., 1990. *Co-operative Organizations and Canadian Society: Popular Institutions and the Dilemmas of Change*. Toronto: University of Toronto Press.

Furstenberg, Friedrich. 1985. "Problems of Member Participation at Different Stages of Co-operative Development," in E. Dufler and W. Hamm, eds., *Co-operatives: In a Clash between Member Participation, Organizational Development and Bureaucratic Tendencies*. London: Quiller Press, pp: 103-117.

Galbraith, John K. 1967 *The New Industrial State*. New York: Signet Books.

Garnett, R.G. 1972. *Co-operation and Owenite Socialist Communities in Britain 1825-45*. Manchester: Manchester University Press.

George, Susan. 1988. *A Fate Worse Than Debt*. London: Penguin.

George, Shanti. 1985. *Operation Flood: An Appraisal of Current Indian Dairy Policy*. Delhi: Oxford University Press.

Giddard. 1991. "Mondragon Update," *Worker Co-op*, No. 4: pp. 15.

Gide, Charles. 1922. *Consumer's Co-operative Societies*. New York: Alfred A. Knopf.

Gill, Manohar Singh. 1983. *Agricultural Cooperatives: A Case Study of Punjab*. New Delhi: Vikas Publishing.

Girvan, Marnie. 1992. "Women in Development Process," pp. 11-13. Proceedings of the *ITB/York University Forum on Gender and Development*. North York: FES York UCE project.

Goldberg, Harvey E. 1972. *Cave Dwellers and Citrus Growers: A Jewish Community in Lybia and Israel*. Cambridge: The University Press.

Gosselin, Gabriel. 1976. "Traditional collectivism and modern associations: the example of South Dahomey," pp. 55-70 in June Nash et. al., eds., *Popular Participation in Social Change*. The Hague: Mouton.

Grenlund, Laurence. 1886. *The Co-operative Commonwealth*. London: Swan Sonnenschein, LeBas & Lowrey.

Hammond-Ketilson, Lou. 1992. "The Saskatchewan Co-operative Women's Guild." Saskatoon: Centre for Co-operative Studies, University of Saskatchewan, proceedings of the Canadian Association for Studies in Co-operation meetings.

——. 1992. "Co-operative Models of Community development: What makes Them Work and Why They Make Sense." Saskatoon, Centre for the Study of Co-operatives, paper presented at ICA Researchers Forum, Tokyo.

Helgesen, Sally. 1990. *The Female Advantage: Women's Ways of Leadership.* Toronto: Doubleday.

Hesselbach, Walter. 1976. *Public, Trade Union and Co-operative Enterprise in Germany: the Commonweal Idea.* London: Frank Cass.

Hindry, J. 1987. *Understanding Japanese Society.* London: Croom Helm.

Hirschfeld, Andre. 1973. "Charles Fourier and the co-operative movement," *Journal of Rural Co-operation,* Vol. 1, p. 11.

Holland, Douglas. 1981. *The Co-operative Movement and Taxation: A Study in Canadian Public Policy.* Toronto: York University, unpublished Masters Thesis.

——. 1986. *Directors in Canadian Co-operatives.* Ottawa: Canadian Co-operative Association.

Holloway, Richard. ed. 1989. *Doing Development: Governments, NGOs and the Rural Poor.* London: Earthscan Publications.

Holmstrom, Mark. 1989. *Industrial Democracy in Italy.* Aldershot, UK: Avebury.

Hyden, Goran. 1980 *Beyond Ujamaa in Tanzania.* Berkeley: University of California Press. 1974. "Co-operative education and co-operative development: The Tanzanian experience," *Agricultural Administration,* Vol. 1 (Jan), pp. 35-50. 1970. "Can co-ops make it in Africa," *Africa Report,* Vol. 15 (Dec), p. 71.

Hymer, Stephen. 1971. "Partners in Development," *NEWSTATEment,* Vol. 1. pp. 4-15.

Iglauer, Edith. 1979. *Inuit Journey.* Vancouver: Douglas & McIntyre.

Ilmonen, Kaj. 1992. *The End of Cooperative Movement? Sociological Affiliation and Morality.* Helsinki: Labour Institute for Economic Research.

Infield, Henrik F. 1947. *Co-operative Communities at Work.* London: Kegan Paul, Trench, Trubnert & Co. 1956a *Utopia and Experiment: Essays in the Sociology of Co-operation.* New York: Kennikat Press.

——. 1956b. *The Sociological Study of Co-operation: An Outline.* Loughborough: Co-operative College Paper No. 3. 1957 "Observations on the nature of co-operative theory," *International Archives of Sociology of Co-operation,* Vol. 1 (2), pp. 3-25. 1958 "Co-operative community and the need for ultimate orientation," *International Archives of Sociology of Co-operation,* Vol. 4 (June-Dec), pp. 46-66.

Illich, Ivan. 1971. *Deschooling Society.* New York: Perennial Library (Harper Row).

International Co-operative Alliance. 1992 *XXXth CONGRESS Tokyo October, 1992 Agenda and Report.* Geneva: International Co-operative Alliance: 77-78.

International Cooperative Alliance. 1967. *Report of ICA on Cooperative Principles.* London: ICA.

Ish, Daniel. 1981. *The Law of Canadian Co-operatives.* Toronto: The Carswell Co.

Jaggi, E. 1974. *Agricultural Co-operatives and Associations in Switzerland.* Oxford: The Plunkett Foundation for Cooperative Studies. Occasional Papers No. 40.

Johansson, Tore & Sven Ake Book. 1988. *The Co-operative Movement in Sweden.* Stockholm: The Swedish Society for Co-operative Studies.

Jones, Derek C. and David K. Backus. 1977. "British producer cooperatives in the footwear industry: an empirical evaluation of the theory of financing," *The Economic Journal,* Vol. 87, (Sept), pp. 488-510.

Jordan, John. 1989. "The Multi-stakeholder Concept of Organization," pp. 113-131 in J. Quarter and G. Melnyk. *Partners in Enterprise: The Worker Ownership Phenomenon.* Montreal: Black Rose Books.

Kagawa, Toyohiko. 1936. *Brotherhood Economics.* New York: Harper and Brothers.

Kanovsky, Eliyaha. 1966. *The Economy of the Israeli Kibbutz.* Cambridge, Mass: Harvard University Press.

Kanter, Rosebeth Moss. 1983. "Power Failures in Management Circuits" *Harvard Business Review,* Vol. 57 (4), pp. 65-75. 1972. *Commitment and Community.* Cambridge, Mass.: Harvard University Press. 1970. "Communes," *Psychology Today,* Vol. 4 (July), p. 53.

Keim, Gerald D. 1978. "Managerial behavior and the social responsibility debate: goals versus constraints," *Academy of Management Journal*, Vol. 21 (Mar.), pp. 57-68.

Kephart, William M. 1976. *Extraordinary Groups: The Sociology of Unconventional Life-Styles*. New York: St. Martins Press.

Knapp, Joseph G. 1979. *Edwin G. Nourse: Economist for the People*. Dansville Il: Interstate Printers and Publishers.

Kohn, Alfie. 1986. *No Contest: The Case Against Competition*. New York: Houghton Mifflin.

Korabik, K. & R. Ayman. 1989. "Should Women Managers Have to Act Like Men? *Journal of Management Development*, Vol. 8, No. 6, p. 20.

Korp, A. 1967a. "Structural reform in the co-operative system," *Annals of Public and Co-operative Economy*, Vol. 38 (Jan-Mar), pp. 17-24. and 1967b. "Co-operative self-help in Austria," *Madras Journal of Cooperation*, Vol. 58, pp. 420-427.

Korten, David C. 1990. *People Versus Government*. Hyderbad, India: Samakhya. 1980. "Community Organization and Rural Development: A Learning Process Approach," *Public Administration Review*, Vol. 40, pp. 480-510.

Kropotkin, Peter. 1989, *Mutual Aid: A Factor of Evolution*. Montreal: Black Rose Books.

Kumar, Satish, ed., 1984 *The Schumacher Lectures*. London: Abacus.

Kurien, V. 1991 "Towards a New World Order," speech in Toronto to the Eighth World Congress of Food Science and Technology. Anand: NDDB.

———. 1992 "Cooperative Leadership and Cooperative Values." Kurien, V. *Cooperative Leadership and Values*. Anand: NDDB.

Kurimoto, A. 1983. *Research Activities-Studies, Project on the Future of Consumer Co-operatives*. Tokyo: Japanese Consumer Co-operative Union.

Laidlaw, Alexander F. 1980. *Co-operatives in the year 2000*. Ottawa: Co-operative Union of Canada.

———. 1974. "The Cooperative Sector." Paper presented in Columbia Mo. to the Graduate Institute of Cooperative Leadership, University of Missouri.

———. 1971. *The Man from Margaree: Writings & Speeches of M.M. Coady*. Toronto: Mc Clelland & Stewart.

Lambert, Paul. 1963. *Studies in the Social Philosophy of Co-operation*. Manchester: The Co-operative Union.

Lamming, G.N. 1983. *Women in Agricultural Cooperatives: Constraints and Limitation to full Participation*. Rome: Food and Agricultural Organization.

Laurence. 1886. *The Co-operative Commonwealth*. London: Swan Sonnenschein, LeBas.

Laurinkari, Juhani. 1986. *Co-operatives Today: Selected essays from selected fields of co-operative activities*. Geneva: International Co-operative Alliance.

Ledesma, A.L., A.Y. Ledesma, A.B. Quizon and A.M. Salinas. 1982, *The Cooperative Experience in Asian Cultures*. Manila: Centre for the Development of Human Resources in Rural Asia.

Lehman, Edward W. 1969. "Toward a Macrosociology of Power," *American Sociological Review*, Vol. 34 (Aug), pp. 453-465.

Leif, Irving P. & Terry Nichols Clark. 1972. *Community Power and Decision Making*. Hague: A Trend Report and Bibliography International Sociologial Association.

Lenin, V.I. 1923. "On cooperation," in *Collected Works*. Moscow: Progress Publishers, Vol. 33, pp. 467-475.

Levi, Yair and H. Litwin eds., 1986. *Community and Cooperatives in Participatory Development*. London: Gower.

Lewin, Roger. 1973 "Matetereka," pp. 189-194 in Lionel Cliffe & John S. Saul, eds., *Socialism in Tanzania*, Vol. 2, Policies. Dar es salaam: East African Publishing.

Lindkvist, Lars G. & Claes Svensson. 1982. "Worker- Owned Factories in Sweden," *Economic Analysis and Workers' Management*, Vol. XVI, pp. 387-400.

Lipset, S.M. 1968. *Agrarian Socialism*. Garden City, N.Y. Doubleday.

Louis, R. 1977. "A United Nations general assembly resolution and the future of cooperatives," *Co-operative Information*, Vol. 77 (1), pp. 1-21.

Lovell, Alyssa. 1989. "Community-Supported Agriculture," pp. 105-109 in C.& J. Plant, eds., *Green Business: Hope or Hoax*. Philadelphia: New Society Publishers.

Lundberg, W.T. 1978. *Consumer Owned: Sweden's Cooperative Democracy*. Palo Alto: Consumer Cooperative Publishing Association.

MacPherson, Ian. 1979. *Each for All: A History of the Co-operative Movement in English Canada, 1900-1945*. Toronto: MacClelland & Stewart (Carlton Library Series).

Manday, E.A. 1977. "A new structure for co-operatives in Tanzania," *Annals of Public and Co-operative Economy*. 48 (April-June): 239-244.

Marcus, Lars. 1988. "Co-operatives and Basic Values," in ICA *Report of the ICA Congress, Stockholm*. Geneva: ICA.:100.

Mariadis, Stavros. 1972. *Groups of Farmers Collaborating on a Non-Statutory Basis*. Athens: Thess aloniki.

Mascarenhas, R.C. 1988. *A Strategy for Rural Development*. New Delhi: Sage.

McRobie, George. 1981. *Small is Possible*. London: Abacus.

———. 1986. "Small is Possible: Towards a Human-Scale Technology," pp. 55-79 in CCSD, ed., *Employmnet and Social Development in a Changing Economy*. Ottawa: Canadian Council on Social Development.

Mead, Margaret. 1961. *Co-operation and Competition Among Primitive Peoples*. Boston: Beacon Press (c1937).

Meghji, Zakia; Clement Kwayu and Ramadhan Meghji. 1985. *The Woman Co-operator and Development: Experiences from Eastern, Central and Southern Africa*. Nairobi: Maarifa Publishers Limited:114-118.

Mehta, S.C. 1975. *Industrial Co-operatives in India*. Delhi: Atma Ram.

———. 1964. *Consumer Co-operation in India*. Delhi: Atta Ram.

Melman, Seymour. 1970. "Industrial efficiency under managerial versus co-operative decison-making," *International Development*, Vol. 6, pp. 47-58.

Melnyk, George. 1985. *The Search for Community: From Utopia to a Co-operative Society*. Montreal: Black Rose Books.

Mercer, T.W. 1947. *Co-operation's Prophet and the Co-operator, 1828-1830*. Manchester: Co-operative Union Ltd.

Miller, Raymond W. 1964. *A Conservative Looks at Cooperatives*. Athens, Ohio: Ohio University Press.

Mintzberg, H. 1983. *Power In and Around Organizations*. Englewood Cliffs,N.J.: Prentice-Hall Inc.

Mitchell, Don and Adrianne Pavo. 1988. "To Zimbabwe with Love from Saskatchewan." *Worker Co-ops*, Vol. 8, No. 1 Summer, pp. 23-24.

Morgan, Dan. 1980. *Merchants of Grain*. New York: Penguin.

Morgan, Gareth. 1988. *Riding the Waves of Change*. San Francisco: Jossey-Bass Publishers. 1980. "Paradigms, Metaphors and Puzzle Solving in Organizations," *Administrative Science Quarterly*, Vol. 25, pp. 605-622.

Morton, A. 1969. *The Life and Ideas of Robert Owen*. New York: International Publishers and Gattrell, V.A C., ed., 1969. *Robert Owen: Report to the County of Lanark and A New View of Society*. New York: Penguin.

Moss, B. 1974. "Parisian producers' association in the nineteenth century: the socialism of skilled workers," *International Archives of Sociology of Co-operation and Development*, Vol. 36 (July-Dec.), pp. 107-127.

Muller, Franz. 1989. "Consumer Co-operatives in Great Britain," in J. Brazda & R. Schediwy, eds., *Consumer Co-operatives in a Changing World*. Geneva: International Co-operative Alliance. pp. 45-137.

Neilson, E. 1986. "Empowerment strategies: Balancing authority and responsibility," in S. Srivastra ed. *Executive Power*. San Francisco: Jossey Bass. pp. 78-110.

Nelson, Harold A. 1974. "Social movement transformation and pre-movement factor-effect: a preliminary inquiry," *The Sociological Quarterly*, Vol. 15 (Winter), pp. 127-142.

Nesbitt, Leonard D. 1964. *Tides in the West*. Saskatoon: Modern Press.

Neubauer, Peter B., ed., 1965. *Children in Collectives: Child-Rearing Aims and Practices in the Kibbutz*. Springfield, Ill.: Charles C. Thomas.

Nisbet, Robert A. 1968. "Co-operation," *International Encyclopedia of the Social Sciences*, Vol. 1, p. 384.

Odhe, Thorsten. 1960. *Iceland: The Co-operative Island*. Chicago: Co-operative League of the U.S.A.

Olson, Mancur. 1965. *The Logic of Collective Action*. Cambridge: Harvard University Press.

Ostergaard, G.N. & A.H. Halsey. 1965.*Power in Co-operatives: A study of Democratic Control in British Retail Societies*. Oxford: Basil Blackwell.

Ostrom, Elinor. 1990. *Governing the Commons: The Evolution of Institutions for Collective Action*. Cambridge: Cambridge University Press.

Palgi, Michal & Menachem Rosner. 1983. *Industrial Democracy in Israel*. Haifa: Centre for the Study of Industrial Democracy and Self-Management.

Pateman, Carol. 1970. *Participation and Democratic Theory*. Cambridge: Cambridge University Press.

Perlmutter, Howard V. 1969. "The Tortuous Evolution of the Multinational Corporation," *Columbia Journal of World Business*. (Jan-Feb).

Pestoff, Victor A. 1989. *Swedish Consumer Policy as a Welfare Service: Organizations in an Negotiated Economy*. Stockholm: University of Stockholm, Department of Business, Studies in Action and Enterprise.

———. 1991. *Between Markets and Politics: Co-operatives in Sweden*. Boulder: Westview Press.

Peters, Tom. 1987. *Thriving on Chaos*. New York: Perennial Library, Harper and Row.

Pfeffer, J. 1981. *Power in Organizations*. Marshfield, Ma: Pitman.

———. 1982. *Organizations and organizational theory*. Marshfield, Ma.: Pitman.

Planning Commission, 1991 *Report of The Committee on Model Cooperatives Act*. New Delhi: Government of India.

Podmore, Frank. 1924. *Robert Owen: A Bibliography*. London: W. Thacker.

Poerbo, Hasan and William Thomas. 1990. "Environmentally Sustainable Development: A Proposal for the Jasinga Area Based on Experience From the Ciamis Project and Studies of Rural Productivity and Non-Farm Employment in West Java." Paper presented to the Workshop on Sustainable Development, Bogor, December.

Poerbo, Hasan. 1991. "Development Consultancy: Agent of Change For a Society in ITB, Bandung Indonesia.

Poisson, Ernest. 1923. *The Co-operative Republic*. Manchester: The Co-operative Union.

Quarter, Jack. 1993. *Canada's Social Economy*. Toronto: James Lorimer & Co.

Quarter, Jack and George Melnyk. 1989. *Partners in Enterprise: The Worker Ownership Phenomenon*. Montreal: Black Rose.

Rabin, A.I. 1965. *Growing Up in the Kibbutz*. New York: Springer.

Rachlan. 1987. "Grass-root Involvement in the Management Process of Agro Development and Land Management in the Citanduy Basin." Paper presented to the International Conference on Local Resource Management for Livelihood Security and Livelihood Enhancement, Bandung.

Raikes, Philip. 1975. "Ujamma and Socialism," *Review of African Political Economy*, Vol. 3 (May-Oct.), pp. 33-52.

Ravoet, Guido. 1992. "Capital Formation and Co-operative Values-The European Experience," *International Co-operative Banking Association*. No. 4: 26.

Rigby, Andrew. 1974. *Communes in Britain*. London: Routledge & Kegan Paul. and Kephart, William M. 1976. *Extraordinary Groups: The Sociology of Unconventional Life-Styles*. New York: St. Martins Press.

Ronfeldt, David. 1973. *Antecingo: The Politics of Agrarian Struggle in a Mexican Ejido*. Stanford: Stanford University Press.

Ross, Steven; Leon J. Kamin and R.C. Lewontin. 1984, *Not in Our Genes*. Harmondsworth: Pelican: 235.

Roth, Warren J. 1976. "Traditional social structure and the development of a marketing cooperative in Tanzania," pp. 45-54 in June Nash et. al., eds., *Popular Participation in Social Change*. The Hague: Mouton.

Roy, Ewell Paul. 1976. *Co-operatives: Development, Principles and Management*. Danville, Ill: Interstate Printers and Publishers, Inc.

Sarkar, A. 1976. "Consumer problems and consumer protection in India," pp. 160-183 in I.C.A., eds., *Consumer Cooperation in South-East Asia*. New Delhi: International Cooperation Alliance.

Satin, Mark. 1978. *New Age Politics: Healing Self & Society. The Emerging New Alternative to Marxism and Liberalism*. Vancouver: White Cap Books.

Saul, John S. 1971. "Marketing cooperatives in a developing country: the Tanzania case," pp. 347-370 in Peter Worsley, ed., *Two Blades of Grass*. Manchester: Manchester University Press.

Saxena, Krishna Kr. 1974. *Evolution of Co-operative Thought*. New Delhi: Somaiya Publications.

Saxena, Suren K. 1985. *Co-operatives and Peace*. Markham Ontario Canada: Saxena and Associates.

———. 1990. "Cooperatives and Women Enterprise Development in India: Note on a Women's Cooperative Bank," *Transnational Associations*, Vol 1, pp. 12-17.

———. 1992. *Cooperatives in India and Pakistan: Some Aspects*. New Delhi: ICA Domus Trust.

Schediwy, R. 1989. "The Consumer Co-operatives in France," in J. Brazda & R. Schediwy eds. *Consumer Co-operatives in a Changing World*. Geneva: International Co-operative Alliance, pp. 671-814.

Schiffgen, Werner. 1975. "Mobilization and co-ordination of co-operative self-help in rural and urban credit services," pp. 12-24 in *Report of 1975 Australian Co-operatives National Convention*. Canberra: The Cooperative Federation of Australia.

Schumacher, Ernst. 1973. *Small is Beautiful*. New York: Harper and Row.

Schwass, Richard. 1990. *A Study of the Implementation of the Ciamis Action Research Project in the Uplands of Citandy, West Java*. Indonesia. PPLH/ITB Bandung, Indonesia: University Consortium on the Environment; Student Publication Series No. 1.

Seibel, H.D. and A. Massing. 1974. *Traditional Organizations and Economic Development Studies of Indigenous Cooperatives in Liberia*. New York: Praeger.

Senge, Peter. 1990. *The Fifth Discipline: The Art and Practice of the Learning Organization*. New York: Doubleday.

Silverman, D. 1970.*The Theory of Organizations*. London: Heinemann.

Singh, S.N. 1992. "Anand Pattern Cooperatives The Indian Experience: A Cooperative Model for Asia. Paper to ICA Researchers Forum, October, Tokyo; and Korten, David C.

———. 1990. *People Versus Government*. Hyderbad, India: Samakhya, P.O. Box 265.

Singh, Mahindu. 1970. *Cooperatives in Asia*. London: Praeger.

Skinner, B.F. 1969. *Contingencies of Reinforcement*. New York: Appleton Century Croft.

Slater, A.G. 1978. "International transfer pricing," *Management Decision*, Vol. 15 (6), pp. 550-560.

Smelser, Neil J. 1962. *Theory of Collective Behavior*. London: Routledge & Kegan Paul.

Somjee, A.H. and G. Somjee. 1978. Cooperative Dairying and the Profiles of Social Change in India. *Economic Development and Social Change*, Vol. 26, pp. 577-597.

Spiro, Melford E. 1975. *Kibbutz: Venture in Utopia*. Cambridge: Harvard University Press (Augmented edition).

Sprudzs, Aleksandrs. 1975. "Cooperatives in Native Communities." Unpublished.

Stager, J.K. 1982. *An Evaluation Study of the Federated Co-operatives in Nouveau Quebec and the Northwest Territories after the Co-operative Development Programs*. Report for the Program Evaluation Branch Department of Indian Affairs and Northern Development. Ottawa: Indian and Northern Affairs.

Stallings, Robert A. 1973. Patterns of belief in social movements: clarifications from an analysis of environmental groups," *Sociological Quarterly*, Vol. 14, pp. 465-480.

Steiner, G. 1975. *Business and Society*. New York: Random House.

Steinhoff, Deborah Ann. 1988. *SEIKYO: Japanese Consumer Co-operatives, Organization and Management*. Sapporo Japan: Hokkaido University, Unpublished Ph.D dissertation.

Stephenson, T.E. 1971. "Conflict in the cooperative retail society," *Annals of Public and Cooperative Economy*, Vol. 42 (July-Sept), pp. 203-217.

Stettner, Nora. 1984. *Chinese Co-operatives: Their Role in a Mixed Economy*. Oxford: Plunkett Foundation, Development Series No. 7:3.

Tannenbaum, A.S. 1968. *Control in Organizations*. New York: McGraw Hill.

Telford, Shirley. 1969. *Economic and Political Peace*. Portland. Oregon: William & Richards. 1973. *Workers Profit Sharing: The Riddle of History Solved*. Portland. Oregon: William & Richards, Publishers.

Terrant, James and Hasan Poerbo. 1987. "Strengthening Community-Based Technology Management Systems," in David C. Korten ed. *Community Management: Asian Experience and Perspectives*. West Hartford Co: Kumerian Press.

The Economist. 1976. "Worker-capitalist dragon seed," *The Economist*. (Dec.11): 86-87.

Thompson, Dorothy. 1971. *The Early Chartists*. London: MacMillan.

Thornley, Jenny. 1980. *The Product Dilemma for Workers Co-operatives in Britian, France and Italy*. Cambridge: Co-operative Research Unit of the Open University. 1981. *Workers' Co-operatives: Jobs and Dreams*. London: Heinemann Educational Books.

Trives, Robert. 1971, "Evolution of reciprocal altruism," *Quarterly Review of Biology*, Vol. 46, No. 1, pp. 35-40.

Tsuzuki, C. 1992. *Robert Owen and the World of Co-operation*. Tokyo: Robert Owen Association of Japan.

Tyagi, R.B. 1968. *Recent Trend in the Co-operative Movement in India*. New York: Asia Publishing House.

Vacek, Gunther. 1989. "The Consumer Co-operatives in Japan," in J. Brazda & R. Schediwy, eds., *Consumer Co-operatives in a Changing World*. Geneva: International Co-operative Alliance, pp. 1026-1105.

Vaillancourt, Pauline Marie. 1975. "Quebec worker production cooperatives." Paper presented to annual meeting of the Canadian Political Science Association in Edmonton.

Verhagan, Koenraad. 1984. *Co-operation for Survival*. Amsterdam: Royal Tropical Institute.

———. 1987 *Selp-Help Promotion: a challenge to the NGO community*. The Netherlands: Cebemo/Royal Tropical Institute.

Viteles, H. 1966. *A History of the Co-operative Movement in Israel*. London: Vallentine, Mitchell Publishers.

Walsh, Tom. 1992. "Funding proposal to Canadian Co-operative Association." Unpublished.

Ward, Michael; Robert Briscoe and Mary Lineham. 1982. *Co-operation Between Co-operatives: A Case Study of Agricultural Co-operatives in the N.E of the Republic of Ireland.* Cork: University of Cork.

Watkins, W.P. 1977. *The International Co-operative Movement: Its Growth, Structure and Future Possibilities.* Manchester: Holyoake Books, Co-operative Union Ltd.

———1986. *Co-operative Principles: Today and Tomorrow.* Manchester: Holyoake Books, Co-operative Union Ltd.

Webb, S. and B. Webb. 1968. "Democracies of producers," in Ken Coates & Anthony Topham, eds., *Industrial Democracy in Great Britain.* London: MacGibbon and Kee.

Webster, F.H. 1973. *Agricultural Co-operation in Denmark.* London: Plunkett Foundation for Co-operative Studies.

Weintraub, D., M. Lissak and Y. Azmon. 1969. *Moshava, Kibbutz and Moshav.* Ithica: Cornell University Press.

Westergaard, Paul W. 1970. "Co-operatives in Tanzania as economic and democratic institutions," pp. 121-152 in C.G. Widstrand, ed., *Cooperatives and Rural Development in east Africa.* New York: Africana Publishing Corporation. pp. 124-128.

Whyte, William Foote and Kathleen King Whyte. 1988. *Making Mondragon: The Growth and Dynamics of the Worker Cooperative Complex.* Ithaca New York: ILR Press.

———. 1991. *Participatory Action Research.* Beverly Hills: Sage Publications.

Wilson, Edward Osborne. 1975, *Sociobiology: The New Synthesis.* Cambridge; Harvard University Press.

Woodward, Warner. 1986. "Participatory Research and Economic Democracy in the 80s: Experience from the U.S.," in Yair Levi and H. Litwin, eds., *Community and Co-operatives in Participatory Development.* London: Gower.

Worsley, Peter, ed., 1971. *Two Blades of Grass.* Manchester: Manchester University Press.

Wright, James F.C. 1956. *Prairie Progress.* Saskatoon: Modern Press.

Yamagishi, M. 1989. "Democratic Administration in the Co-operatives," in Kurimoto, ed., *Proceedings of the International Forum on the Vision of the Consumer Co-operative Movement towards the 21st Century.* Yokohama Japan: Co-op Kanagawa.

Zald, M. and R. Ash. 1966. "Social movement organizational: growth, decay and change," *Social Forces,* Vol. 44 (March), pp. 327-341.

INDEX